T0305253

SPANISH AND LATIN AMERICAN TRANSITIONS TO DEMOCRACY

SPANISH AND LATIN AMERICAN TRANSITIONS TO DEMOCRACY

Edited by

CARLOS H. WAISMAN AND RAANAN REIN

sussex
ACADEMIC
PRESS

BRIGHTON • PORTLAND

Organization of this volume
© Carlos Waisman and Raanan Rein, 2005.
Text © Sussex Academic Press, 2005.

The right of Carlos Waisman and Raanan Rein to be identified as Editors of this work has
been asserted in accordance with the Copyright, Designs and Patents Act 1988.

2 4 6 8 10 9 7 5 3 1

First published 2005 in Great Britain by
SUSSEX ACADEMIC PRESS
PO Box 2950
Brighton BN2 5SP

and in the United States of America by
SUSSEX ACADEMIC PRESS
920 NE 58th Ave   Suite 300
Portland, Oregon 97213–3786

British Library Cataloguing in Publication Data
A CIP catalogue record for this book is available from the British Library.

Library of Congress Cataloging-in-Publication Data
Spanish and Latin American transitions to democracy / edited by
Carlos H. Waisman and Raanan Rein.
    p. cm.
    Includes bibliographical references and index.
    ISBN 1-903900-73-5 (hardcover : alk. paper)
    1. Spain—Politics and government—1975– 2. Spain—
Economic conditions—1975– 3. Democratization—Spain.
4. Latin America—Politics and government—1980– 5. Latin
America—Economic conditions—1982– 6. Democratization—
Latin America. I. Waisman, Carlos H. (Carlos Horacio), 1943–
II. Rein, Raanan, 1960–
DP272.S67 2005
320.917′561′09048—dc22

                                                2005005583

Typeset and designed by G&G Editorial, Brighton
Printed by MPG Books, Ltd, Bodmin, Cornwall
This book is printed on acid-free paper.

CONTENTS

PREFACE

COMPARING TRANSITIONS IN SPAIN AND LATIN AMERICA

This volume compares the political and economic transitions that have occurred in Spain and Latin America over the past three decades.

This comparison is a natural one, for three reasons. First, the transitions in the two regions have been similar in some basic respects (even though there have been substantial differences as well), and they have taken place in the same historical period: namely, the last three decades of the Twentieth Century. Second, Spain and Latin America do not just share a language, a culture, and a common history as objective traits. Their citizens view themselves as part of the same Iberian civilization. Third, the Spanish transition was one of the first in the current wave of democratization, and it has been considered a model for similar processes in many parts of the world. In many ways, it became the standard by which the success of other cases was measured. For countries that initiated a similar itinerary later, Spain had to be the obvious reference point and trendsetter.

The transitions in Spain and Latin America shared some basic characteristics. In the polity, they involved three "tasks" (to use the classical Marxist language). The first involved the dismantling of the institutional apparatus of the Old Regime, and implied two processes: Reaching basic agreements ("pacts," as they became known in the literature) among major political forces, about the process of transition itself and the characteristics of the new institutions; and putting these new institutions in place, i.e. writing or updating constitutions, and promulgating new laws.

Second, the transition presupposed coming to terms with the legacy of the authoritarian past. This meant much more than changing the laws and rewriting history textbooks. In Spain and some Latin American countries, the pre-existing regimes had been highly coercive and committed major violations of human rights. The issues of whether this ugly past should be investigated and subject to judicial adjudication became a salient part of the transitional political agenda. Third, it was necessary to legitimate new democratic institutions. The exercise of civil rights and the taste of political liberties in situations in which these had been curtailed for a long time were exhilarating experiences. However, the legitimation of political institutions is inherently linked with their efficacy. In order to become exclusive in citizens' minds as the government formula, the new democracies had to show their ability to deliver in economic and social policy areas: employment, inflation, provision of health, education and social services, etc.

Nor were these transitions merely political. They were correlated with large-scale processes of economic liberalization. This entailed the dismantling of pre-existing autarkic economies (whose institutions had been quite similar in the two regions in the 1950s and 1960s) through privatization, de-regulation, and opening-up to trade and investment. In some cases, e.g., Spain and Chile, this transformation had begun in earnest before political change, and continued during it. In other cases, such as Argentina or Brazil, the political transition preceded intense economic liberalization.

There is the potential for the clash between these economic and political processes, because the establishment of market mechanisms in previously semi-closed economies, even if successful, produces, in the beginning, major changes in the welfare of major social classes and in many regions. Privatization of public firms leads to workers' layoffs, de-regulation drives some firms out of the markets, the opening-up of the economy renders some industries unviable and turns the regions that house them into rust belts. It made sense to fear that the resulting discontent could affect the legitimacy and stability of the new democracies, but they have proved to be quite robust in this regard.

Finally, the transition involves cultural tasks. In a narrow sense, this implies the need to revamp curricula and textbooks in schools, remove barriers to freedom of the press and expression, etc. In a broader sense, the coming to terms with the past and the legitimation of the new democratic institutions imply the strengthening of the public sphere and the generation of a political culture that allows and fosters pluralism, debate, and toleration. In both Spain and Latin America, the construction of this culture was hampered not only by the pre-existing authoritarian regimes, but also in many cases by cultural traditions that exalted monism, uncritical acquiescence to religious and political dogmas, and intolerance. Cultural change is a process still under way, especially in Latin America.

On the other hand, the Spanish and Latin American transitions also featured some important differences. The first is the nature of the pre-existing regime. The Franco dictatorship was the outcome of a bloody civil war, and was one of the longest-lasting regimes in the world. It presided over massive coercion in its first period, was highly institutionalized and dominated by an elaborate ideology, not just anti-communist but also anti-liberal, and had substantial backing within the society. Latin American military regimes, on the other hand, came into power following internal conflicts whose intensity was considerably lower, were less coercive in relative terms, were more weakly institutionalized, developed at most vague anti-communist mentalities, and attracted support of a contingent and instrumental type. Mexico, whose authoritarian regime was party-based and supported by a state-corporatist apparatus, was quite different from both Francoism and the military dictatorships in the rest of Latin America. In comparison with the other cases in the region, the regime of the *Partido Revolucionario Institucional* was less coercive, more institutionalized and based on a more legitimate ideology (revolutionary nationalism) and enjoyed considerable legitimacy.

A second difference has to do with the way in which Spain and Latin American countries reckoned with the past. The central issue in this regard was the punishment of human rights violations. In Spain, these violations had taken place decades before, most perpetrators and their victims were dead, and collective stocktaking had been taking place, sometimes silently, for a generation. In Latin America, on the other hand, both victims and victimizers were alive and the interpretation of the past in the public sphere was only just beginning with the onset of democratization. Consequently, the demand for justice was one of the most salient matters in the early stages of the transition. Outcomes varied, from the appointment of truth commissions to a blanking out of the past trauma, and from trials to political amnesty. In any case, the revision of the past and the clamor for truth and judicial review is still at the center of public debate.

Third, unlike Latin America, Spain experienced, in addition to the political and economic processes discussed above, a national transition, which involved the nature of the nation state. This transition entailed, first, a shift in the conception of the nation — from an unitary one that had imposed Castilian language and culture to the rest of Spain to a pluralistic definition that recognized regional cultural differences and collective identities. Second, there was a radical change in the nature of the state, from a highly centralized type to a regime that devolved authority to the regions and recognized their autonomy. The centrality of the national question and the existence of strong regional nationalisms in parts of Spain (Euzkadi, Catalonia) lacks any counterparts in Latin America, where the considerable cultural pluralism that exists in some societies has not generated, thus far, significant national identities or secessionist movements. The violent strategy followed by ETA, again, does not have parallels in Latin America.

Finally, the international context was different in the two regions. The Spanish transition took place in the final stages of the Cold War, and Spain was a strategic asset for the Western powers. The democratization of Latin America, on the other hand, began when Communist regimes were already in profound crisis, and the consolidation of the new democracies took place after the collapse of the Soviet Empire. Due to these differences, Western powers cooperated much more actively with the Spanish than the Latin American transitions.

The papers in this volume will aim to light over important aspects of the complex processes of moving from authoritarianism to democracy and from neo-mercantilism to a market economy. This volume is the product of the Woodrow Borah International Colloquium on Transitions from Dictatorship to Democracy, which took place at the Institute for Latin American History and Culture of the University of Tel Aviv on May 25–27, 2003.

Lastly, we would like to thank Uri Rosenheck, Rosalie Sitman, Gabriela Williams, and Lisa Ratz, as well as Anthony Grahame and the staff at Sussex Academic Press, for the work invested in this project. Thanks are also due to the S. Daniel Abraham Center for International and Regional Studies at Tel Aviv University for its support for the publication of this book.

Introduction
Latin American Transitions in the Spanish Mirror

Carlos H. Waisman

The Spanish Transition as a Paradigmatic Case

In both academic and popular debates about transitions to democracy and a market economy in Latin America and Central and Eastern Europe, Spain remains the paradigmatic case. In the academic "transitological" literature, comparisons with Spain, when not manifest, are usually latent,[1] and the same could be said about public discourse. Those who followed the demise of the Soviet Union will remember the continuous references to the Spanish pattern, and the contemporary Latin American press is full of invidious references to Spain's accession to the club of rich nations and to traits of the Spanish political transition, such as the role of King Juan Carlos or the Moncloa Pact.

The reasons for the centrality of the Spanish case are clear. First, the transition in that country was one of the first in what came to be known as the "third wave". Second, Spain, like most of Latin America and much of Central and Eastern Europe, was a nation lacking strong democratic traditions. Third, its democratization was, as in Latin America, part of a larger process involving substantial economic conversion, from a semi-autarkic to an open market economy. Finally, the outcome of Spain's economic and political transition appears to have been an unqualified success. The data below illustrates this last point.

1. While the transitions in the other regions was in full swing (and about a decade and a half after its inception), Spain exhibited a market economy in the process of successful integration into Europe (today it has the tenth highest per capita GNP in the world).[2] The country has had a respectable rate of economic growth: In 1998, its per capita GNP was 56% of that of France;[3] twenty years before, shortly after Spain put forward its candidacy for membership in the European Community, it was 42%.[4]

1

Latin Americans (and Latin Americanists) find the comparison poignant because, at the very beginning of Spanish economic liberalization in the mid-1960s, the country's economy, based on import-substituting industrialization, looked very much like that of Latin American countries. And it was quite backward, to boot: Its GNP was 73% of Argentina's, similar to the Chilean, 123% of Mexico's, and twice that of Brazil.[5] By 1998, the corresponding proportions were 157%, 293%, 172% and 308%. Spain had clearly raced ahead of the Latin American pack.[6]

2. Indicators of welfare (income distribution and provision of health and education) in Spain have been quite satisfactory, except for the rate of unemployment, which tended to be higher than in most West European nations. In 2000, the country's Gini index was 32.5, not as good as that in a highly egalitarian country like Sweden (25), but incomparably better than in Latin America, where this index was 53 in Mexico, 57 in Chile, and 61 in Brazil.[7] Also in 2000, Spanish life expectancy was 78.9 years (only slightly lower than in Sweden, where it was 79.7), considerably higher than in Latin American countries (75.3 in Chile, 73.4 in Argentina, 72.6 in Mexico, and 67.7 in Brazil).[8]

In the domain of education, the differences between Spain and most of Latin America are also substantial. In Spain, the percentage of the population aged 25–34 that had completed high school was 53% at the turn of this century (again, substantially worse than in Sweden, where it was 87%), a proportion matched by Chile (54%) but much better than in Argentina (36%), Brazil (28%), and Mexico (26%).[9] Data on the quality of education are hard to come by, but in a recent test of student achievement in mathematics and science administered to eighth graders (TIMMS, Trends in International Mathematics and Science Study), Spanish scores, while not spectacular, were much higher than those of Chile and Colombia, the only Latin American countries to participate in the test.[10]

3. Since its establishment, Spanish democracy has been relatively robust despite being marred by continuing ETA terrorism, the Tejero coup attempt of 1981, and the GAL affair. There is no question that basic attributes of the democratic regime (high levels of participation and contestation, and political rights) are firmly established in the country. As for the rule of law, it is still relatively strong in comparison with Latin America, in spite of the GAL murders and the financial scandals of the 1980s.[11]

Two decades after the inception of the transitions in Latin America, and fifteen years after the beginning of the Central and Eastern European transitions, none of these countries' trajectories especially in Latin America, appear as successful when examined against the Spanish standard. This can be seen by comparing the Spanish outcomes with those of the three largest third-wave democratizations in this region plus Chile (in many ways the best performer in the group).

There have been important variations in economic performance within Latin America. In terms of the growth of per capita GDP, Chile has done well in the aggregate; Argentina and Brazil not so well (the former engulfed in a major crisis at the turn of the new century), and Mexico has grown spectacularly since joining NAFTA. However, the extent to which these countries have carried out the transition from semi-closed and state economies to the open-market model is variable. With the exception of Chile, most have done so in partially, with progress frozen somewhere in the middle of the process. Privatization is more advanced in Argentina or Chile than in Mexico, both latter countries have opened up their economies more than Argentina and Brazil, and fiscal responsibility is in most cases problematical. Again, with the possible exception of Chile, none approaches the extent of economic conversion carried out by Spain.

However, in all cases, the intense economic and social inequality that has always been characteristic of Latin America persists. In fact, in most countries this inequality has intensified recently, because of economic liberalization and the failure to implement effective compensatory policies. The provision of health, education, and pensions is still unsatisfactory, as the data above have shown.[12]

Democratic regimes exist almost everywhere in Latin America, but their quality is not comparable to that of Spain at the same point in time. High levels of participation and contestation are the norm, but so are relatively high levels of corruption and deficient institutionalization of the rule of law (again, except for Chile). In most countries in the region, governments and major social and political forces are not consistently subordinate to the law. Typically, their approach to the rule of law is pragmatic and contingent. The judiciary in many countries on the continent is extraordinarily slow, and its objectivity and competence are questionable. In some cases, it is widely considered venal. Following are some comparative data in relation to these issues.

Civil rights and political liberties

Table 0.1 shows Freedom House ratings for several countries at the end of the authoritarian regimes, at a point in which the new democracies were well established and under consolidation. It indicates substantial improvements everywhere, but there are interesting differences. In the two decades from the end of the Franco regime to the mid-1990s, when democratization was transforming Latin America, Spain's ratings became similar to those of the established democracies of Western Europe and North America. None of the Latin American countries we have been following registers a similar performance: At the end of the Twentieth Century, ratings for Argentina, Brazil, Chile, and Mexico were still much lower than in Spain (particularly in Brazil and Mexico). Indeed, Uruguay is the only Latin American nation showing a transformation similar to that of Spain, and this is why it is included in the table. Costa Rica, the only long-lasting democracy in the region, showed ratings similar to those of advanced democracies throughout, but as it does not qualify as a transitional polity, it has been omitted.

Table 0.1 Civil Rights and Political Liberties in Spain and Latin American Countries, 1975–2000 (Freedom House ratings) ★

Country	Year	Rating
Spain	1975	5.5
	1995	1.2
Argentina	1982	6.5
	1990	2.3
Brazil	1973–4	5.5
	2000	3.4
Chile	1987	6.5
	1999–2000	2.2
Mexico	1990	4.4
	1999	3.4
Uruguay	1984–5	5.4
		1.2

★ Ratings on a 7-point scale, 1 being "free."

Source: http://www.freedomhouse.org/ratings/index.htm.

Table 0.2 Levels of Corruption at the Turn of the Century, Spain and Several Latin American Countries ★

Country	Corruption Index	Irreg. Pmts.	Legal Corruption
	2001	2000	2000
Spain	7	6.1	6.3
Argentina	3.5	4.0	4
Brazil	4	4.1	4.7
Chile	7.5	6.2	5.2
Mexico	3.7	3.7	3.2

★ The Transparency International Corruption Index is based on a 10-point scale (in which 10 is the highest level of transparency). The indices of irregular payments to government officials and to judges, reported in the *Global Competitiveness Report* vary on a 7-point scale (7 being the most transparent). All these indices are based on evaluations made by academics, business firms, and credit rating agencies.

Sources: Corruption index, Transparency International 2001 (http://www.globalcorruption-report.org/); irregular payments and corruption in the legal system, World Economic Forum, *Global Competitiveness Report 2000* (New York: Oxford University Press, 2000), pp. 247, 249.

Table 0.2 shows data on levels of corruption, based on surveys of judges (academics, business firms, and credit-rating agencies) at the turn of the century. In all these indicators, Spain ranked more or less at the level of the United States, and so did Chile. The other Latin American countries in our group showed quite substantial levels of corruption.[13]

Finally, Table 0.3 includes estimates of the strength of the rule of law in these countries at the turn of the century, also based on evaluations by judges. Again, Spain ranked at the level of the United States, while Latin American countries, Chile included, had lower rankings. One of these indicators, judiciary independence, reveals important differences within the Latin American group, with Mexico and Argentina ranking below Chile and Brazil. Had the survey on protection of property rights been taken after the default in Argentina, then it too would have had a much lower ranking in this respect.

Table 0.3   Rule of Law in Spain and Several Latin American Countries, 2000★

Country	Independence of The Judiciary	Protection of Property Rights	Independence of Public Servants
Spain	5.5	6	4.1
Argentina	2.9	4.5	2.9
Brazil	4.3	5.2	2.9
Chile	4.5	5.5	3.2
Mexico	3	4.2	2.8

★ On a 7-point scale, 7 represents the highest level of rule of law. The third column estimates public servants' independence from political pressures.

Source: *Global Competitiveness Report 2000* (New York: Oxford University Press, 2000), pp. 248, 240, 237.

The Peculiarities of the Spanish Transition

The previous survey raises an obvious question: If, a generation ago, Spanish economic institutions and the level of development were within the Latin American range, and its authoritarian regime was harsher than the ones in Latin America, why were the outcomes of the double transition so different?

The simplest way to deal with this question is to take Spain seriously as a model, and try to understand its peculiarities *vis-à-vis* Latin America. This will allow us to gauge to what extent these, or equivalent factors, were present in the Latin American cases. I will argue that five factors, three social and two political, three internal and two external, facilitated the Spanish transition. The social factors are: the strength of the civil society; the effect of the memory of the Civil War among elites during the

5

foundational period of Spanish democracy; and the positive exemplary effects of European capitalist democracies, deriving from the existence of a common collective "European" identity. The political factors are: state strength and the active cooperation of European countries and the United States, which was substantially based on strategic considerations derived from the Cold War. Most of these factors have been discussed in other related literature, but one of them, state effectiveness, has not. I will argue that this is a central difference between the Spanish and Latin American cases.

The strength of civil society, which Victor Perez-Diaz has analyzed,[14] is the foundation of the image of the Spanish economic and political transition as ideal-typical. In particular, this factor explains why elites, representing economic and political forces that had fought an intense civil war in the 1930s and were opponents of the authoritarian regime established in its aftermath, have revealed an unexpected capacity to recognize each other's legitimacy, negotiate agreements based on reciprocal concessions, stick to these agreements, and live with their consequences.

Alexis de Tocqueville called this phenomenon the "art of association,"[15] i.e., a feature that renders a society a *civil* society. The term refers to a dense web of voluntary associations representing all major interests and values in society. The web is viable as long as it is not controlled by the state, and has the ability to promote and protect the interests and values of its constituent units through institutionalized negotiation rather than confrontation.[16]

Of course, the violent characteristics of the Basque conflict indicate the weakness of civil society in that region of Spain, but Euzkadi is the exception that highlights the norm. In all the other regions, including Catalonia, national and regional conflicts, in some cases intense, have been processed and (thus far) resolved within the institutional channels of the democratic state.

This civil society silently came into being within the Franco regime, as an unintended consequence of three factors. First, the social and economic changes that followed the 1959 stabilization plan and subsequent liberalization programs, i.e., the development of capitalism. Second, the pressures from the US and Western Europe, whose economic aid stipulated as a condition some respect for the autonomy of the Church and other associations. Finally, the penetration of demonstration effects from Western Europe, and the close contact between Spaniards and other Europeans in the 1960s and 1970s, that resulted from guest worker and tourist flows, and the opening of Spain to external cultural influences. This strong civil society was the ground upon which two processes essential to the transition could grow: One, referring to past events whose repetition should be avoided, was the collective elaboration of the memory of the Civil War. Two, referring to a future to be attained, was

6

the demonstration effects emanating from Europe. These two framed the beginning and end of the transition roadmap.

The second factor was the acceptance by major social groups of the radical social transformation associated with economic liberalization, in which, as in Latin America, there would be social and regional losers. The gradual development of a consensus about this matter is especially interesting for the comparison undertaken here. In Spain, as in some countries in Latin America, past economic ideologies of the radical Left and Right had been hostile to the institutions of a market economy. This applies to socialist and communist ideological and programmatic preferences, as well as to the economic institutions and mentality of the early Franco regime, whose orientations toward radical import substitution and autarky were similar to those of Argentina, Brazil, or Chile in the immediate Postwar period.

The construction of a shared memory of the Civil War (see Paloma Aguilar's analysis[17]) is a recurring theme in the conception of Spain as a model. This memory was a powerful controlling factor in elite behavior. Right and Left had contrasting understanding of the causes and effects of the Civil War and different evaluations of the Franco regime, but these understandings and evaluations led to a common consequence: The realization that failure to compromise could have an unbearable cost, leading to the resuscitation of old demons, and result in devastating consequences. This factor did not determine specific substantive outcomes, but it constrained the repertoire of forms of action in the major social and political forces. It operated as a veto, banning not only the resort to violence, but also intransigent attitudes, something especially important in a society whose political culture had, in the past and in some groups, applauded uncompromising behavior.

The positive demonstration effects emanating from Western Europe were based on the pre-existence of a shared identity. Spaniards understood themselves as members of a common civilization with the rest of Europe; none of the major social and political forces in the country could conceive of a future separate from that of its neighbors. This perception had a consequential corollary: The acceptance of the economic and political institutions created by Western Europe after World War II as the only reasonable model for Spain. The belief that there was no future for the country outside of the European Community conferred instant legitimacy on an institutional package consisting of an open market economy, a sustainable welfare state, and a liberal democracy.

No major social force thought that alternatives to these institutions were desirable or possible (the communists, even if disavowing the East European model, pursued socialism as a distant goal, but realized that radical strategies would backfire by rendering them politically irrelevant). This meant that very early on in the process, Europe's economic and political frameworks attained the highest possible form of legitimacy, where institutions are accepted not on the basis of rational calculation, but "naturally", without questioning, to use Blondel's phrase.[18] This contrasts starkly with the Latin American and some of the East European transitions, where the new economic and political institutions were only accepted on a contingent basis, for their legitimacy was much more dependent on the test of efficacy for group interests' than was the case in Spain.

Let us now discuss the two political peculiarities of the Spanish transition.

The first, which is centrally important for the comparison with Latin America, is state strength or capacity, a factor not usually emphasized in studies of the Spanish transition. It refers to the effectiveness with which policies can be generated and implemented. State capacity is, of course, independent of political institutions: Both democratic and authoritarian regimes vary in the extent of the effectiveness of their states. Low effectiveness may be the product of bureaucratic incompetence, lack of appropriate material resources, inadequacy of the laws or rules within which it works, a high level of corruption, or the state's insufficient autonomy *vis-à-vis* elites and other strategic forces in the country.

Effective open-market economies and democracies presuppose a substantial level of state capacity: They depend on the rule of law, which only a strong state, and one insulated from strategic elites, can guarantee; the ability to extract revenue from society; and the adequate management of areas reserved for the state (such as defense, health, education, and welfare). Finally, a market economy cannot function without the effective regulation of markets, a task only the government can perform.

There is little doubt that, when examined in comparative perspective, the Spanish state has displayed considerable effectiveness during the transition and consolidation phases. A crucial indicator of state strength is the capacity to extract resources from society through taxation. Data on expenditures as well as tax evasion reveal that in Spain, government expenditure as a percentage of GNP was 19.8% in 1972, at the end of the Franco regime. It grew to 31.5% in 1985, an increase of 60% in the first decade of the transition.[19] Tax revenue kept rising during democracy, from 22.1% in 1980 to 28.3% in 1997 (an increase of 28%), a figure considerably higher than that of the US in the same year (19.8%).[20] In comparison, tax receipts at the end of the century constituted only 11.2% of GDP in Argentina and 12.8% in Mexico. In this respect, Chile did much better than the other Latin American countries we are considering: Its tax revenue then were 18.9% of GDP, more or less in line with the US.[21]

Tax evasion is also highly indicative of state strength. According to estimates by judges, evasion is relatively low in Spain (4.3 on a 7-point scale, in which 7 indicates minimal evasion), while the scores are 5.2 for Chile (better than in Spain) but 2.3 for Brazil and Mexico and 2.1 for

Argentina.[22] In this latter case, the estimate is that evasion amounts to about 50% of potential tax revenue.

The active cooperation of the European Community and the US is the last of the five distinctive factors of the Spanish transition. The relationship between Spain and the European Community was one of reciprocal attraction, where the main Spanish input was identitarian and purposive, while the main European input was material. For the US, a successful economic and political transition in Spain was a significant strategic goal in Europe. From the 1960s to the 1980s, the EC and the US actively cooperated in order to help Spain overcome the straightjacket of protectionist and neo-mercantilist, Latin American-style policies; set up the institutions of a market economy, and establish and consolidate a democratic state.

At the "material" level, this support took three forms. One, direct economic aid from various sources, furnished by the US since the stabilization program of 1959, and structural and cohesion funds provided by the European Community since the Spanish accession. These were large transfers, focused on the "poor" members of the Community, and at the turn of the century, represented about a third of the European Union budget. Two, the EC provided jobs for Spanish guest workers in the 1950–1970s, and markets for Spanish goods from the 1960s on. Finally, there was a direct institutional transfer: Spain adopted the institutional frameworks developed by Europe for the management of the economy and the organization of government. European assistance included advice to Spanish parties and governments about operating within the new institutions (e.g., the party-to-party guidance offered by sister organizations in Europe).[23]

Obviously, this cooperation was the consequence of strategic considerations; Europe was the central theater of the Cold War. Preventing the economic destabilization of Spain and blocking the establishment of a pro-Soviet regime in the post-Franco era was a central concern for NATO. Thus, Spain has been fortunate in existing in a good neighborhood. It also benefited from hosting major NATO military bases and, oddly, from having a substantial communist legacy (whose potential, as usual in such cases, was magnified by fearful Western elites).

It is difficult to over-emphasize the importance of this factor in facilitating the double transition, especially in relation to the social dislocation produced by the dismantling of the autarkic economy and the establishment of open market institutions.

The difference to Latin America in this regard has been radical. The fact that autarkic industrial policies would lead to stagnation in places such as Argentina or Chile, at the outer periphery of the Cold War, appears to have had limited strategic significance for the US and its major NATO allies. It was only in the 1970s, when leftwing socialist Salvador Allende came to power in Chile and revolutionary rumblings were heard

in Argentina and Uruguay, that major Western powers realized that political processes in Latin America were still significant for the global balance
of power.

Why Latin America is Different

This brief comparison leaves little doubt about the pertinence of these five
factors in explaining the different outcomes of the double transition in
Spain and in Latin America. There are several reasons for the difference.

One, Latin American civil societies do exist but in general are not very
strong. Since the demise of authoritarian regimes, associations and social
movements representing interests and values of all kinds have thrived
throughout the region. Old-standing organizations, such as business associations, trade unions, the Catholic Church and Protestant denom-
inations, as well as newer social movements representing the poor and the
excluded (e.g. the MST landless movement in Brazil, the "picketeers" in
Argentina, indigenous communities in Chile), have thrived. Moreover,
associations that express "post-materialist" values, akin to those flour-
ishing in advanced industrial societies, from environmental groups to
movements expressing sexual identities, have appeared.

However, the strengthening of civil society is thwarted by the preva-
lence of social dualism.[24] This was always a central trait of Latin American
societies (except, until a couple of decades ago, in the "richest" ones,
Uruguay and perhaps Argentina), but dualism is being reinforced everywhere because of economic liberalization. I have previously argued[25] that
privatization, de-regulation, and the opening-up of the economy increase
the differentiation in society, both vertically and horizontally:
Polarization between the affluent and the deprived widens, and so does
the gulf between "winners" and "losers" within each social class, and also
between economic sectors and regions of the country. Both upward and
downward mobility is intensified, to the extent that the Marxist image of
affluence and misery growing at the same time in different poles of the
society is eminently applicable to this situation. Competitive sectors, or
those shielded from foreign competition (e.g., producers or providers of
non-tradable goods) expand, while the least competitive branches of the
economy, or those most dependent on the consumption of strata nega-
tively affected by economic liberalization, contract. Regions that house
the growing sectors thrive, while those that have specialized in activities
that now appear non-viable turn into rust belts or their agrarian equiva-
lents. Of course, capitalism produces continuous social differentiation
everywhere but, in societies with effective political institutions, governments can implement countervailing economic and social policies. Here
we again meet a crucial factor that distinguishes the Latin American from

10

the Spanish transition. In most of Latin America, weak states have difficulty in collecting enough revenue to finance their expenditures. The usual consequences have been high levels of inflation (in the past) or drastic budget cuts (in the recent period), and the poor and the excluded are always the primary victims of both policies.

A political environment of this kind is not conducive to the strengthening of citizenship, i.e., to the mobilization and organization of citizens who make demands and offer supports. Mobilization and participation is the "glue" of a strong civil society. In contrast, the Latin American milieu is characterized by deprivation and dependency, the conditions that foster clientelism. Clientelism, a relationship in which politicians are the principals and clients the agents, is the reverse of citizenship. This is why the processes described above have revitalized the strong clientelistic tradition characteristic of Latin American societies and politics. Of course, these trends are weaker in the more "democratic" countries, such as Chile, Uruguay and Costa Rica (especially in the former, because its stronger state is capable of implementing effective social policies), but there is little ground for optimism with regard to the strength of civil society in the rest of Latin America.

Two, the weight of the past has not constrained elite behavior as effectively for the economic and political transitions as in Spain. Except for Costa Rica, major internal turmoil and/or authoritarian regimes have existed in the recent past throughout Latin America, but there are major differences within the region with respect to the weight this factor bears on current elite behavior. In some cases, the elites have developed, as in Spain, a set of compatible understandings about the causes and consequences of these conflicts and regimes, and these understandings constrain, to some degree, their current behavior. Argentina and Chile are cases in point: In both countries, different social and political forces have clashed over the evaluation of the "dirty war" or the Allende administration and the ensuing military regimes, but they have agreed on the need to heed the lessons of the past, and behave within institutional channels. In other cases, like Mexico, Brazil, or Peru, the rejection of authoritarianism *in toto* is less generalized, and it is even a less significant determinant of current elite behaviors. But even in Argentina or Chile the past turmoil and dictatorship, although undeniable negative, did not match the scale or trauma that Spain encountered in the Civil War, nor the subsequent repression and international isolation under Franco.

However, in most countries, the weakness of this controlling mechanism, compared with Spain, has not been very consequential thus far, for governments and major social and political forces have generally refrained from committing major violations of constitutional norms. The closing of the Peruvian Congress by President Fujimori, and the coups and attempted coups in Ecuador, Paraguay, and Venezuela, appear as exceptional events in a region where the norm is the existence of low-quality but stable democratic institutions.

Three, the demonstration effects of successful market economies and liberal democracies have been important in the Latin American transitions, especially after the demise of the competing institutional complex: state socialism. The Spanish example in particular has become a cliché. However, unlike the case of Spain, these effects were not mediated by common cultural ties with economic and political communities in which the new democracies could integrate.

Mexican society and economy have been transformed by NAFTA, the North American Free Trade Agreement. In the 1990s, Mexican exports more than quadrupled, and the ratio of manufacturing to total exports doubled,[26] but NAFTA is merely a free-trade zone that does not entail the formation of a political or cultural community. Furthermore, Mexicans and Americans do not view themselves as carriers of the same civilization. Such a cultural pull exists within Mercosur or the Andean community, which may also give origin to common political institutions, but these are instances of integration among transitional economies and polities, rather than, as in the case of Spain or Portugal and the European community, processes of institutional upgrading based on demonstration effects.

Four, state capacity is a major determinant of the differences we are analyzing. The data presented earlier indicate that, with the exception of Chile, the major Latin American states have a limited capacity with which to obtain resources from their societies and allocate them effectively, and to guarantee the rule of law. This fact undermines the effectiveness of the newly established open market institutions; prevents states from ameliorating the situation of the poor and excluded, thus reducing dualism and generating the conditions for the expansion of citizenship; also it is an important determinant of the low quality of the existing democracies. Therefore, state weakness goes a long way toward explaining the difficult and uncertain nature of the double transition.

Finally, external centripetal forces are much weaker in Latin America than they were in Spain. It is clear that neither the U.S. nor the European Union are actively involved in managing the double transition in the region in order to ensure high-quality economic and political outcomes. At most, they see Latin America as an external arena, where markets and opportunities for investment may be found. In the absence of identity commonalities, there are no substantial transfers of resources to Latin America (something akin to the structural and cohesion funds received by Spain). Moreover, some of the more developed countries' trade policies (such as agrarian subsidies, especially in Europe) are actually detrimental to the region.

The reason for the situation is that, after the demise of Communism, the current strategic environment does not create any specific impulses to reshape Latin America among the major powers. The Cold War was fought in almost every continent, and its actors were states. Even if Latin America was located at the periphery of that conflict, major powers still had strategic reasons to pay attention to the region, at least in some circumstances. Latin America remains quite irrelevant in relation to the emerging conflict between the US and other Western nations and Jihadist Islam. At most, it may become a target for terrorist actions – indeed, it has been so – or perhaps a haven for fugitive militants, but it is unlikely to become a significant strategic battleground in this new conflict.

Prospects for the Latin American Transition

Latin America remains a heterogeneous region, and prospects vary from country to country. However, only very few (Chile, and perhaps Uruguay and Costa Rica) seem to have developed an adequate institutional foundation for a market economy and a liberal democracy. At the other extreme, in Colombia, a situation amounting to state failure seems a realistic prospect, and Bolivia and Paraguay are mired in very low-quality capitalism and democracy. Most other countries are somewhere in between: They have partially liberalized economies, democratic polities in which civil rights are not strongly institutionalized, and weak states with a deficient capacity to guarantee the rule of law, regulate the economy effectively, and manage the rudiments of a welfare state.

Of the five factors discussed, the strength of civil society and the strength of the state are the only ones that could change in the near future, and the quality of Latin American economic and political outcomes will ultimately depend on performances in these two areas. Economic and social policies will be critical in this regard. If governments can manage to avoid the temptations of populism and clientelism, strengthen the fragile foundations of the new market economies, improve the institutional foundations of health and educational systems, and build sustainable welfare states, a virtuous circle could be set in motion. Economic performance would improve substantially in the long term, and the reduction of social fragmentation would lead to the strengthening of civil society and the expansion of citizenship. The feedback of these processes would strengthen both civil society and the state.

However, sustaining such policies and implementing them with a certain degree of success presupposes a level of state strength rare in contemporary Latin America. Nations unable to carry out these tasks with a modicum of effectiveness are likely to remain at the margins of modernity.

13

Notes

1 See Larry Diamond, *Developing Democracy: Toward Consolidation* (Baltimore: Johns Hopkins University Press, 1999); Samuel P. Huntington, *The Third Wave: Democratization in the Late Twentieth Century* (Norman: University of Oklahoma Press, 1991); Juan Linz and Alfred Stepan, *Problems of Democratic Transition and Consolidation* (Baltimore: Johns Hopkins University Press, 1996); Guillermo O'Donnell, Phillippe C. Schmitter, and Laurence Whitehead, *Transitions from Authoritarian Rule* (Baltimore: John Hopkins University Press, 1986); Adam Przeworski, *Democracy and the Market* (New York: Cambridge University Press, 1991).

2 World Bank, *World Development Report 1999–2000* (New York: Oxford University Press, 2000), p. 231.

3 Id., pp. 230–231.

4 World Bank, *Poverty and Human Development* (New York: Oxford University Press, 1980), p. 69.

5 Taylor, Charles L. and Michael C. Hudson, *World Handbook of Political and Social Indicators* (New Haven: Yale University Press, 1972), p. 316.

6 World Bank, *World Development Report 1999–2000*, pp. 230–231.

7 Naciones Unidas, *Informe sobre Desarrollo Humano 2002* (Madrid: Ediciones Mundi-Prensa, 2002), pp. 194–195. No data were available for Argentina.

8 Ibid., pp. 149–150.

9 World Economic Forum, *Latin American Competitiveness Report 2001–2002* (New York: Oxford University Press, 2002), p. 66.

10 For Spain, the average scores were 487 for math and 517 for science. Chilean scores were 392 and 420, and Colombia's 385 and 411. *Latin American Competitiveness Report*, p. 74.

11 On these issues, see Víctor Pérez Díaz, *Spain at the Crossroads* (Cambridge, MA: Harvard University Press, 1999), pp. 70–102.

12 For a survey of inequality in Latin America, see World Bank, *Inequality in Latin America: Breaking with History?* (Washington, D.C.: World Bank, 2004).

13 On this topic, see Simon Johnson, Daniel Kaufmann and Pablo Zoido-Lobaton, *Corruption, Public Finances and the Unofficial Economy* (Washington, D.C.: World Bank, 1999), and Joseph S. Tulchin and Ralph H. Espach (eds.), *Combating Corruption in Latin America* (Baltimore: Johns Hopkins University Press, 2000).

14 Víctor Pérez Díaz, *The Return of Civil Society: The Emergence of Democratic Spain* (Cambridge: Harvard University Press, 1993). See also Felipe Aguero, *Soldiers, Civilians and Democracy: Post-Franco Spain in Comparative Perspective* (Baltimore: Johns Hopkins University, 1995); Victor Alba, *Transition in Spain: From Franco to Democracy* (New Brunswick: Transaction, 1978); Andrea Bonime-Blanc, *Spain's Transition to Democracy: The Politics of Constitution-Making* (Boulder: Westview Press, 1987); Raymond Carr and Juan P. Fusi Aizpurua, *Spain, Dictatorship to Democracy* (Boston: Allen & Unwin, 1981); Robert M. Fishman, *Working-Class*

Organization and the Return to Democracy in Spain (Ithaca: Cornell University Press, 1990); Montserrat Guibernau, *Catalan Nationalism: Francoism, Transition, and Democracy* (New York: Routledge, 2004); Jose M. Maravall, *The Transition to Democracy in Spain* (London: St. Martin's Press, 1982); José Ramón Montero, Richard Gunther and Mariano Torcal, "Democracy in Spain: Legitimacy, Discontent, and Dissafection" (Madrid: Centro de Estudios Avanzados en Ciencias Sociales, Instituto Juan March, 1997); Cristina Palomares, *The Quest for Survival After Franco: Moderate Francoism and the Slow Journey to the Polls* (Brighton & Portland: Sussex Academic Press, 2004); Víctor Pérez-Díaz, *Spain at the Crossroads*; Paul Preston, *The Triumph of Democracy in Spain* (London: Methuen, 1986); and Donald Share, *The Making of Spanish Democracy* (New York: Praeger, 1986).

15 Alexis de Tocqueville, *Democracy in America* (New York: Doubleday, 1969), p. 517.

16 Carlos H. Waisman, "Autonomy, Self-Regulation, and Democracy: Tocquevillean and Gellnerian Perspectives on Civil Society and the Bifurcated State in Latin America", in Richard Feinberg, Carlos H. Waisman and Leon Zamosc (eds.), *Civil Society in Latin America* (forthcoming).

17 See Paloma Aguilar Fernández, *Memoria y olvido de la Guerra Civil Española* (Madrid: Alianza Editorial, 1996).

18 Blondel, Jacques, *Comparing Political Systems* (New York: Praeger, 1972), Ch. 4.

19 World Bank, *World Development Report 1987* (New York: Oxford University Press, 1987), pp. 246–247.

20 World Bank, *World Development Report 1999–2000* (New York: Oxford University Press, 2000), pp. 256–257. No data for Brazil were available in this source.

21 Ibid.

22 World Economic Forum, *Global Competitiveness Report 2000* (New York: Oxford University Press, 2000), p. 239.

23 See Pilar Ortuno Anaya, *European Socialists and Spain: The transition to Democracy 1959–77* (New York: Palgrave, 2002).

24 This discussion is based on Carlos H. Waisman, "Civil Society, State Capacity, and the Conflicting Logics of Economic and Political Change," in Philip Oxhorn and Pamela Starr (eds.), *Market or Democracy?* (Boulder: Lynne Rienner, 1998). See also Ahrend Lijphart and Carlos H. Waisman (eds.), *Institutional Design in New Democracies* (Boulder: Westview Press, 1997, pp. 235–237.

25 Ibid.

26 See World Economic Forum, *Latin American Competitiveness Report 2001–2002*, pp. 138, 140.

PART I

INSTITUTIONAL AND CULTURAL DIMENSIONS OF THE SPANISH TRANSITION

1

IMAGINED MEMORY AS THE WEIGHT OF THE PAST
POLITICAL TRANSITIONS IN SPAIN
Enric Ucelay-Da Cal

In recent years, there has been abundant discussion of the role of "memory" in the configuration of long-term socio-political attitudes. Nora's compilation of French "Lieux de Mémoire", by inviting historians to study monuments and calendar celebrations, and evaluate their emotional impact over time, inspired doctoral dissertations throughout Europe. Established in the mid-1980s, this critical fashion was also fed by Hobsbawm's "invention of tradition," as well as by Anderson's proposal to understand nationalism as "imagined community." Today, such influential works clearly represent interpretative orthodoxy at work. Their historiographic importance is so overwhelming that it bears serious reexamination.

What is "memory"? According to standard dictionary definitions, memory is the individual and collective recollection of the past, as well as certain forms of organization that such retrieval implies. Memory is also the personal and social rituals that can accompany the recollection of significant events. The dictionaries, however, do not differentiate between the detailed quality of such recollection, its accuracy as measured retrospectively against sources, and its emotional intensity. The power of memory, especially if reinforced by reiteration, is so strong that it easily develops into moral certitude, oblivious of what can be dismissed as pointless detail or even malicious mischief; once embarked upon such a course, the strength of conviction can take on a clearly constitutional meaning. All political systems ultimately refer to a founding mythology, which at best can only resist intense analytic scrutiny by denouncing interpretative nihilism.

Memory's capacity to distort – a concept as old as Freud – was perhaps the central aspect of the reinterpretation sought by French and British analysts at the end of the last century. Hobsbawm and Anderson purported that such distortion was advantageous to those in power, although it is clear that any protest movement must weave a sort of fiction of what could happen to justify their predictions. The question, therefore, is how important is a fact that is inherently contra-factual to a political understanding? How "real" are the suppositions on which self-confident political "realists" base themselves? This paper will attempt to present the problem of intense selective memory in a relatively closed political situation. Over time, in progressively acute crises, politicians have believed that their policies regarding régime change have been based on the rational assessment of previous events. In truth, their choices are derived from crucial misunderstandings of foregoing options. I shall argue that such "rational" assessment stems in fact from ideology, and that any other interpretation would be Machiavellian (defined as the politician systematically thinking one thing, saying another, and doing a third). This is both psychologically untenable for the individual leader and ineffective as a communication base.

All régime changes per force somehow refer to the origins of those institutions being rejected. If that which is overthrown is necessarily deemed illegitimate (at least partly, otherwise the present transformation would itself be lacking in legitimacy), the origins of the *ancien régime* are themselves questionable. If nothing else, there is a need to relate to the legal and practical precedent they set: the political genealogy of the political system being eliminated may serve as a discreditable beginning that justifies current actions; more perversely, this genealogy may serve as an example. Thus, the last coup or revolution qualifies the nature of its successor. Paradoxically, revolutionaries, conspirators and politicians share a common view of the nature of the previous change, and their own immediate intentions as well as their public statements and later evaluations must be adjusted accordingly.

To develop this observation, I shall discuss the five "transitions" which have marked Spanish politics between December 1874, when a "pronunciamiento" (pronouncement of military revolt) shut down the experiment in republican army rule *á la* MacMahon and reestablished the primacy of the main branch of the Bourbon dynasty with a liberal parliamentary system, and at present, with a monarchy and democratic government. The remaining four "transitions" occurred in the twentieth century: the coup by general Primo de Rivera that overthrew the parliamentary system in 1923, the overthrow of the monarchy and the proclamation of the II Republic in 1931, the Civil War of 1936–1939, resulting in the Franco régime, and, finally, the establishment of the current system in 1976–1978. In all cases, the major players miscalculated the preceding process, thus qualifying both their strategic and tactical decisions.

Celebratory, Condemnatory, and Tactical Memory

Since the collapse of the Soviet system, the terms "memory," "identity," and other related terms have become buzzwords in political science and historiography, thrown about with relative abandon, as if their meaning was clear and easily defined. Nevertheless, just as many simultaneous "identities" can exist in a person or persons at any time, politics use varied and even exclusive types of remembrance. Several historians, including Radcliffe in "Gijón under the II Republic", or Aguilar in The "Democratic Transition" of the late 1970s seen from Madrid", have attempted to follow the use of the past in constructing a "civic religion" (to use Comte's term) or a "civic culture" as posited by Almond and Verba. Such studies, however, do not differentiate between degrees of use of the images, merely emphasizing the ritual invocation of historic events and the alterations that public reference to the past might undergo in times of political stress.

Surprisingly, given the importance of metaphor and simile in such ideological codification, there has been relatively little recourse to critical theory of literature, beyond the reckless borrowing of formulae such as an "imaginary." Perhaps the emphasis of postmodern cultural studies on ostentatiously restrictive models with their forbidding neo-philosophical vocabulary has not appealed to historians, while political scientists with their own jargon, are even less disposed to an alternative discipline. In any case, historians, adamantly adhering to the facts but otherwise rather eclectic in their choice of interpretative models, might consider learning from the practitioners of cultural studies, while communicating their own preoccupations to that rather historicist, but scarcely factualist, discipline, which might also gain from the exchange.

To employ the language of literary critical theory, narratives can be constructed around a past event, the choice of which, by highlighting a certain set of chronological events, is a creative act. This produces a storyline, which is ennobled by being defined "historically" significant and above the chaotic flow of infinite mundane occurrences, i.e., life's daily events. Cultural studies, traditionally dependent on French concepts, term these narratives "discourses." All modern social movements attempt to harness history in this "discursive" fashion. In Spain, dynastic legitimists, exalted Catholics, Republicans, enthusiasts of working-class movements, as well as Catalan, Basque and other nationalists, have all tried to create alternative chronologies to the allegedly false, "statist" version of collective history. This official version jousts with sophisticated and popular versions for the retrospective unity of each respective cause. During the last two centuries, this has produced a considerable body of partisan historiography. As Boyd has shown, the proliferation of various historical narrations repeatedly made it difficult to establish a "national" and/or "standard" history enjoying sufficient consensus so as to be unquestioned by a majority of citizens (or political consumers), and flexible enough to incorporate or discard details, as political fashions wax and wane, as happens in more stable political systems. On the contrary, Spain has suffered numerous rival "civic religions" (including traditional or fundamentalist versions), but to date has not achieved a functional "civic culture" able to standardize schoolbook explanations and amend the terms of historiographic or "poli-sci" debate. Instead, Spain has suffered from a civil war culture, in which one-sided and predisposed arguments are the norm, and interpretative positions regarding the past are judge by party affiliation or political friendships.

Major political events, such as régime change, are thus awarded greater or lesser importance, depending on the ideological perspective of each historical date. In any event what becomes common to all "discourses" must necessarily be integrated as either positive or negative: it must be explained and evaluated from the prejudiced perspective of a particular cause and of the inherited past. At its simplest, any narrative concordant with a "discourse" is presented as a confrontation between the forces of good and evil, with a diabolical battle as a teleology; the "good" engaged in an ascendant struggle to realize the "chiliasm", the reign of God and goodness on earth, must like all heroes, pass through a myriad trials and defeats before attaining the collective goal. Conversely, the agents of evil defend what amounts to "hell on earth." This binary option can be understood as a celebratory or a condemnatory memory. In other words, an historic date which, from a determined political perspective, is perceived either as a "good" step toward the ideal end, or as a "bad" step backward, to be overcome through faith and perseverance. Logically in this context, every celebration is also a condemnation of what was defeated. In a political climate such as Spain's, where resentment and rancor over continued civil war have plagued society long after the events, time offers no cure, no healing which could permit the quarreling sides to join hands in a shared remembrance. The past is linear, but the memory to which it is harnessed is essentially circular and unforgiving.

Both celebration and condemnation are "discourses" that unite a cause and establish a defensive circle and differentiate between inside ("good") and outside ("bad"). Accordingly, they are an appeal to the rank and file, a formal invitation to the doubtful to join. Such discourses affirm the potential openness of an unending, all-inclusive circle, and are intended more to assuage guilty consciences than to be actively applied. Such memory serves an immediate political purpose; it is incantatory, magical, not analytical. It reminds all participants of the long-term meaning of their cause, and underlines the moral significance of the group's strategy. But it cannot be used to design tactics, because it would produce immediate distortions in judgment. Therefore the leadership needs an alternative view of crucial events of the past, of major political inflections, which change the course of collective development. Those seeking to alter political evolution by radical change of some kind must employ a tactical memory, which, from whatever sources, closely replicates the "real" motives and options behind past régime change, so as to better distinguish the probabilities behind immediate choice in the present or near future.

Undoubtedly, this is a real problem. How does leadership move beyond the certitudes of celebratory/condemnatory memory, so as to best assess potential tactical memory? This paper argues that, in Spanish politics, leaders tend to look back only as far as the last major régime change. They interpret the most recent change through a mixture of fact and fiction, of both kinds of memory, and combine simplistic, moralistic perceptions with a cynical awareness of dealings taking place behind the scenes. As a result, each régime change tends to be "a take" on the immediately preceding change, lacking any serious reflection on political patterns.

1874: A Military Coup to Establish Parliamentary Order

A recent study estimated that over the last two centuries in Spain experienced some five hundred coup attempts, including approximately forty plots with some measure of credibility. The invasion of Napoleon, backed by constitutional justification (the Bayonne Constitution), coincided with an internal coup (the "motín de Aranjuez," the overthrow of Godoy and Fernando VII usurping his father) that sent the country into upheaval, marked by military occupation, internal warring and foreign intervention. The civil war between liberal and traditionalist "patriotas" against the "josefinos" ultimately resulted in armed confrontations between royalists and independents in the American colonies. Urban Spain was formally pacified in 1814, yet civil war continued on Spanish "Tierra Firme" until the royalist cause was defeated in 1824. The counterexample of the American struggle inspired numerous liberal military revolts in the Peninsula, and a three-year liberal régime was crushed by French (royalist) occupation after 1823. The liberal model of uprising stimulated absolutist armed protest against Fernando's rule, placing the Crown in a difficult position. Fernando's death in 1833 created a succession crisis, with high political stakes during seven years of renewed civil war between the defenders of a "traditional" monarchy and "progressives" and "moderates" who believed in a liberal solution. Spain's "liberal revolution," from the mid-1830s to 1874, was thus a confusing conflict between factions, often spilling into open combat, marked by a potpourri of coups. There were so many coups that Spanish historiography distinguishes between a strict "golpe de Estado" (coup d'état) and a "pronunciamiento", a change by implication, in which the mere threat of action in a manifesto achieved the desired effect.

The descriptive simplicity of classic histoire "événementielle" or the cheerful tempering of chronological celebration, poorly reflects such political turbulence. The usual way to make sense of such chaos is to impose a rudimentary periodization that misperceives much of the liberal infighting and the variety of political positions among both liberals and strict traditionalists. In this regard, Catholic dynastic legitimists had a single explicit point to make: no governmental power in modern Spain has been able to boast undisputed legitimacy. This is still true today. The exercise of power, rather than any longstanding or widespread consensus, has provided the authority to rule: de facto has been consistently de jure. Naturally, any group wielding power has indignantly denied such a premise. Most historical explanations prefer external criticism, as if this were somehow more ethical. There is therefore no intellectual tradition of systemic loyalty, beyond the immediate benefits of short-term align-ment. Even when arguing such radical interpretations however, historians, as members of a professional association, always have tended to seek government jobs (as functionaries in universities, for example), and by extension, approval. This is the longstanding structural paradox of the "business of memory" in Spain.

Spain experienced a stable parliamentary monarchy from 1875 to 1923. However, the origin of the "restoration" (which enthroned Alfonso XII) was a military coup, led by General Martínez Campos in Sagunto on 29 December 1874. Although its antecedents can be discerned in previous military actions, the Sagunto coup exhibited a basic pattern, which deter-mined the future of régime change for the following century in Spanish politics. First, Martínez Campos acted impulsively, jumping the gun and directly contravening agreements or orders coming from the "alfonsista" leadership. While most Hispanic cultures share a certain anthropological conviction, that defines clever improvisation as somehow morally and practically superior to careful preparation, the coup derived its strength from a perceived political vacuum. The government, under General Serrano as head of State, was in effect provisional, but unlike the gobierno provisional of 1868–1870, there did not appear to be any clear direction. Following a monarchy under Amadeus I of Savoy (elected 16 November 1870 – abdicated 11 February 1873), and a rapidly evolving succession of republican governments (11 February 1873–3 January 1874), political opinion was unable to instill faith in the people. Republican governments, especially "cantonalist," were measured against the 1871 Paris Commune, while the military régime that followed also seemed to parallel later French events. Thus, beyond the usual illegitimacy inherently asso-ciated with all modern Spanish governments, the Serrano *República de los duques*, an emergency wartime alternative with Sagasta as prime minister (3 September–29 December), bore an additional burden of doubt. Lacking a systemic description, being neither Republic nor Monarchy, nor even a *sui generis* proposal for some kind of conceptual future, it was doubly illegitimate by Spanish standards. While any specific formula of government might be loathed, the lack of a systemic approach is especially abhorrent in Hispanic eyes. As elsewhere, ambiguity is essential in Spanish politics, but, in a society in which the law represents the pinnacle of science and knowledge, it must always be categorizable and definable in legal terms.

The perceived political vacuum was thus a clear advantage to the rebels, but it permitted Martínez Campos to appear as leading coup maker. By making a formal statement, he could cast a possible consensus for generic change to become an active consensus for régime change. The ambitious general could take a situation that was politically "exhausted," and promise "parliamentary order" which could gather enough support from diverse political opinions to become credible. He could then get on with fighting the civil wars in Spain against the Carlists and in Cuba against the independentists, reaching some kind of conclusion, between 1876 and 1878. Foreign observers, such as German historian Treitschke, saluted Alfonso XII as example of the successful monarch. These three easy levels of implication leading to the 1874 coup thus determined the paradigm for all future structural change in the Spanish State. All successive changes would be formulated in these terms. The question was not only 'when?' but also 'how?'

1923: A Military Coup Against Parliamentary Disorder

Until revamped by the socialists in the late 1980s, Spain's administration has traditionally been divided into two parallel structures, one civil and the other military. Provinces had both civil and military governors, a reminder of how nineteenth century liberalism was uncomfortably grafted onto the pre-existing military trunk, grown under Bourbon auspices and French influence in the eighteenth century. Until the 1874 "Restoration" and the Constitution of 1876, captain-generals had unchallenged authority to dismiss civilian officials if they challenged army superiority. Conservative leader Cánovas del Castillo considered as his first job the channeling of the generals into regular party politics through non-elective senate seats, thus allowing the law makers to have control over the legislature, scrutinized only by brave newspapermen, journalism having become the standard method of socio-political promotion. But Cánovas' success was relative – by establishing essentially corporative rules, the army and navy controlled their respective ministries and military spending, which granted them ultimate leverage on the budget and its proportionate investment. The understanding was indeed functional, in that the coups basically ceased, the last being a republican failure in 1887; the custom of plotting, however, continued, and the threat of military action was never far from politics.

It was the "long government" of Sagasta (1885–1890) that created a certain juridical coherence between the "Whig" conquests of the "Glorious Revolution" of 1868–1869, and the "moderado" counterrevolution led politically by Cánovas. The liberals reinstituted trial by jury, habeas corpus, common commercial and civil law codes, encouraged the freeing of slaves , reimposed universal male suffrage, and eventually, later in the 1890s, granted autonomy to the Antilles, although by then such overseas reform was hopeless. But, as Cánovas himself rather cynically pointed out in 1888, while the conservatives had reinstituted the Crown with its promise of stability, the liberals failed to initiate uncorrupt elections that would enable the parliamentary system to expand socially and prosper. Thus "systemic loyalty" was confused with dynastic fidelity. Republicans and Carlists were excluded from the arrangements. They were included in parliament with the express hope of "turning them round" individually, as opinion makers, rather than effectively integrating the opinion they represented, a task considered impossible. As long as compliance was a working form of representation, this succeeded. But, over time, expanding corporative politics, the pressure of civil society (especially in Catalonia), and the increased demand for party participation in parliament beyond the pattern of "notabilities" or "fuerzas vivas", all made effective legislative reform impossible.

The colonial wars of the mid-1890s constituted a huge effort: Spain dispatched to Cuba some 200,000 men, the largest army to cross the Atlantic from Europe to America. These wars sowed the seeds of political insubordination and popular uniformed activism among low-ranking officers, a style born of the "españolista" volunteer units in the Antilles, and previously unknown to Spanish politics. After 1898, civilian rule was endangered by the mid-ranking military, rather than by older high-ranking generals, who increasingly followed trends set by lower-ranking officers. Furthermore, much military activity created a vociferous press, capable of exerting considerable pressure both on constitutional parties and on ex-constitutional opinion. The increasing intervention of Spanish forces in Northern Morocco, a formal protectorate after 1912, further complicated the issue of political militarism, as army factions clashed over the benefits vs. costs of colonial war. After late 1916, intra-military squabbling became a crucial factor in regular politics, greatly affecting the rise and fall of governments. In 1921, a costly defeat in the Riff even implicated the Crown: the following year Spaniards could choose between alternative options of the fate of Greece, where a similar debacle led to the downfall of the monarchy, or that of Italy, where paramilitary subversive groups reached an agreement with the king and organized a new cabinet, eventually forging a distinctive dictatorship.

General Miguel Primo de Rivera instituted a self-defined "dictadura", alluding to a Cincinnatus-type of brief emergency rule. The two-tier system of Spanish administration gave military provincial governors (and, above them, regional commanders or captain-generals) considerable latitude in matters of public conduct, which was ultimately understood to be a military responsibility, rather than a police matter dependent on the civil governor. Primo de Rivera contrived his coup from his regional command in Catalonia. After 1917, Barcelona's labour troubles sparked increasing activism among military authorities, who took over the civil police, until they controlled most non-elective civilian posts. The 1922 attempt by the conservative Sánchez-Guerra to reestablish civilian control clearly contributed to his downfall later that year, a situation which Primo, commencing his Barcelona post, used to good advantage. Violent social conflict and terrorism by rival unions facilitated the lack of a civil governor, and Primo was unchallenged during the fateful summer of 1923, until he conducted his coup on 13 September.

The central government was in liberal hands from December 1922, but García Prieto's cabinet, with Santiago Alba the prominent figure in Foreign Affairs, was a weak coalition with an unstable majority in parliament. The government was generally considered incompetent in handling both a new wave of terrorism and a major series of strikes, as well as mutinous sentiments among troops embarking for Morocco; Catalan and Basque radical nationalists publicly supporting an alliance with Riffian "rebels." Accordingly, Primo knew he was working in a perceived political vacuum. Given his eloquence, Primo successfully persuaded extremely diverse political elements to cooperate and accept a military coup led by himself. He was capable of talking enemies (such as Catalan regionalists and Spanish nationalists in Catalonia) into agreement, and of bringing opposing military factions to near consensus. Alfonso XIII acceded or was pressured into connivance with the conspirators. Primo succeeded because he promised unprecedented reform. He vowed to clean up the worst problems in lawlessness, bureaucratic inefficiency and corruption, and to pass legislative reforms that parliamentary backlog had impeded – all within three months. Strictly speaking, he was not proposing to form a government at all, but an emergency military cabinet, lacking parliamentary status, a "military directorate" understood to be a temporary dictatorship charged with sanitizing government institutions.

Primo could offer such a solution, capable of garnering considerable support for limited change, across the political spectrum, because of Dato's mediocre political leadership. In 1913–1915, conservative premier Dato, faced with the collapse of the liberal party as a cohesive parliamentary bloc followed by the immediate splintering of his own conservative party, dealt with parliamentary instability and party fragmentation by ruling by royal decree and extending the Cortes' vacations as long as legally possible. Primo appeared when parliament was on summer recess; hence the king technically had the power to create a substitute government that need answer only to the king, not to the Cortes. The king's decision to suspend the constitution was legally questionable, but could be justified by the state of emergency, if the Directorio adhered to the announced short-term schedule. The crunch came a few months later, when the presidents of the Chamber and the Senate reminded the monarch that constitutional law dictated that both houses be assembled. Primo forced the king's hand and took the plunge. After November 1923, the dictatorship began to exclude sectors that had joined Primo's reform program with varying degrees of enthusiasm, but now distanced themselves or were pushed aside by others willing to gamble on the eventual legalization of the new political situation. Primo used the worsening military situation in the Moroccan protectorate during 1924–1925 that increasingly monopolized the dictator's attention, as an excuse for his growing indifference to his domestic program.

Primo's gamble paid off in the second half of 1925. The dynamics of the social base of Riffian leader Abd el-Krim forced him to advance beyond the stalemated limits fixed by the Spanish, and attack the French protectorate. This in turn meant French backing for Primo and a joint offensive. The defeat of the Riffians marked Primo's highpoint, which he celebrated by declaring the Directorio a "Civilian Government," progressively announcing details about summoning a "National Assembly" which would "consult" with the new cabinet regarding the future constitution of Spain. Here Primo overreached himself. By what legal authority did the self-proclaimed dictator normalize government without recognizing the Constitution? On what juridical basis did he presume to supersede the previous basic law? What guarantees did a "constitutional monarch" who reigned outside the still legal, but "suspended," Constitution, offer?

The perception of the coup as a break with established legal custom, the audacity of calling the improvised emergency political situation a "dictatorship," all the visible aspects of Primo's initiative in 1923, which may have indeed seemed brilliant in terms of a three-month operation, began to play against the extension of his rule. As soon as Primo's juridically undefined situation became the precursor for some future extended régime, his rule took on aspects of a *fuite en devant*. Opposition, at first sparse, grew, to become an invisible fixture in all political considerations.

By going too far, Primo had broken the unwritten code of constitutional custom, an unspoken agreement that conservatives and liberals succeeded each other in government and as the parliamentary majority. The liberals had waited for Primo's declared emergency situation to resume the natural order: a new liberal government, to be followed by the conservatives who felt that after the dictatorial interlude, their turn had come. Now both had nothing to lose. In June 1925, with the king's assistance, the liberals, followed by a liberal-conservative coalition in January 1929, tried to imitate Primo's coup in reverse, that is, to declare that the dictator was operating in a legal vacuum, and restore a modified version of the 1876 Constitution. Despite appearances, such a "constitutional based" approach meant the eventual judgment of the monarch. This, in turn, meant that dissident liberals (Santiago Alba, specifically threatened by Primo's manifesto in 1923 and forced to flee) and republicans could negotiate with radical nationalists and anarcho -syndicalists, all enemies of the dictatorship. After all, who could oppose the return to "constitutional liberties" (freedom of the press and freedom of assembly, free elections, the right for labour to organize)?

This meant that the desire for immediate change could extend to a full-scale régime change. Everyone knew that the heir to the throne was a hopeless hemophiliac (like his youngest sibling), and his next brother was deaf, due to a childhood ear infection. Any proposal for abdication or a monarchy without the current king meant, in practice, establishment of a republic. Any alternative would necessarily mean a messy succession struggle. Alfonso thought he could use this unfortunate dynastic fact as a threat, but his game of playing both sides during the Dictatorship left him with scant personal credit. "Constitutionalists" and liberals both believed the monarch should be curbed, and both kept their distance or demanded a higher price than Alfonso was willing to pay, at least until there was little alternative. The king finally acted openly against Primo in 1929, after the dictator had inexplicably abandoned both his project to implement a new constitution, which would somehow perpetuate his "system," and his promised retirement.

1931: A Civilian Coup to Reestablish Parliamentary Order

The republicans supported the liberals and "constitutionalists" during the dictatorship. But they also profited from this secondary role. In 1926, in preparation for the liberal coup that failed, the diverse republican families were able to unite with the excuse of celebrating the anniversary of the brief 1873 Republic. Thus the "historic" republicans, like Lerroux or the followers of novelist Blasco Ibáñez, were able to join hands with "new" republicans, like Manuel Azaña, newly recruited from the liberal reformism of Melquíades Álvarez. The Catalan republicans, with their own special line, also participated. In the shadow of liberal initiative and conspiring, Spanish republicanism, after periodic attempts, was able to implement successfully a united campaign under circumstances that proved extremely favorable. Furthermore, as they insisted on the unification, they also inherited the network of conspiracy (especially among military officers, particularly artillerymen, who resolutely resisted Primo's military reform plan) that the liberals and the "constitutionalists" left behind as they progressively turned to political action and abandoned insurrectional tactics. The remains of the "constitutionalist" plot led by Sánchez Guerra in early 1929 (who was arrested, court martialed for treason and acquitted, signaling military displeasure with the dictator) were taken over by Lerroux's Andalusian Lieutenant Martínez Barrio; General Goded used the republican presence as a negotiating point with the king, forcing the monarch finally to drop Primo at the beginning of 1930.

The dismissal of the dictator, particularly considering how it was achieved, proved disastrous for Alfonso. The "primorriveristas" were outraged at the unceremonious ousting of their hero and cooled toward the king (the dictator's eldest son, who devoted himself thereafter to righting the alleged wrong, founded the infamous Falange in 1933). The transition was a planned operation, which had to produce a new government headed by Cambó, head of the Catalan regionalists and the outstanding internal opponent of Primo; Cambó was backed by Gabriel Maura, and carefully prepared a broad conservative party throughout Spain, which could guarantee genuine reform, starting with regional change. But, when he returned from Paris, Cambó discovered he had cancer. Without explaining his reasons (cancer was synonymous with death and Cambó was not betting on recovery), the Catalan leader refused the responsibility, and Maura supported him. Alfonso was forced to turn to General Dámaso Berenguer, who offered no convincing political warranty and had no real talent for the job. Berenguer's immediate response to the urgency of transition was to procrastinate, and he quickly lost what political capital he might have had. The mechanical transition to "constitutional normality" became an open question, a visible political vacuum that threatened the continued rule of the crown. Both liberals (after some discussion between their leaders, including Alba) and the "constitutionalists" refused to participate in "normal" legislative elections, and adhered to the dangerous threat of a constituent parliament. The republicans were delighted, and enjoyed following their lead, while rebuilding contacts in preparation for an armed revolt to counter any electoral development.

The tactical struggle over elections between Berenguer, supported by conservatives, and the demands of liberals and "constitutionalists," permitted the republicans to expand. Ex-monarchists (like the liberal Niceto Alcalá-Zamora or the conservative Miguel Maura) became opportunist converts. They believed that monarchic substitution was impossible. The only hope for an orderly future would be a Republic "without price," in the sense that the core of the 1876 Constitution would be preserved, by changing the nature of the Head of State, and correcting those aspects of executive or legislative practice known to be defective. This was an undisguised call for régime change by consensus, hence the supposition that it could be carried out without a price.

At the same time, the republicans, including the newly converted, hedged their bets and, in a famous meeting in San Sebastián in August 1930, prepared for rebellion according to the usual pattern, as in 1926 and 1929. Despite previous failures, the plan once again amended Primo's coup by expecting military civilian collaboration in the revolt. Due to disagreement in republican ranks, two "revolutionary committees" were established, one in Madrid and one in Barcelona. These two separate committees manifested a deeper incompatibility between the defenders of the "cost-free" moderate Republic and the more radical partisans of "a revolution within the revolution," aimed at producing a "syndical Republic." The latter accepted the agenda for revolt but intended to rechannel it farther left. This discrepancy helps explain the well-known confusion over the date of the uprising in mid-December 1930, which splintered the initiative, and facilitated Berenguer's response. But, once again, Berenguer's scant political talent lost him his momentary gains: the execution of military leaders, although juridically justified, alienated popular support, and definitively dismissed any possibility of "normal" elections. Berenguer resigned, and an unusual interim followed during which Sánchez-Guerra (who had publicly stated he would never again serve the king) attempted to piece together a cabinet with some of the "newest" republican conspirators, who refused him, knowing that such a step gave them greater power. The result, in February 1931, was a new cabinet with representatives from all major monarchist groups, a classic Catalan trump, engineered by Romanones and Cambó, with Admiral Aznar, titular head of the 1926 liberal revolt, at the front. The new Aznar government promised Catalan autonomy, the future dispersal of power, and municipal elections. The left could not resist the political prizes (republicanism was built on local patronage), which assured skeptics that due electoral process – first municipal, then provincial, and finally, legislative – would follow. But the coalition of monarchists had tricked the leftists. Without the "constitutionalists," burned out by Sánchez-Guerra's inexplicable midnight escapade, all reference to constituent change was forgotten, in lieu of a promise of mere "normal" legislative reform.

The municipal elections were meticulously presided over by an "inexperienced" interior minister, who demanded faultless behavior from monarchists, but was indulgent toward the left. To almost everyone's surprise, in the 12 April 1931 election, socialist-republican candidates

31

won in most major urban centers, with the exception of some rural capitals. On Tuesday morning, 14 April (no newspaper was published on Monday at the time), there was considerable expectation. The left wing of the republican coalition – in Barcelona, the CNT and those republicans who communicated with the anarchosyndicalists, elsewhere with greater socialist intervention – took the initiative, and began to provoke "revolutionary" seizures of mayoralties, according to what was deemed a popular "plebiscite." Although the socialists in the Basque town Eibar were the first to do so, the maneuver really began with the occupation of Barcelona's municipal hall, and the proclamation of a "federal" republic, followed by a similar operation in the provincial government building, in which the Catalan Republic and Iberian Confederation were added on for good measure. Radio broadcasts spread the good news. The republicans and their allies convoked the "masses" to a festive participation in the change of the political system.

This activity, much of it coordinated by telephone (for example, in La Mancha), presented the Aznar government with a no-win situation: the government could open fire on the happy demonstrators, forgetting about constitutional "normality" and the next elections, or it could give up. Either way, it lost and the republicans won. Perhaps the most perfect coup in Spanish history due to its being invisible, the proclamation of the Republic established the myth of a happy beginning, the official holiday celebrating the foundation of a new system, and veiled the reality of a calculated civilian masterstroke. From its inception, the new republican régime was confronted with the contrast between the perception of change and the subtle methods by which it had been realized.

1936: The Simultaneity of Military and Civilian Options

Not surprisingly, it was not long before someone tried to apply to the new republican "provisional government" the same trick that had brought it to power. The left wing of the republican movement – particularly the anarchosyndicalists, and their "ultra-republican" allies, envious of socialist participation in the new cabinet – understood success as a call to renew the prospect of "a revolution within the revolution" and a "syndical Republic" which would not require elections and political parties to participate in parliament. Beginning on May 1 in Barcelona, anarchosyndicalists took to the streets as an alternative to the voting booths: a few days later, on May 11, they instigated a series of church burnings from Madrid to much of the South, intending to alienate Catholics and conservatives from the moderate "newest" republicans such as Alcalá-Zamora and Miguel Maura. They were extremely successful. Although the anarchosyndicalists obtained certain goals such as the unicameral legislature and the anticlerical articles of the new constitution, these measures were basically sops, delivered by Azaña, who, after October, replaced both the ex-monarchists and the "historic" Lerroux as the leading figure, firmly allied with the socialists. Any federal structure was ruled out, once the Catalan left acceded to an autonomy only for itself rather than a generalized, systemic devolution. This meant that the anarchosyndicalists – or their "revolutionary" leadership – were trapped in a hostile position toward the new institutions, and maintained constant pressure from the streets with terrorist activities and three major revolts in 1932–1933, until finally, after the socialists had disengaged from Azaña, Lerroux was elected in December of that year. Aside from any illusions harboured by enthusiastic militants at the base level, the anarchosyndicalist revolt was never designed to triumph, but rather to apply pressure. The anarchosyndicalists inherited the failed pattern of civilian military interaction pioneered by liberals and "constitutionalists" against the dictatorship, and which the republicans had attempted, with equal lack of success, against Berenguer and the Monarchy in 1930. It was not a favorable combination, and after their initial impact during the first month of republican rule there were clear limits to what the libertarians could accomplish.

Surprisingly, this same pattern of civilian revolt and military coup, while emphasizing different parts of the formula, served as the basis for all the conspiracies of the II Republic, both of the left and the right. The 1931 revision of electoral law created a tendency toward large, unitary candidacies, one of the many ways (unicameralism, a weak Head of State) the republicans attempted to correct the flaws of the old régime. This resulted in a lopsided, uneven voting pattern. First, in the June 1931 elections, the left was over-represented in relation to its real sociological constituency, and later, in November 1933, the same happened to the right. The right's frustration with what was perceived as their exclusion led to an insurrectional response – the August 1932 revolt of general Sanjurjo. Defeat of this revolt taught the right the value of unity, as was evidenced by their victory at the polls the following year. The overconfident left, convinced that it "was" Spain and feeling superior, was plagued by infighting, and the fall of the electoral parties that had been forged in 1929–1931. Divided in the 1933 election campaign, the left lost, and expressed its resentment in the October 1934 revolt, which, at least in Catalonia, had hoped for army clemency in what was to be a magical replay of the foundational celebration of the 14 April. Electoral defeat thus resulted in a failed revolt, but the anger of repeated defeat produced electoral unity and a new victory. For the left, the "Popular Front" was the miracle-worker, which put everything right in February 1936.

An instable background with serious implications for the survival of republican institutions was behind this almost ritualized exchange of polls and guns shared by both left and right. The weakness of republican parties that had allowed Azaña initially to triumph also caused the socialists to emulate the plurality behind republicanism. However the socialists were not strict republicans, and had their own ideological agenda, which went beyond systemic loyalty to the Republic. Similarly, Lerroux's apparent triumph in 1933 actually brought the CEDA to the foreground, and as opposed to the socialists, this coalition had serious demands for redesigning the republican system. The backward and forward effect of oscillating votes made the slow stabilization of the Republic imperceptible, even unwelcome to both sides that were drawn into a process of rapid polarization. By the spring of 1936, while the socialists tore themselves apart discussing the best kind of revolution, even as they relished and took for granted the triumph of the "Popular Front," the right was determined to launch a pre-emptive counter-revolution. All the parties opposed to the spread of frentepopulismo agreed that this would bring the process initiated in 1931 to a full, definitive stop.

The conspirators had one major structural problem: they could establish only a broad negative goal. The only issue they agreed on was the overthrow of the Popular Front government, its parliamentary majority (which they were sure had been obtained by underhand politics) and perhaps the President of the Republic (since April, Azaña). Beyond that, there was no clear objective and many favored a new sort of Republic (like Portugal, perhaps Mola's preference), while others favored a monarchical solution, but could neither decide on the candidate (ex-king Alfonso, his son Juan, the elderly Carlist pretender, or his proposed "regent"), nor the means by which the new monarch would be proclaimed (constituent Cortes, as Sanjurjo seemed to want, a classic restoration, or a more direct instauration, as the neo-royalists advocated). As a result, the key conspirators decided to aim for military unity, while avoiding all discussion of positive aims, i.e., which system should replace the loathed Popular Front. The decision that was reached attained firm concurrence among officers – demanding much political ambiguity – and postponed resolving the political content of the uprising until after victory, when appropriate representative figures would be convoked. Some major figures of the hard right – rival monarchists Goicoechea and Calvo Sotelo, and financier Juan March – were tapped for funding, and were kept abreast of developments, but were not allowed to participate in the decision-making process.

The initial premise was that the chaos obliged the army to invoke, province by province, unrestricted emergency powers regarding public order, with the military governor removing his civil colleague and taking charge. The conspirators judged that the government was illegally encouraging social violence, and had lost its constitutional mandate; it was a political vacuum by inference, comparable to Primo de Rivera's accusation against the Liberal Union cabinet in 1923. But it also represented the challenge of 14 April 1931 in reverse: in the face of countless demonstrations, the army was quick to open fire, and indiscriminately carried out arrests, detaining anyone suspected of hostility, regardless of rank. Just as General Goded had successfully negotiated in December 1929, he might have done the same with President Azaña, to force the government to withdraw (perhaps even the presidency) without bloodshed, but regardless of his intentions, Azaña refused him an audience.

Azaña and premier Casares Quiroga underestimated the extent of support for the coup (relying on information from extreme left-wing officers) and trusted police tactics. They envisioned a colonial military rebellion, which could be isolated by police commandos. In any case, police action against mid-level leaders in Melilla apparently ignited the coup on Friday 17 July, which then proceeded haphazardly over the next two days. The dilatory nature of the uprising – probably a reflection of doubt among less committed officers – allowed for a variety of street reactions by syndicates and by left-wing parties. Azaña, realizing that police force was not an option, moved to replace Casares with the third constitutional authority, the president of the Cortes, Martínez Barrio, a moderate republican with good contacts across the ideological center. Barrio was the perfect choice to insist on the utmost importance of legal procedure. Martínez Barrio spent the night between Saturday and Sunday on the phone convincing numerous commanders to stall. But renowned rebel Mola refused to compromise. Barrio assured the "loyalty" of the Northern coast, and more importantly, the railroad line from Alicante-Cartagena and Valencia to Madrid. This assured defense of the capital, even if the situation should get desperate. His success guaranteed the failure of the coup and defined the territorial division of what quickly turned into civil war. Over the coming weeks, both sides – believing in opposed but symmetrical ideas of betrayal – tended to arrest and execute those that had responded to Martínez Barrio's call. On Sunday the 19th July, leftist socialist Largo Caballero, with communist support, threatened mass opposition to the Barrio cabinet in Madrid, and Azaña folded, naming a trusted follower as new premier, and sending Barrio to control the Valencian lifeline.

Because of the fragility of the conspiracy's political program, the coup had to move fast to succeed; once stopped, the response had to be equally swift to conquer. The incapacity of both sides to win and their common unwillingness to surrender produced the war. The relevance of the internal Spanish conflict was magnified by the lack of contemporary crises in the vicinity other than the Palestinian revolt against the British. The republican cause retained the formal legitimacy of its electoral and parliamentary origins, even if these were questionable. The dispersal of political power in the summer and fall of 1936 served as the basis for considerable innovation – if not constitutional, at least administrative – which was awarded some consistency by the Largo Caballero government (September 1936 – May 1937). Largo tried to forge a "particularist alliance" whose recognition of new entities or autonomies other than Catalan (Euzkadi, Aragon, Asturias, and the reorganization of provincial bodies) was to provide the basis for a new kind of unity. The republicans' real problem was that while they maintained a certain institutional continuity, the collapse of the armed forces (heightened by Casares' famous last decree, which dissolved the bond between officers and men, intended for rebel areas, but applied only in republican territory) meant that their main task was to reinvent a working military organization, strategically capable of large-scale offensive operations.

The rebels had the exact opposite problem: they had military resources and a command structure, somewhat dispersed but functional, but no political organization to speak of. Sure of their triumph, the rebels avoided such a possibility, as they expected to take charge of the administration swiftly. During August-September 1936, the rebel generals preferred to work through a loose Junta in expectation of the rapid seizure of Madrid. When Franco was chosen as "Generalissimo" (or, more accurately maneuvered himself into the position) on October 1, the "nationalists" still hoped to fight their way to Madrid, and they fostered this hope until the following spring. The demands of war, the need to finance logistics, to humour foreign supporters, and to act within international rules, all forced the "nationalists" to reinvent the State, understood to be an *Estado Nuevo*, a revolutionary break, quite ironic, given the left's historic defense of continuity. The "nationalists" accomplished this by expanding the military provincial administration as needed, to the point that, at the beginning of 1938, the Junta Técnica del Estado became the "Spanish State" with a "formal" government. This process of subtle regeneration, like an amphibian that regrows a limb, facilitated the peculiarity of Franco's dictatorship, at the expense of divergent monarchist options, the "nationalist" cause felt no urgent need to articulate any constitutional basis. For years, at least until the "Fuero de los Españoles" in 1945, various specific measures for given institutions and a generic Labour Program passed for "Fundamental Laws," and even later, "franquismo" remained a juridical jumble, with a *sui generis* legal justification.

1975–1977: Civilian Negotiation and the Necessary Fiction of Non-Exclusion

Franco's régime was a remarkably efficient organ of repression. However by its very effectiveness, and the unassailable position of the *Caudillo* that was its core, it was paradoxically doomed, however long it might last. "Franquismo" was hindered, by its birth and nature, from significantly expanding its social base. Hence the dictatorship could continue, but was incapable of reproducing itself without changing into something else.

In many ways, the changes under franquismo reflected what, in the 1950s, Daniel Lerner called the "crisis of rising expectations" in the face of "the passing of traditional society" in the Middle East. Perhaps, in this sense, it would be better to focus on the Mediterranean Basin as a whole, rather than on an exclusively European context. In the case of Spain, such hopes of corporative and personal advancement, the dream of simultaneously becoming citizens and consumers, of reaping the assets of urbanization and its conveniences, while leaving behind the discomfort of old-fashioned agrarian living, with its restrictive behavioural codes, intensified under Primo's dictatorship and flourished under the II Republic. At the same time, the aggressive anticlericalism of the republicans provoked a burgeoning of neo-traditionalist religiosity, even Catholic "fundamentalism," which presided over the process of urbanization initiated during the civil war, and which continued unabated at least until the 1970s. From this perspective, the 1936–1939 civil war takes on less epic proportions than usually perceived as the struggle between the Popular Front ideal of merging democratic forms and socialist content to battle fascism, and the National Front model of a conservative-fascist alliance against any social progress. The Spanish conflict augured future Mediterranean internal conflicts, born of World War II, in France, Italy, Yugoslavia, and Greece, and of decolonization, such as the French Algerian War, or even the Lebanese civil war of 1976–1990 and the internal Algerian struggle of the 1990s.

This understanding of the Spanish civil war also makes it easier to understand the franquista decision to pursue economic development, in marked contrast to its peninsular and ideological neighbor, Portugal which, under Salazar which feared the consequences of growth and urbanization, and actively idealized rural underdevelopment as a matter of Lusitanian identity. In Spain harsh repression and strict controls proved capable of eradicating the challenge of any guerrilla-like "resistance" in the countryside. Once proven, such techniques guaranteed that dissent born of changing circumstances would remain localized in working-class areas and among students, leaving the armed forces completely apart. As a result, the dictatorship considered modernization a risk worth taking. Francoist politics and its faction struggles should be seen in terms of control of the rhythm of growth: for example, the Sección Femenina, whatever its ideological message, extensively enlisted women into public service. This gamble on the advantages of development indicated that the dictatorship would become obsolete. This, despite leftist disbelief, was the expectation of the Opus Dei technocrats that dominated Franco's cabinets after the 1950s. Even the most regressive influences, such as admiral Carrero Blanco, premier from June 1973 until his assasination by an ETA bomb in December, despite appearing "continuista", were trapped in this context. Carrero's program is comparable to later "developmentalist" strategies of systemic preservation, like *Le Changement* in Tunis in 1987. When faced with an Islamic fundamentalist challenge, Ben Ali displaced the elderly founder Habid Bourguiba, suppressed the fundamentalists and launched market reforms, to the sustained cheers of Western investors.

The "democratic transition," thus, was a sociological encounter, instead of a political exchange. This is why it succeeded. If it had depended on dynamics parallel to the fall of the Greek or Portuguese dictatorships in 1973 and 1974, the result could have been a political reaction, a victory for what was then facetiously called *El Búnker*. To begin with, the vast majority of the Spanish "new left," which appeared around the "Wunderjahr" of 1968, was born of the "new Catholicism" and the *aggiornamento* of the Vatican Council II. The children of "fundamentalist" *franquistas* went far beyond the religiosity of their parents, until they rediscovered the heroisms of the old left and the myth of the great "lost cause," the republican vision of the civil war. Secondly, the "opposition," although imbued with theoretical Marxism, was in fact aspiring to equality in the means of consumption, including electoral rituals, which seemed the energetic, youthful negation of the dictatorship's elderly and sclerotic patriarchalism. Led by middle-class youth, or those aspiring to this status, the "opposition" was terrified of anything truly violent and destructive: there were no angry masses burning down churches like in 1936, but syndicalists and revolutionaries enjoying priestly sanctuary from the police while meeting in parish centers, under the understanding gaze of a *cura comprometido*. Only the ETA, on both sides, denied this indulgent code and pointedly increased the brutality of their murders, as the etarras, "poli-milis" or "milis," argued for the statu quo ante, a return to the position of rejection dating from the war, and demanded direct negotiation with the "poderes fácticos", specifically the army. The "opposition," behind its revolutionary chatter, was bluffing: yield to democratization, or else we summon "the people" to the streets. Fortunately the new king, Juan Carlos I, and many members of the régime's political apparatus, especially those born in the 1930s (Adolfo Suarez was born in 1932, the king in 1938), were also bluffing: agree with our conservative solution, or else the tanks will roll. It was a marriage of necessity, based on the exclusion of all those, left or right, who retained an activist re-expulcation of the past war, who truly sought mass street action or military control. This implied that the generation then in its fifties, which had lived under the dictatorship (within or without) awaiting its chance, was swept aside by a flood of ambitious thirty-somethings. Once the deal was done in early 1977, everybody could come on board: the functionaries of the *Movimiento* retained jobs and pensions, the armed forces modernized American-style (to the benefit of younger, more professional officers, but also to the advantage of the more technical services – navy and air force), while the "new left" would receive teaching jobs. That was a sufficient critical mass. ETA, GRAPO, and other ultra-right terrorists remained out of the picture, but the core would be dense enough to remain, despite the permanent irritant of occasional bombings and murders.

One major aspect remained unresolved, even after the June 1977 elections: the problem of regional autonomies, heightened by Basque nationalist terrorism. The solution, once the basic agreement was reached, was to recover the memory of the 1930s, but in a careful, selective way. Negotiations of agents for the Suarez government with the Catalan president-in-exile in the summer and fall of 1977 yielded a surprise: the republican sub-State of Catalonia, with its titular president-in-exile, was recognized as legally valid, producing a specific *ruptura* for the Catalans, which flattered their sense of self-importance, and paved a way to redesign the political system so as to multiply levels of political representation, simultaneously allowing for a vast increase in public jobs. While an Estado de las Autonomías presented a potential solution to Basque terrorism (albeit not very successful, as it turned out), the regions of Spain with more or less historic claims to specificity could be integrated into an articulation that was neither centralist, nor federal, nor confederalist: *ni sí, ni no, sino todo lo contrario* (neither yes nor no, but on the contrary). In the meantime, the various Castilian-speaking regions could also happily fracture themselves along ancestral claims, satisfying what was then called "coffee for everybody," as opposed to concessions to over-weening, potential "separatism" in "historic communities," which viewed themselves as "nationalities" or even "nations." The result was what Spaniards call a "ceremony of confusion", with enough ambiguities to satisfy any opinion. The obsessive reiteration of the Franco régime in "Spanish" identity and nationalist values (which had much to do with the use of equivocal symbols for personal dictatorship, at the expense of such conservative rivals as the monarchists) had served to bring such rhetoric into disrepute, and eased the change to eclecticism.

The "democratic transition," thus, was the arrangement of 1931, but successfully implemented. The republic "without cost," which could unite all possible "constitutionalists," was now reproduced in reverse, as a monarchy where even the most hardened republicans admitted that Juan Carlos would make an excellent president for a Third Spanish Republic. The Catalan "differential fact" was explicitly recognized in 1977 as in 1931–1932, and served to redefine the very nature of Spain, the "problema de España, deliberated since the "Generation of '98."

Future Stability

By 2003, according to radical explanations in the left-wing Spanish press, the country seemed perched on the brink of a sixth transition. Democracy has been venerated as a value, preached to tots in kindergarten. As such, it can be considered internalized, although exactly what is meant by such rhetoric, however popular, is more difficult to ascertain. For all the repeated insistence on democracy, Spain still visibly lacks systemic loyalty, or a common civic culture that might sustain similar feelings of collective belonging.

But after Aznar's stunning victory in 2000, with his re-election as incumbent and a full majority in parliament, the PP made such sentiment a key issue in both its marketing strategy and its program for improvement. Nevertheless, Aznar was no more successful than Spanish leaders before him. His dogmatic sermonizing turned systemic loyalty into what seemed like a party slogan, a partisan interest vehemently rejected by all those who also disliked the PP appeal, especially outside the Castilian and/or Spanish heartland where *aznarismo* seems to generate its greatest allure. Aznar has insisted that "Spanishness" be recognized, after almost twenty years of particularist reaffirmation. Such insistence produced tremendous protest, asserting that the populares were a reincarnation of franquismo, particularly after Aznar aligned Spain with the Bush-Blair coalition against Iraqi Ba'athism, a departure from the usual Spanish alliance with the European French-German axis. While Aznar harassed the socialists in 1993–1996, confident of his ability to blame his predecessors for all that went wrong during his first term, the period after 2002 has been a kind of revenge, a time of retribution for the socialists, much to their satisfaction. Beneath both the protests against the ecological disaster in Galicia in late 2002, and the vast street demonstrations against the Iraq war during the following year, there was a palpable crisis of representation, where participation is understood as tangible, real and good, while political or institutional personification is allegedly false and unresponsive to immediate popular demand. It remains to be seen what this bodes for Spanish constitutional life.

The short-term effect has been clear enough. After the November 2003 regional elections in Catalonia, the Catalan Socialists outmanoeuvred the long-time dominant coalition of Nationalists and Christian Democrats, in power successively since 1980, by forging an alliance with the Left Nationalists (Esquerra), long taken for granted by hegemonic Catalanism. Repercussions on Spanish politics as a whole were immediate, given the open challenge to the PP affirmation of "Spanishness". The general elections, held in March 2003 a few days after Islamic extremists executed a brutal bomb attack in Madrid, heralded a change. It resulted in a new socialist government, led by Rodríguez Zapatero, which adamantly espoused a willingness to redefine institutions. This willingness included the constitutional organization of the State, as a function of openness, thereby channelling the covert demand for greater participation into what would remain basically representative structures. The long-term implications of weak systemic loyalty and underlying doubts of political legitimacy, however, promise to be a challenge, even within a European framework.

References

Paloma Aguilar Fernández, *Memoria y olvido de la Guerra Civil Española*, Madrid, Alianza, 1996.

Miguel Alonso Baquer, *El modelo español de pronunciamiento*, Madrid, Rialp, 1983.

Sebastian Balfour, *Deadly Embrace: Morocco and the Road to the Spanish Civil War*, Oxford , Oxford University Press, 2002.

Shlomo Ben-Ami, *The Origins of the Second Republic in Spain*, Oxford (UK) /New York, Oxford University Press, 1978.

——, *Fascism from Above: the Dictatorship of Primo de Rivera in Spain, 1923–1930*, Oxford , Clarendon Press, 1983.

Carolyn P. Boyd, *La Política pretoriana en el reinado de Alfonso XIII*, Madrid, Alianza, 1990.

——, *Historia Patria: Politics, History and National Identity in Spain, 1875–1975*, Princeton (NJ), Princeton University Press, 1997.

Irene Castells, *La utopía insurrecional del liberalismo: Torrijos y las conspiraciones liberales de la década ominosa*, Barcelona, Crítica, 1989.

Gabriel Cardona, *El poder militar en España hasta la guerra civil*, Madrid, Siglo XXI, 1983.

José Cepeda Gómez, *Los pronunciamientos en la España del siglo XIX*, Madrid, Arco Libros, 1999.

Manuel Espadas Burgos, *Alfonso XII y los origenes de la Restauración*, Madrid, C.S.I.C., 1975.

J. Fernández López, *Militares contra el Estado. España: siglos XIX y XX*, Madrid, Taurus, 2003.

Helen Graham, *The Spanish Republic at War, 1936–1939*, Cambridge (UK) / New York, Cambridge University Press, 2002.

David Gilmour, *The Transformation of Spain: from Franco to the Constitutional Monarchy*, London / New York, Quartet Books, 1985.

J. Lleixà, *Cien años de militarismo en España*, Barcelona, Anagrama, 1986.

Paul Preston, *The Triumph of Democracy in Spain*, London / New York, Methuen, 1986.

Javier Tusell, *Radiografía de un golpe de Estado: el ascenso al poder del general Primo de Rivera*, Madrid, Alianza, 1987.

E. Ucelay-Da Cal and S. Tavera, "Una revolución dentro de otra: la lógica insurreccional en la política española, 1924–1934", *Ayer, monographic issue Violencia y política in España* (J. Arostegui, ed.), n° 13, 1994, pp. 115–146.

E. Ucelay-Da Cal, "Buscando el levantamiento plebiscitario: insurreccionalismo y elecciones", *Ayer, monographic issue Política in la Segunda República* (Santos Juliá, ed.), n° 20, 1995, pp. 49–80.

——, "Moderni sogni girondini: Italiani, portoghesi e catalani nella rivoluzione repubblicana spagnola (1923–1938)", *Quaderni del Circolo Rosselli, monographic issue: Carlo Rosselli e la Catalogna Antifascista* (A. Landuyt, ed.), 2, 1996, pp. 67–86.

Paddy Woodworth, *Guerra sucia, manos limpias. ETA, el GAL y la democracia española*, Barcelona, Crítica, 2002.

2

KEY FACTORS TO UNDERSTAND THE SPANISH TRANSITION

José María Marín Arce

Spanish transition must be considered a process without a watershed in the passage from dictatorship to democracy. Even the death of Franco in November 1975, a relevant symbolic event in Spanish contemporary history, did not constitute a turning point in the beginning of the transition. Social change, a process essential in understanding how the transition happened, already gained pertinent relevance during the last days of Francoism. In face of the regime's immobility, the democratic opposition and social movements experienced significant growth, and consequently a slow but irreversible societal democratisation process began, contrasting with the regime's attitude, which, particularly since early 1975, obstructed any possibility of political openness and liberalisation.

Thus, the transition towards democracy was really not surprising, but rather the logical result of a path taken years earlier, one that would culminate in December 1978 with the approval of the Constitution, and in March 1979 with the holding of the first general elections in an already normalised democratic system. Nevertheless, these dates are arguable. It must be assumed that the culmination of the transition did not occur prior to at least 1982, when the Spanish Socialist Workers' Party (PSOE in Spanish abbreviation) came into power and the fear of a military coup against the still fragile democratic system began to dissipate.

Thus, obviously there is no clear stage between the Francoist regime and the democratic system. Transitions, as well as some revolutions, have a beginning and an end that are not easily delimited, and thus cannot be studied as a simple series of events that seem predetermined. Furthermore, the study of the Spanish democratic transition should not be limited to a

43

process of institutional change, but must be understood as a wider political and social process.

A certain interpretation, quite widespread among several historians, considers that the transition from dictatorship to democracy took place in a context of civil society demobilisation, practically without any pressure "from below". This allowed the political elites a wide range of action, with the result that the protagonists of political change were mainly the reformist sectors coming from Francoism.

Some years, ago as a result of new studies based mainly on archives from the Administration and from trade union organisations, a new interpretation has emerged: it gives more relevance to social movements, and emphasises the significance of social and political mobilisation for the transition development, particularly for the pace of the democratisation process.

During the last years of Francoism, a new type of mobilisation appeared, characterised by its adaptability It ranged from strikes and mass demonstrations to petitions, manifestos published by workers, intellectuals, professionals, as well as boycotts, concerts, recitals, performances, forums, besides an endlessness number of protests against the dictatorship. This mobilisation gradually gained "spaces of freedom" that were separated from dictatorship, and were not the result of the regime's liberalisation process. On the contrary, during the State years 1969, 1970, 1971 and 1975, the regime's institutions remained immutable. The most reactionary Francoist sectors (the so-called "bunker") managed to transfer power to the most progressive sectors, while the regime simply retaliated against democratic opposition with repression, particularly against the Spanish Communist Party (PCE), the Spanish Trade Union Centre (CC.OO. from the Spanish name of Workers Commissions) and the extreme left parties.

It is generally acknowledged that since the sixties, Francoism eased, allowing more freedom and showing some tolerance towards the different opposition sectors. This might be true in the case of the so-called regime's political families or for the opposition's most moderate groups, which were allowed to appear in the mass media as long as they were rigorously controlled by the regime itself. However, as regards the opposition's most leftist groups, fundamentally working class groups and parties that sustained the student's movement, repression grew exponentially from the early seventies to mid-1977. By examining the figures of the prosecuted people and the trials held by the "Court of Public Order" (Tribunal de Orden Público *TOP*) from its establishment in 1963 to its abolishment in 1976, the spectacular increase of trials since 1973 becomes manifest. Between 1964 and 1976 22,600 proceedings were initiated, directly or indirectly involving more than 50,600 people, of whom 9,000 were sentenced. These are, indeed, large numbers that reveal on the one hand the regime's stern attitude, and on the other hand the extensive scale of the opposition movement, which some historians considered to be minority groups. Another interesting fact is that 49% of prosecuted people by the TOP were from the working class, and 22% were students. This corroborates the argument that the bulk of democratic opposition was essentially composed of working class and student movements, and that the primary purpose of the TOP special jurisdiction was to retaliate strongly against working class dissident behaviours.[1]

Although a great number of people were prosecuted, the mechanism mainly used during the dictatorship was arrest by the *Brigada Político-Social* (BPS) and by the Guardia Civil. The constant "states of emergency" sheltered them, enabling them to detain suspects in police stations for more than 72 hours, during which the detainees were very often tortured. For example, a report of International Amnesty on the State of Emergency in the Basque country during May, June and July 1975, reveals that more than 2.000 people were arrested, most of them belonging to the working class, and no less than 500 remained detained for several weeks.[2]

The decree established by the state of emergency affected not only the two Basque provinces, but also the whole of Spain, though to a much lesser extent. In addition, the 1966 Press law was decreed and "governmental authorities were enabled to censure the press and any publication, television and radio broadcasts, as well as to cancel any show that might alter public order".[3] News in the Basque Country were practically non-existent during the three months of State of exception. Not a single piece of news concerning the State of exception, not a single testimony or comment about arrests, trials or ill treatments, nothing at all but official news and some comments on industrial disputes appeared in press agencies.

Another cliché that appeared incessantly was the "progressive policy" regarding the Press. Since the so-called 1966 *Fraga law*, most of the press had used the possibilities this law offered in order to achieve greater openness demanded by society. However, these possibilities were in fact quite limited, and they depended on the good will of the Minister of Information or of the Civil Governor. The law maintained a tight control over the press and imposed a kind of self-censorship through fines, suspensions, kidnappings or prosecutions of journalists.

In 1975, the democratic press endured persistent harassment by the government, which however did not manage to crush seditious publications. Their numbers rose continuously enjoying the solidarity and support from most of the press associations. The list of magazines and newspapers that suffered sanctions is endless, as well as the number of journalists who were arrested, fined, and what is worse, trailed by the TOP. In the late 1975, the board of directors of Madrid's Press Association issued a communiqué in which it denounced the numerous government sanctions against the press, the escalation of violence against newspapers and journalists, the increase of death threats, assaults and attacks as well as reprisals against journalists who insisted in maintaining their informative objectivity and professional dignity".[4]

Thus this presumed "openness" that the government so proudly displayed did not exist in the media, not even in the cinema, despite the so-called "nudity law", which was nothing but a series of rules of demo-cratic censorship, published in February 1975 in the Official State Gazette (BOE in Spanish abbreviation). The sole innovation of the law was that "nudity was admitted provided that the film cohesion required it, but was excluded when aimed to raise passions of normal viewers or when resulting in pornography".

Actually, the regime's repression did not succeed in crushing the ever-growing opposition, or in restraining the rise of participation in any kind of demonstrations; The legitimacy of Francoism began to collapse and repression could no longer be as broad or as indiscriminate as it was in the post-war years. Furthermore, though the memories of war and fear of repression persisted among a large part of the population, the younger generations considered Francoism as outdated rather than a dictatorial and police regime. Even their estimation of General Franco was that of a ridiculous and doddering character, rather than a bloodthirsty dictator, as he was still considered by the generations that endured the Civil War and the long post-war period.

Following the death of Spanish Prime Minister Carrero Blanco in 1973, democratic opposition began to organise. That same year, the Assembly of Catalonia became the only body of anti-Francoist opposition in Catalonia, and the Junta Democrática was launched in 1974. Also in that year, industrial disputes reached unprecedented figures: according to official data, 700,000 workers on strike, and numerous conflicts took place, particularly in Barcelona, Asturias, Madrid and the Basque Country. Concurrently, the working class movement's organisation improved, culminating in the 1975 trade union elections, where CC.OO. candidates were highly successful and a significant part of the vertical union structures were defeated by trade unions. It was precisely these trade union structures that created an unprecedented strike process in Spain, which began shortly before Franco's death and would not diminish until mid-1977.

Although it was obvious that democratic trade unions, particularly CC.OO., had become the opposition's most important mechanism of demonstration to end dictatorship,[5] this does not imply that the trade union movement was extremely important at the end of Francoism, nor that trade union organisations were able to rout dictatorship and to impose its termination by themselves. Nevertheless, they did have, partic-ularly the CC.OO., a significant capability for influencing the public

46

order. This was due not to organisational strength, but rather because of the political character of the regime and the difficulties involved in negotiating with the Vertical Union that made every conflict a matter of public order and a political challenge to the Francoist regime. Since the two main trade union weapons, strike and demonstration, were forbidden (although used very frequently by workers), they were considered public order conflicts that guaranteed police intervention to crush assemblies or demonstrations and to arrest trade union's leaders. Consequently, political clashes against dictatorship swiftly took on the guise of strictly industrial disputes, by demanding the release of arrested people, reemployment for the dismissed and the right to demonstrate, gather and strike, as well as full trade union freedoms.

CC.OO.'s strategy, mainly promoted by the PCE, was to put a radical end to Francoism adopting a working class dimension and leadership by popular sectors, avoiding a "pseudo-democratic" end led by the Spanish bourgeoisie. The way of imposing democracy was one the PCE had advocated since 1970 in its political "freedom pact". Briefly, the intention was to combine popular mobilisation with the establishment of a grand coalition against Francoism. Mobilisations would begin with a general strike staged by the productive sectors, which would lead to a National Strike, in which all citizens would join. The National Strike would impose a "provisional government" that would decree political freedoms and call constitutional elections.[6]

This approach was certainly too rigid to correspond to the country's political and social reality. Neither workers nor citizens were in favour of such a radical method, but rather supported a slow and gradual political transition. Nor could opposition parties accept such a process in which CC.OO. and the communist party would be the main agents of political change. Nevertheless, most of the democratic parties and trade unions participated in this general strike strategy to force the severance from the Franco regime. Both the *Junta Democrática*, a PCE's organ and the *Convergencia Democrática* Platform, in which the PSOE and the UGT (Spanish Trade Union Centre) participated,[7] demonstrated in favour of severance from the Franco regime, for the opening of a constitutory process and for a popular mobilisation that would culminate in the general strike. The socialist trade union even went beyond traditional communist proposals, by claiming the need for a revolutionary general strike that would get rid of Francoism, impose political and social freedoms as well as workers' emancipation, and finally abolish the capitalist system.[8]

According to this policy, aimed at a general strike, the trade unions took advantage of an opening presented by upcoming negotiation of approximately two thirds of collective agreements, the validity of which was to expire on December 1975. In early 1976 a spate of strikes was launched throughout the country. Logically, strikes began in those sectors and areas with longer traditions of labour conflicts and where most of clandestine trade union organisations, particularly CC.OO were established. In early 1976, the notable strikes were held in Barcelona, with Baix Llobregat and Sabadell's general strikes; in Madrid, where strikes affected more than 500,000 workers in almost all productive sectors (metal, construction, insurances, bank, graphic arts, Correos [The Post Office], Telefónica, RENFE [railway], public transports, etc.); and in the Basque Country, where more than half a million of workers went on strike in March. Nevertheless, these were not the only centers of industrial disputes, since strikes extended to other areas such as Valencia, Asturias, Navarre, Seville, Valladolid, Córdoba, Galicia, etc.

One of the most important consequences of this strike movement, which peaked in early 1976, was the organisation of an unprecedented political mobilisation that culminated in the Amnesty Meeting , called by several opposition unitary organisations, to which thousands of demonstrators flocked in the summer of 1976. At the same time, democratic opposition was slowly emerging. Political parties, still illegal, called press conferences; trade unions held their assemblies in churches and in the Vertical Union premises; the world of arts and culture declared itself against Francoism; and the University, lost by Francoism, had become a real "freedom area" in which opposition parties acted publicly. Neighbours associations and neighbourhood movements were also an opposition stepping-stone and the seeds of social mobilisation. Furthermore, an important part of the press became a vehicle to publicise the yearning for freedom of the majority of the society. This whole process of clashes with the dictatorship, which involved not only the workers' sectors, had already began to surface in 1975 with actors, university teachers, Health workers and students going on strike, as a result of the closing of the Universidad de Valladolid.

Facing this ongoing mobilisation came from a sector of the population, which perhaps was not a majority, but which nevertheless had an especial relevance in urban areas and in the main industrial centres throughout the country. The first Monarchy government, led by Arias Navarro, reacted roughly against this workers' mobilisation. Navarro expressed his inflexibility arresting and prosecuting of workers' leaders under the anti-terrorist decree-law, through ousting factories and companies, breaking up demonstrations violently, applying military rules to transport workers who were on strike (Metro [underground], RENFE, Correos, Telefónica, as well as some civil servants such as the Fire Brigades, local police, etc.). Above all, he expressed his rigidity through the thousands people who were dismissed by executives trying to stem the flow of strikes (60,000 people suffered reprisals in Madrid on January 1976).

This policy of continuous repression against the working class movement, of using public order forces as the sole solution to industrial disputes, could only lead to tragedy. And the tragedy took place in early March 1976, in Vitoria. When 20,000 workers went on general strike, the police broke up an assembly of strikers in a church, causing the death of 4 workers and several injured people. Sánchez Torán, Barcelona's Civil Governor, remembers: "It had to happen . . . and it finally occurred in Vitoria. So many confrontations between demonstrators or strikers with police forces had to explode somewhere, sooner or later".[9]

The events in Vitoria, and the violent incidents that took place in Montejurra, caused the Arias government to lose credibility, and ended by his losing the King's support, who compelled him to resign in June 1976. The truth is that very few believed in the democratising intentions of Navarro, not even when he tried to differentiate himself from the "bunker". Navarro's Minister of Foreign Affairs, José María de Areilza, relates that in a meeting of the Joint Commission Government-Movement National Council, Arias had the floor and said "I am simply accused of wanting to maintain Francoism, touching it up slightly but without any main modification"; "then followed something amazing," says Areilza and Arias emphasised: "Well, yes, it is true. What I wish is to keep Francoism. And as long as I stay here in power, I will be nothing but a strict perpetrator of Francoism". Monarchy was not even mentioned. Nobody talked about the King's Message. No one came up with the real issue, which is the pressing democratic reform demanded by the Institution feasibility.[10]

One of the transition's characteristics to bear in mind is the extent of uncertainty and improvisation that marked the attitudes of both the government and the opposition during 1976 and 1977. Therefore, there is no sense in considering democratic change as the result of a political operation outlined by the King and the reformist sectors of Francoism. Many historians have already rejected this interpretation that ascribes meticulous planning for political change to political actors. According to Tussell, "The belief that some of the main protagonists had a detailed plan besides their good resolves is simply inaccurate. Very often, original purposes had to be changed: for instance, neither the King nor Suárez ever considered, at first, the feasibility of legalising the Communist Party, though they fulfilled it. All these were spontaneous decisions, taken in an unforeseeable context that was determined not only by demonstrations, but even by a single newspaper article".[11]

In my opinion, that capability of adapting to events as they developed, without following strictly a pre-settled script, was the key to the success of the transition. That capacity to adapt, of trying to understand what was really going on and to satisfy the demands of society's majority for freedom and democracy characterised Suárez's political action, which contrasted with that of his predecessor Arias Navarro.

The Arias government was unable to take note of social reality and the range of working-class demonstrations throughout the first quarter of 1976. Not even Fraga, the former Minister of Interior who, together with former Minister of Foreign Affairs Areilza, represented the reformist view of the first Monarchic government, realised the political importance of social mobilisations. Furthermore, he consented to play the role of the oppressor the Premier had assigned him. According to Fraga, "politics are accomplished in official offices, not in the streets", for it was necessary to dismantle any mobilisation in order to achieve his reformist plans. He tried to restrain the opposition, so that the government would make the concessions it considered more convenient. Besides, social mobilisation was nothing but a matter of public order to Fraga. In his memoirs, this belief is clearly mentioned: when referring to Friday, 9th January 1976, as the underground strike was still proceeding and with an alarming situation in Madrid (roughly 350.000 workers on strike), Fraga states "I was hunting hares and partridges with my diplomatic colleague, the Duke of Maura . . . After the second beating, the news on the Guardia Civil's radio counselled me to come back to Madrid. The sound was awful, but I understood that thousands of people were demonstrating in Calle Sagasta. I went there, but the demonstration was taking place elsewhere, in Plaza del Ágata . . . That night, I attended the Mayte's Theater awards".[12]

Another example of Fraga's political attitudes is the way he considered the incidents of Vitoria, which is reminiscent of the traditional resort to "conspiracy" that were so characteristic of Francoism: "A dubious group of leaders – according to the Minister of Interior – . . . They had a go in Vitoria; their arrest and transfer to Madrid brought the matter to an end. Nevertheless, they had their day; though instead of triumphal, their day was bloodstained. Vitoria was lending itself to this kind of experience, inspired by the Soviets in 1919 and 1968 Paris".[13] Such a serious matter, which engenders obvious national and international repercussions, was settled as if it were a street brawl, and without associating the events with the Basque Country's General Strike that took place two days later, and which Fraga mentions in his memoirs but without any comment at all.

In my opinion, Suárez's main accomplishment was that he understood the need of proceeding little by little, satisfying society's demands of freedom, as well as giving impetus to the political change process from the very legality of the regime.

Very soon, Suárez showed his willingness to boost the democratic reform and to contact and reach agreements with all the groups from the opposition. Nevertheless, together with this clearly progressive and democratising policy, he also developed another policy, which was to isolate politically the PCE and the CC.OO., and to prevent demonstrations. In an extraordinary study on the transition in Alicante, Francisco Moreno Sáez disclosed that throughout the first Suarez government, the real obsession of both the Ministry of Interior and Civil government was to counteract the clear leadership of the PCE. According to his research, the PCE had "a total control" over the opposition movement, and "led every kind of mobilisations".[14] Other recent monographs, which have turned to government sources, emphasised the importance that Arias and Suárez attached to the repression of the working-class organisations. These studies also proved that police services were accurate in reporting about operating capacity and activities of left groups and parties, particularly communist ones. These reports continued until 1979–1980, that is, some years after the legalising of the political parties in question.[15]

In early autumn 1976, trade unions already realised that the Suárez government was seeking to postpone as long as possible the union reform and to carry out its own political reform project. Nevertheless, the trigger that stirred unionists were the economic measures that the Council of Ministers adopted on October 8th 1976, and more concretely the suspension of article 35 on the Industrial Relations Law and the new norms on collective negotiation. Unionists answered this so-called aggression with a call for a general 24-hour strike on November 12th 1976. The government paid especial attention to this call, and aimed to prevent it at all costs in order to thwart the strengthening of the unions and to keep an image of control over the political situation, which was important in order to avoid more troubles in the Cortes' debate on the Political Reform Law. The Ministry of Interior's orders to civil governors constitute a very good example of the interest the government had in quashing the strike:

"From early November" – recalls the governor of Barcelona – "we received an avalanche of telex from the Interior Police Directorate, asking for information and proposing measures of security forces designed to deter any disorder. This constituted an evident symptom of the worry that marked Madrid due to the unfortunate call for a general strike in the midst of the political reform process the government had already prepared. Considering all the measures to be adopted, the most operational were the extensive deployment that the Guardia Civil headquarters had foreseen for the conflict areas, as well as the concise telex the Interior Police Directorate sent with the following instructions: (1) Arrest as many pickets as possible. (2) Arrested people will be detained for 72 hours, as stated by law. (3) Minimum fines will range between 200,000 and 300,000 pesetas. (4) Once the 72 hours have expired, arrested people will appear before a judge. We also have a complete dossier on the Spanish Communist Party, its tactics and strategies, its propaganda, organisation, militants and mass actions."[16]

In his Memoirs, the Minister of Interior, Rodolfo Valentín Villa, describes the thorough preparation to quash the strike. A crisis Cabinet was called, in which all Ministerial Departments, as well as other entities such as *Correos* were represented. The Spanish Television played a crucial role: Martín Villa stated that the essential element was that the *Metro* should work properly, for television would handle the rest.[17] As a matter of fact, the government succeeded in transmitting the idea that the strike failed thanks to the media. Nonetheless, huge crowds flocked to the workers' mobilisation (figures differ according to the sources: almost 2 millions according to the trade unions, and barely 500,000 according to the government). However, the strike did not succeed in bringing the country to a standstill, nor to stop Suárez's political reform law, nor to avoid the government decrees that again introduced unfair dismissals (obviously with severance pay) and wage freezes.

Although this was the day in which the country experienced the most important social struggle of the previous forty years, the November 12th mobilisation certainly did not become the hoped for general strike that was supposed to force the severance from Francoism. It must be remembered that Spain had no tradition of general strikes (not even in 1917 or in 1934) and that the opposition's unionist organisations, which had just come into existence following the fall of Francoism, were aware of their weaknesses and of the difficulties of launching such an action from secrecy of the undergound. Consequently, these organisations limited the strike to mere industrial claims, related directly to the government's economic measures.

Nevertheless, the strike served a serious warning to the government, which could not perform the reform without the workers' support and the fringes of democratic opposition. It should be taken into account that the strikes throughout 1976, from January to the November 12th COS call, had a huge significance, not only due to the political nature of many of the conflicts , but also because of the high number of workers that participated. Figures clearly reveal the significance of those workers' mobilisations: according to the Spanish Trade Union Organisation, in 1975, slightly more than half a million workers were involved, and subsequently 10 million working hours were lost; whilst in 1976, these figures were multiplied by 7 and by 11 respectively, thus 3,600,000 strikers were involved and 110 million working hours were lost, another issue that arose was the dilemma between reform and severance. Did the triumph of the reformist path denote the severance failure? Was the Suarez's reformist pathway a sort of intermediate path between the possibility of an extreme right coup and the danger of a Marxist revolution? It must be said that such a dilemma never existed, since the severance suggested by the opposition never implied a political transformation with a revolutionary attitude. No social changes were suggested, nor any State reorganisation; not even a purge of some sectors from the Administration or State institutions, close to Francoism, such as the Army, the police, or the administration of justice. In fact, the Suárez reform mode approached the severance positions, while at the same time democratic opposition moderated its attitudes, relinquishing the idea of the creation of a provisional government and finally accepting the Monarchy.

Once the political reform law was approved, the referendum called and the PCE legalised, the political agenda increased in tempo. Elections were called very soon, on June 15th 1977, and Francoist institutions were promptly dismantled. The TOP was abolished on December 30th 1976; the right to demonstrate was regulated on March 4th 1977; on March 30th the labour law was passed, which legalised trade unions organisations and abolished the Spanish Trade Union Organisation; and on April the 1st the National Movement was closed down. Also in that spring, the amnesty decree was enlarged, which enabled the release of many members of ETA; the Spanish State ratified a series of international pacts regarding civil, politic and unionist rights.

In practice, as stated by Carme Molinero and Pere Ysàs, the fundamentals of the severance thesis had come true, and the majority of the great demands of the anti-Francoist opposition became a reality; the dismantling of Francoist institutions had begun, political freedom was established and free elections were called.[18] Javier Tusell considers that there had been a consented reform, with real effects of severance, which changed the fundamental basis of the political system, but without involving major social ordeals.[19] Despite all this, several acts of political violence took place and affected the transition process between 1975 and 1979. They claimed 331 deaths, from extreme right groups (23), from ETA (174) and from GRAPO (52), as well as from police forces (81).[20]

Notes

This work is a modified version of the French text "La mobilisation politique et sociale pendant le post-franquisme et la transition" published in Anne Dulphy et Yves Léonard (dir.): De la dictature à la démocratie: voies ibériques, Brussels, Presses Interuniversitaires Européennes, 2003.

1 Juan José del Águila: *El TOP. La represión de la libertad (1963–1977)*, Barcelona, Planeta, 2001, pp. 261 and 268.

2 Javier Domínguez: La lucha contra el franquismo. En sus documentos clandestinos (1939–1975), Bilbao, Desclée de Brouwer, 1987, p. 449.

3 *Decree-law order in Council 4/1975 of April 25th.*

4 *Informaciones*, September 11th 1975.

5 Manuel Redero San Román and Tomás Pérez Delgado: "Sindicalismo y transición política en España" in Manuel Redero San Román (ed.): *La transición a la democracia en España*, magazine AYER, no. 15, Madrid, Marcial Pons, 1994, p. 199.

6 *Manifiesto programa del partido comunista de España*, 1975, pp.144–145. Political statement of the PCE's Executive Committee, January 1976, Mundo Obrero, 14/1/1976.

7 The Convergencia Democrática Platform was composed of: The Basque

Consultative Council (Partido Nacionalista Vasco, Acción Nacionalista Vasca, Partido Socialista de Euskadi, CNT de Euskadi, Solidaridad de Trabajadores Vascos and UGT de Euskadi), Izquierda Democrática, Movimiento Comunista de España, Organización revolucionaria de Trabajadores, Partido Carlista, Partido Gallego Social-demócrata, PSOE, Reagrupament Socialista i Democràtic de Catalunya, Unión Democrática del País Valencia, UGT and Unión Social Demócrata Española.

8   *UGT*, no. 358, April 1975.
9   Salvador Sánchez Terán: *De Franco a la Generalitat*, Barcelona, Planeta, 1988, p. 40.
10 José María Areilza: *Diario de un ministro de la monarquía*, Barcelona. Planeta, 1977, p. 82.
11 Javier Tusell: *Historia de España en el siglo XX*. Vol. IV, *La transición democrática y el gobierno socialista*. Madrid, Taurus, 1999, p. 31.
12 Manuel Fraga Iribarne: *En busca del tiempo perdido*, Barcelona, Planeta, 1987, p. 30.
13 Manuel Fraga, op. cit., p. 38.
14 Francisco Moreno Sáez: "La transición en Alicante, vista desde el Gobierno Civil (1973–1977) in *Calendura*, no. 3, July 2000, Elche (Alicante).
15 Carmen R. García Ruiz: *Franquismo y transición en Málaga (1962–1979)*. Published by the Universidad de Málaga, 1999.
16 Salvador Sánchez Terán, op. cit., p. 188.
17 Rodolfo Martín Villa: *Al servicio del Estado*, Barcelona, Planeta, 1984, pp. 56–57.
18 José María Marín, Carme Molinero and Pere Ysàs: *Historia Política de España 1939–2000*, Madrid, Istmo, 2001, pp. 274–275.
19 Javier Tusell: *Historia de España*, Madrid, Taurus, 1998, p. 771.
20 Cayo Sastre García: *Transición y desmovilización política*, Universidad de Valladolid, 1997, p. 148.

3

REGIONS, NATIONS AND NATIONALITIES

ON THE PROCESS OF TERRITORIAL IDENTITY-BUILDING DURING SPAIN'S DEMOCRATIC TRANSITION AND CONSOLIDATION

Xosé-Manoel Núñez

Regionalism has generally played an ambiguous role in European history. On the one hand, regional identities helped fashion the nation states that emerged in the nineteenth century.[1] Yet the persistence in Spain of territorial identities forged during the pre-modern period also contributed to the emergence of several sub-state nationalisms. They opposed the existence of a Spanish nation as identified with the territory of the State, and advocated self-determination for their specific territories. In fact, regionalist forerunners generally precede or accompany sub-state nationalisms Thus Spain is a good case study in the ambiguous processes of region-building and nation-building.

To give a clear definition of what is meant by a region seems as complicated as providing a definitive answer to the question of what is a nation. There is no clear-cut agreement regarding one single definition of a region: they are economic entities, historical territories, frontier areas and geographical units bound by natural features. But they are also forms of collective identity that are imagined by intellectuals and region-builders and then spread to the general population via social actors. The social construction of regions has also led to the "rediscovery" of unique histories, traditions, languages, or even disappearing local ethnicities. Some scholars (Moreno 1997, pp. 11–23; Petrosino 1991) hold that regionalism has three characteristics that are also present in minority nationalisms. They involve: (1) the shaping of a territorially bound collective identity;

(2) the existence of a centre/periphery conflict within the state that may be culturally, economically or politically based; and (3) the existence of social mobilisation and/or political organisations of a territorial character. In this way regionalism and minority nationalism can be considered as two parallel products of ethno-territorial conflict and social mobilisation, with diffuse lines of demarcation but common elements underlying both: (a) ethnic mobilisation, and (b) claims on a territory that is considered a political unit.

This article will examine the relationship between region-and nation building, focusing on the political dynamics of regionalism in Spain since 1975, as well as the theoretical and doctrinal aspects of regionalist discourse. Recent research in the social sciences, and historical research in particular, have moderated the classical assertion that region-building and nation-building were opposite processes. In some cases they even have espoused the opposite thesis: nation-building may also imply region-building, since the former may be heavily dependent on the latter. Not all forms of collective identity have equal dimensions, and not all expressions of local or regional identity are infused with immediate political consequences. For example, the claim to self-determination lies exclusively in the realm of nationalism and national identities. Although some forms of regional identity may lead to a conflict with the national identity given certain factors and circumstances, not all of them do. Regional identities may be sustained by a (more or less invented) historical tradition, or they may be founded on common cultural traits fostered by the prior existence of collective political institutions. The relationship between nation- and region-building is not static, but rather is subject to constant change. Moreover, the basic discussion on nationalism in current research can also be applied to regions, regional identities and political regionalism (Applegate 1999). Are nations/regions given, pre-existing entities, or rather a construct of nationalist/regionalist doctrines and movements? What came first: the regions or the regional identity? Why are some regions successfully constructed (or, if one prefers, invented) while others are not? Do regional identities complement or oppose national identities?

Our point of departure will begin with the assumption that regional identities were constructed during the modern period by several actors (the state, local elites, institutions and political movements). These actors developed the criteria necessary for defining a region as a community, and in some cases proposed a certain level of collective political rights, but never sought the right of self-determination and full sovereignty. In the course of this construction process regionalists have been forced to appeal to elements that are very similar to those used by (sub-state) nationalists. But in contrast with them, regionalists always have maintained their belief in the existence of a larger nation that enhances their region, and may even see regional identity and regionalism as a step in the process of consolidating the nation as a whole. The Spanish case shows how one region-building process may turn into nation-building while another may not; how both identities shift and may even become contradictory over time; and how different social actors have constructed different concepts of the region (Núñez 2001a).

The focus of our paper will be the process of region-building that has taken place in Spain since the implementation in 1978, of the new decentralised state structure known as the *State of the Autonomous Communities*. The extension of regional claims to several regions that were not among the "historical nationalities" where sub-state nationalism had thrived prior to the Civil War (Catalonia, the Basque Country and Galicia) was initially seen as a means of avoiding territorial imbalances and sentiments of discrimination in regions that had not voiced demands for home-rule (Castile, Aragon, Valencia, etc.). However, the implementation of autonomy has contributed to creating regionalism from above, as seen in the emergence of several regionalist parties built on an almost non-existent historical tradition prior to 1975. In addition, the new process of region-building resulting from the implementation of the new state structure has meant a redrawing of regional borders. This meant shaping new territorial entities that rapidly became institutionalised as all the autonomous communities were granted legislative and executive competencies. As a result, new territorial identities were gradually promoted among the Spanish population.

The national question remains one of the unsolved problems of Spanish democracy 25 years after the framing of the 1978 Constitution. This issue and the permanent challenge posed by the persistence of peripheral nationalist claims to full sovereignty, particularly in the Basque Country, tend to obscure another key characteristic of Spain: it is a perfect example of a multiplicity of concurrent ethno-territorial identities (Moreno 1997). Within the Spanish State of Autonomous Communities, ethno-nationalist demands and independence movements coexist with regionalist parties and regionally based political claims. The outcome is a complex mosaic of territorially based identities (Núñez 2003).

The Transition Process: A New Opportunity Structure for Political Regionalism

The political solution to the national question achieved in the Constitution of 1978 established a complex framework that combined the notion of Spain as a single political nation with autonomy statutes to all regions. Part VIII of the Constitution created the so-called *Estado de las Autonomías* (State of the Autonomous Communities), which was developed more fully in several subsequent articles.

The new state was initially conceived as a decentralised structure composed of seventeen "autonomous communities" that reframed the pre-existing fifty provinces. In many cases they clearly matched the previous "historical regions" (which had had no administrative recognition whatsoever during the Franco regime). Most of them began on the basis of the so-called "Pre-autonomies", which were temporary representative bodies constituted in 1977 and 1978, before the Constitution was ratified. They were based on the various illegally constituted Assemblies of regional parliamentarians, first established in the Basque Country and Catalonia after June 1977 and subsequently in many other regions, concluding with Madrid in May 1978. The process was in fact tolerated by the Democratic Centre (UCD) government, since local branches of this party and the Socialist Party (PSOE) also took part in shaping these assemblies of elected parliamentarians (Funes Martínez 1984). From then on the steps towards legitimising them progressed. Moreover, the units integrating Spain's future regional map were defined in the course of negotiations between the provincial representatives that participated in these assemblies. Thus new regions emerged, such as La Rioja (formerly the province of Logroño), Cantabria (formerly the province of Santander) and Madrid (whose representatives where not accepted by the assembly of Castile-La Mancha), while other regions like Murcia and Castile were split losing some of their provincial units. This map was subsequently approved by the bumpy and improvised implementation of "pre-autonomic regimes" through law decrees issued by the Government between September 1977 (for Catalonia) and October 1978 (for Castile-La Mancha), and subsequently ratified in the 1978 Constitution. Thus, between 1979 and 1983 each of the pre-autonomy regimes developed its own home rule statute.[2]

From the outset, the autonomous communities were more or less explicitly divided into two groups. The first was composed of the so-called "historical nationalities": Catalonia, the Basque Country and Galicia – regions that had approved a home rule statute by referendum prior to the Civil War. The other group consisted of the remaining fourteen regions. In reality the extension of a decentralised state structure to the entire Spanish territory was the result of a political agreement among the various political actors that participated in shaping the Constitution. The Basque and Catalan nationalists pressed for self-government for their communities within the framework of a multinational state that could adopt a federal or confederation structure. This demand was unacceptable to the right-wing parties, mainly composed of "reformists" from the Francoist state apparatus, as well as for a good portion of the UCD, the party that led the first phase of the democratic transition. It was adamantly rejected by the People's Alliance [AP] headed by former Franco minister Manuel Fraga Iribarne. These actors were not ready to modify their vision of Spain as one indivisible united nation, and would only tolerate a slight amount of administrative decentralisation. In theory, the left advocated a federal solution. But the centrist UCD party was eager to reach a compromise with moderate Catalan nationalists by seeking a more flexible position, partly due to the divergent positions on the regional question among its different factions (Meilán Gil 2003, pp. 53–54).

In the end, the right to achieve autonomy was extended to all regions, but there would be different routes toward home rule and varying levels of autonomy were established. Sovereignty was held by the Spanish state, which then transferred broad powers to the autonomous communities and strengthened them with legislative and executive powers in many areas. At the same time, the central state maintained legislative pre-eminence in many other areas and a monopoly on nationwide taxation (with the exception of the Basque Provinces and Navarre).

One of the key characteristics of the 1978 Constitution is its ambiguity in defining certain crucial concepts. On the one hand, it states that Spain is the sole existing Nation, and hence the sole collective entity with full sovereignty; but on the other hand it recognises the existence of "nationalities" and regions, without clearly establishing the difference between a nationality and a nation. Article 2 of the Introductory Section of the Constitution reads:

> The Constitution is based on the indivisible unity of the Spanish Nation, the common and indivisible Fatherland of all Spaniards. It acknowledges and guarantees the right to autonomy for the nationalities and regions that constitute it, and the maintenance of solidarity among them.[3]

Two different paths for achieving autonomy were also delineated. One was the "fast track" defined by Article 151 and reserved for the "nationalities" (Catalonia, the Basque Country and Galicia), later joined by Andalusia. The other was Article 143, which defined a "slow track" for the rest of the regions (though Valencia, Navarre and the Canary Islands have advanced far more rapidly than the other ten). By mentioning the existence of "nationalities", the Constitution intended to satisfy peripheral nationalist demands that the new territorial structure of the state explicitly include recognition of the "qualitative" historical, cultural and social peculiarities of specific territories.

The "State of the Autonomous Communities" was initially conceived as a negotiated solution, and was accepted by the main peripheral nationalist parties as a first step towards consolidation of regional self-government. Nevertheless, a majority of Basque nationalists did not accept the framework drawn up by the 1978 Constitution, as it failed to recognise the traditional Basque "historical rights" (a kind of modernised version of *Fueros*) in a manner that affirmed Basque sovereignty. This caused a "legitimacy deficit" that still lingers today. At the other end of the spectrum, some parties that participated in framing the Constitution were not convinced of the long-term survival of the autonomy system. Conservatives were opposed to the term "nationalities" and were reluctant to accept bilingualism in certain autonomous communities. By contrast, the final goal for part of the Socialist party and the rest of left-wing parties was federalism.

In spite of broad acceptance by a majority of the Spanish population during the process of implementation, the State of the Autonomous Communities contained several ambiguities that eventually caused problem areas requiring permanent bargaining among the political parties, the central state and the regional governments. Thus, the system did not establish any detailed delimitation of the spheres of competence of the central state, the autonomous communities and the municipalities. Also left unsettled were many other details regarding the crucial area of public financing for the system. Finally, there was no provision for a parliamentary forum that would allow the regions to cooperate and become co-participants in government tasks. In addition, there was no mechanism for the participation of the autonomous communities in the formulation of Spain's European policy after the country joined the EEC in 1986. These deficiencies made the evolution of the system heavily dependent on short-term agreements and negotiations between the central government and the nationalist and regionalist parties.

Unexpected Actors: "Autonomist Regionalisms"

The system of autonomous communities also unexpectedly contributed to the rise of "regional claims" and regionalisms not only in Catalonia, the Basque Country and Galicia, but throughout Spain. From the beginning of the transition process new parties, organisations and platforms emerged with the objective of strengthening regional identities, seeking to foster the achievement and subsequent enlargement of self-government within a decentralised state structure.

To a certain extent these autonomist regionalisms are a new incarnation of pre-war regional movements, and in fact reproduce some of the characteristics of historical regionalism present during the first third of the twentieth century (Núñez 2001a). The nature of the pre-war regionalist movements was not clear. On the one hand they stressed their allegiance to the common Spanish Fatherland and presented themselves as a new way of incorporating the local identities into a joint project for regenerating or reshaping Spanish identity. On the other hand, they also elaborated a repertory of historical, ethno cultural and mythical images that would serve as the basis of new ethno-nationalist discourses opposed to what had been the common heritage of Spanish "regionalised" nationalism. Moreover, a rather peculiar dynamic emerged out of a combination of imitation effect and fear of State discrimination that favoured the Basque Country and, particularly, Catalonia (i.e., initiating a discourse that emphasised territorial grievances). Diverse territorial regionalisms re-emerged and voiced their autonomy demands throughout Spain whenever peripheral nationalist pressure on the Central State happened to open a door for reforming the state structure in the direction of decentralisation (1917–19, 1931–36).

Post-1975 political regionalisms emerged in the course of a sort of chain reaction caused by the imitation effect produced by peripheral nationalisms that "showed the political path" that regions should travel in order to gain power. At the same time, most regions have insisted on their particular "Spanishness" and protest against "unfair" discrimination by the State in favour of Catalonia and the Basque Country, which are perceived as seekers of unique privileges and therefore subject to accusations that they lack solidarity. But there is now a further factor encouraging the emergence of "autonomous regionalisms" – the fact that the consolidation of a decentralised political system created an additional arena for political competition (regional parliaments, meso-territorial level administrations and elections, etc.). Regional elites began to experience increased access to power and resources within a suitable institutional framework, and therefore opposed central elites, who were more interested in achieving a stable democratic order (Genieys 1997). In other words, regional administrations were imposed from above, and often did not have any corresponding regional awareness among the mainstream of their respective populations. The exceptions were Catalonia, the Basque Country, Galicia, the Canary Islands and Valencia, according to survey data from the beginning of the transition.[4] But the existence of new regional administrations and the emergence of new arenas of political competition at the meso- territorial level also caused regionalism to be promoted by both the new political and the traditional elites – some even tied to the late Franco era. Regionalism offered low opportunity costs and numerous advantages in the short term, while also allowing the "recycling" of old local elites who could be transformed into newly legitimised ones. This was of the utmost importance since no municipal elections were held until the Constitution was passed in May 1979. Thus, no real removal of late Francoist local elites had taken place before the Constitution was passed.

During the late Franco period, paradoxically occurring parallel to the increasing official reluctance to recognise any administrative or political content for the more culturally defined notion of region, certain academic elites began to suggest the need to promote regional decentralisation purely on a functional basis. They were mainly active in the fields of Geography and Economic Planning, influenced by the theories of

Gunnar Myrdal and the geography of territorial development and regional economic analysis. Particularly since the implementation of a State policy regarding local poles of economic development, some political elites in the Spanish provinces came to consider these academic and intellectual tenets as updated formulae for territorial management. This philosophy was adopted by the presidents of *Diputaciones*, as well as town-councillors and mayors. According to its supporters, decentralisation should favour a more functional territorial unit that would be larger than the provinces and could therefore facilitate the task of territorially based economic planning. The borders of the regions were not necessarily to be defined in historical or cultural terms, but rather on the grounds of strategic planning and territorial interests (Garrido López 2002, García Alvarez 2002, pp. 356–69). This coincided with a timid recovery of certain signs of cultural distinctiveness in several regions, which was tolerated and even fostered by institutions such as the provincial *Diputaciones*, but did not necessarily include demands for political autonomy. Still, in April 1976 some fifty-five parliamentary representatives of the last Francoist *Cortes* gathered around the former Catalan Minister of the Franco government, Laureano López-Rodó, to shape a "regionalist faction" that advocated the institutional recognition of the Spanish regions while renouncing federalism. During the transition process "functional" neo-regionalism emerged as a new repertory of arguments for regionalist claims that were backed by law experts, geographers and economists.[5]

A parallel development arose from the official doctrine of regional affirmation that had been tolerated by the Franco regime since the mid-1940s. It was represented by institutions such as the *Instituto de Estudios Asturianos* (IDEA) in Asturias (1947) or the *Institución Fernando el Católico* in Zaragoza (1943), which in a disjointed but effective manner studied regional traditions, folklore, dialects and cultural diversity. This was understood as a particular contribution to the common Spanish heritage; a way of helping national identity take stronger root among the population by appealing to local images and symbols intended as complementary frames of meaning capable of promoting Spanish identity, particularly in regions where ethnic distinctiveness was accepted as a matter of fact (Lamikiz 2002). Similar to what had happened in the nineteenth century, the effect of this "Spanish regionalism" was paradoxical and, to a certain extent, even contradictory. On the one hand, it was intended to be apolitical, to avoid challenging the loyalty of Spain's regions and provinces to a common national project. In fact, this cultural undertaking was understood as a means of enriching Spanish culture. But it also provided peripheral movements with a repertory of literary images, cultural icons and historiographical discourses that could lay the basis for political regionalism and even lead to denying the "Spanishness" of their territories as a whole (Garrido López 1999, pp. 21–83; San Martín-Antuña 2002, pp. 235–71).

This process can be observed in several regions, from Aragon to Asturias, and was reinforced by the political opportunity structure created by the new Law on Local Government that was finally passed in November 1975. The mobilisation of these new and unexpected actors – "neo-regionalisms" or autonomist regionalisms – may be understood as a complex reaction of local political elites and some segments of the Spanish public opinion to a twofold phenomenon. First, the pressure exerted by peripheral nationalisms, particularly by Basque and Catalan nationalism, threatened to lead towards home-rule statutes or to gaining some areas of sovereignty for their territories. The initial concessions made after 1975 by the first post-Franco government consisted in granting the establishment in Catalonia of *Mancomunidades* (regional associations of provincial institutions or *Diputaciones*), and setting up a special committee to study the reestablishment of the Economic Agreements for the Basque provinces of Biscaye and Guipúzcoa. This was the beginning of a process that would lead ultimately to the achievement of home-rule for the Basque Country and Catalonia. The provincial elites of other regions saw this as a "privilege" that left them at a disadvantage, for which they blamed the Central Government. Thus, a chain reaction rapidly spread throughout the rest of Spain. The phenomenon involved a complex variety of factors, as many regions desired to follow the path towards decentralisation initiated by Catalonia and the Basque Country. Decentralisation was perceived as synonymous of further democratisation and reallocation within the new political opportunity structure, and some regional spokesmen feared "discrimination" of being considered second class territories liable to receive fewer resources from a State that favoured the more developed peripheries.[6]

This blend of protest against "unfair discrimination", mixed with a demand for equal privileges equal to those regions that claimed to be culturally distinct, was also fostered by another factor. At the end of Francoism, Spanish nationalism was profoundly discredited and delegitimized as a political discourse in the Spanish public sphere (Núñez 2001b). Regardless of its political orientation, it had lost its appeal as a doctrine transmitted by the dictatorial regime. Hence, Spanish nationalism could adopt a regionalised form, following its ancient pre-1936 traditions. It was present on the left, which voiced a preference for a federal state according to the old regenerationist tenets of reforming the state from the provinces up; and on the right, which defended the *Fueros* and the pre-liberal essence of Spain, based on the principle of unity within territorial diversity, usually maintained by conservative-traditionalist thought. Thus paradoxically, one of the discursive repertoires where Spanish patriotic tenets could best be expressed was the claim for regional

63

decentralisation, as long as it was symmetrical and granted equal treatment to all regions and territories of Spain. Moreover, the coalescence of local elites around the common demand for home-rule made it possible for both new and old political and intellectual elites to find an appropriate vehicle for conducting social mobilisation and achieving power. Opposition regional parties also used regionalism to erode governmental support by exploiting territorial unrest for the sake of their own electoral purposes.

In other words, regionalisation created a new political arena, which both at the discursive and at the political-administrative level enabled local elites to become engaged in a new competition for resources and power. Moreover, the extreme fragmentation of the Spanish party system during the first years of the Spanish Transition also made it possible for new organisations to emerge and to attempt to consolidate themselves within a fluid context. For instance, between October 1976 and June 1977, 59% of the 151 new parties registered at the Ministry of Government were regional in their focus. Moreover, this regional fragmentation also affected the major Spanish parties, from the UCD to the several federations of Christian-democrat parties and the socialist camp (Heras Planells 1997). Equally important, the local branches and regional groupings integrated within the UCD and PSOE, as well as the parties located on the left of the spectrum, were among the leading forces supporting regional autonomy. In some regions like Cantabria and La Rioja they adopted this position against the express wishes of their own party's national elites.[7] Constituted in 1976, the Iberian Socialist Conference included several nationalist and regionalist parties of socialist orientation that emerged during the late Franco era and the first months of the Transition period. Some of these short-lived organisations gradually merged with PSOE regional branches after 1977. As a consequence, many of the regional structures of the Socialist Party were imbued with strong regionalist tenets (Gillespie 1991).

This complex mix involved mobilisation structures, ambiguously framed "territorialised" discourses, and political opportunity structures, along with the instrumental use of territorial grievances as a basis for the elaboration of new ethno-territorial discourses. The phenomenon can be discerned in such instances as the protest by Cantabria and La Rioja against the "unfair competition" of the Basque Economic Concerts; the protests in Aragon against the use of the Ebro river as a source of water for other Mediterranean agricultural areas such as Catalonia; or the demand for a more balanced economic development that could propel forward the economies of backward areas such as Castile or the Canary Islands. These claims, along with the rapid advance of the decentralising process since 1976 and the sudden visibility of the "regional question" in the public sphere, resulted in a further unanticipated outcome. A rapid increase of regional consciousness was already noticeable by the end of the 1970s and the beginning of the 1980s, even in territories such as Castile and Leon, where the percentage of people opting for home-rule against centralism increased from 32% (1976) to 53% (1979). The demonstrations held in Andalusia (December 1977), Valencia (October 1977), Castile (April 1978) and Aragon (April 1978) included impressive numbers of participants, and in some cases reached the point of becoming the largest mass demonstrations in the history of these regions. All this seemed to indicate that regionalism from above also received an unexpected echo from below, fostered by the uncertainty of the political conditions of the democratic transition.[8]

Some regionalist parties emerged before the 1978 Constitution had been approved. Opposition to neighbouring sub-state nationalisms was a decisive factor in this forward impulse. The Aragonese Party [PAR] was founded in December of 1977 by a handful of Zaragoza's conservative oriented bourgeoisie and professionals, some of them former members of previous local Francoist institutions, while others had been local UCD leaders who had joined an independent list to stand at the 1977 elections. They succeeded in getting one parliamentarian elected in the province of Zaragoza. Their political aim was to proclaim regional identity yet at the same time, they strongly expressed their opposition to neighbouring Catalan nationalism. In fact, Navarre and Aragon regionalists were among the first to condemn the introduction of the term "nationalities" into the Constitution, due in part to its ambiguity (since Spain should be the only nation), but also because it created a distinction between "regions" and "nationalities" that was considered discriminatory by regionalists. Therefore, the PAR sought home-rule for Aragon based on a principle of equality with Catalonia. Every region should receive similar treatment and an equal degree of self-government delegated from the Central State.[9] This position was maintained in subsequent years once the State of the Autonomous Communities began to be implemented. In the eyes of the regionalist President of Aragon in 1987, the development of the decentralised system established by the Constitution should lead to an equality of powers among all regions. The existence of the Spanish nation was not to be questioned, as the PAR preferred to focus on economic considerations and demands for more authority and power from the Madrid government (Gómez de las Roces 1988).

A stronger degree of explicit anti-Catalanism was also a characteristic of the Valencian right wing and regionalist party, Unión Valenciana [UV], founded in 1981. Its main concern was the defence of Valencia's particular regional identity against the so-called "Catalan cultural imperialism". It reached the point that this party supported academic standardisation of the Catalan Valencian dialect as a distinct language from Catalan. The social network behind Valencian regionalism derived mainly from the clubs and traditional associations involved in organising the local celebrations of the *fallas* in the city of Valencia, and included a blend of populist appeal, regional traditions and Spanish cultural affirmation (Hernández i Martí 2002; Cucó 1996).

Other regionalist parties relied on a more local discourse. The Regionalist Party of Cantabria [PRC] founded in 1978, originated in the intellectual and political unrest that occurred around the Association for the Defence of Cantabria Interests (ADIC) during the first years of the Transition. The purpose of the PRC was to achieve for Cantabria – formerly the coastal Castilian province called Santander – the status of a separate autonomous region distinct from Castile. In order to defend the need for regional decentralisation, this party expressed a series of somewhat chaotic political goals and ideas, blending arguments from Christian personal thought and from pre-war regenerationism.[10]

However, these parties and other regionalist options hardly presented a well-defined regionalist creed, at least from a theoretical point of view. They mainly consisted of pluralistic but conservative platforms with very diffuse and improvised ideological principles, relying on the mobilising appeal of condemning the privileges that the Central State gave the historical nationalities, combined with demands for funds from the Government in Madrid for further improvement of their regions.[11] This inter-class appeal was common to all regionalist parties, and a good example is the purely "functionalist" approach to regional policy adopted by La Rioja Party, founded in 1982. So far it seems to be focussed on counteracting the competition of the neighbouring Basque Autonomous Community in the area of industrial policy and financial powers, and on presenting "a new way of doing politics in defence of a territory, leaving aside the outdated ideological positions that tend to encapsulate politics". This approach is meant to defend La Rioja from the constant "aggression that has been levelled" against its social, historical and cultural characteristics.[12]

Only in the case of the main party in Navarre, the strongly conservative Navarre People's Union [UPN, founded in 1979], can a specific regionalist tradition be traced back to the nineteenth century. It was maintained throughout the Franco era thanks to the survival of the Navarra's foral institutions, in conjunction with enduring traditional postulates – since Navarre has been a historical stronghold for Carlism. The UPN founding ideology, as expressed in the writings of one of its early leaders, constitutes a blend of Spanish nationalism interpreted in a "provincial" way with extremely conservative tenets, mixed with fiercely anti-Basque statements. At present these ideas have been transformed into a conception of the Spanish nation based on traditional "regional liberties" that supposedly date back to the late Middle Ages and were preserved under the Spanish monarchy. This creed is also reinforced by the strong opposition to Basque nationalism, which has endeavoured to assimilate the region into the Basque Country (Medrano Blasco 1984). At present the UPN advocates a defence of the specific identity of Navarre, a nationality in the sense established by the Spanish Constitution. The key characteristic is the continuance of the *Fuero*, and participation in a pluralistic Spanish nation defined as "a community of sentiments, interests and cultures" from which "Navarre does not want to be separated".[13]

Unión Alava [UA], the regionalist party of the Basque province of Alava, has somewhat similar characteristics. It was founded toward the end of the 1980s after splitting away from the provincial branch of the right-wing People's Party (PP). During the first half of the 1990s it maintained the third place in Alava politics. The historical roots of UA date back to the pre-war fears of the overwhelmingly Spanish-speaking population of Alava concerning possible integration into the Basque autonomy. This was manifest in the interpretation of the regionalist legacy as a provincial claim opposed to the "hegemony" of other Basque provinces, and also as a defence of the provincial autonomy maintained by the *Fueros*. But Alavese regionalism may also be interpreted as a form of legitimising a local variant of Spanish nationalism. Hence, UA has taken to defending the Spanish language, "discriminated" against by the linguistic policy of the Basque Government, but it does this under the banner of the so-called "Alavese language". The defence of the unity of the Spanish nation, consecrated by the 1978 Constitution, is perceived as being compatible with a reverend preservation of regional liberties as legitimised by history, and identified with a progressive understanding of individual rights. Since the Popular Party has gradually increased its support in the Basque Country, the only way for UA to distance itself from the Spanish conservatives after 1998 has been to demand that the province of Alava become a new Autonomous Community.[14]

In spite of their confusing ideological principles and variegated political character, the new autonomic regionalisms have proven themselves to be very able and pragmatic improvisers, and in this sense they have benefited from a favourable political opportunity structure that can be summarised along three lines. First, the electoral system adopted by Spanish democracy since 1977 – the so-called D'Hont system – moderately favours proportional representation, allowing small parties competing in the regional arena to win a seat in the regional parliaments. Until the 1990s they also benefited from the instability of the Spanish party system, a fact that has made it possible for sub-state parties to emerge and gain significant support (Alcántara and Martínez 1999). Second, regionalist parties flourished and expanded between 1982 and 1989 thanks to the spectacular demise, after the 1982 parliamentary elections, of the UCD, the main Spanish centre party during the Transition.

This party had collected a good number of local elites from the late Franco period, for which a conversion to regionalism became the best way to reorient their political activity and retain their influence after 1982. Third, autonomous regional governments and institutions benefited from a period of expansive public expenditures (1982–1992), which served to implement a sort of micro-welfare-state at the regional level. This took place with little cost to the regional governments since they had the power to spend but did not have to collect taxes directly.[15] This demonstrated to citizens the positive effects of regional institutions and according to official surveys, was subsequently expressed in the high rates of approval of the system of autonomous communities two decades after its implementation (Mota-Consejero 1998).

Table 3.1 Election results for regionalist parties in five autonomous communities, 1983-2003 (regional elections only)
(% of valid votes)

	1983	1987	1991	1995	1999	2003
Aragon	20.64	28.48	24.68	20.46	13.25	11.20
Valencia	—	9.24	10.41	5.72	3.95	2.97
Navarre★	23.51	31.18	34.95	49.90	46.76	49.09
La Rioja	7.52	6.49	5.38	6.66	5.75	6.84
Cantabria	6.77	12.29	6.36	14.63	13.51	19.47

Source: Spanish Ministry of Governance (Ministerio del Interior).

As a consequence of these favourable opportunities, meso-territorial parties either emerged or were reinforced by new members. Thus, almost two thirds of former UCD members in the region of Navarre entered UPN after 1982. Similarly, many local UCD representatives from Aragon, a number of whom had already occupied posts in some of Franco's administrations, subsequently joined the PAR. Something similar happened in 1990–92 after the final defeat of the centre party [CDS] led by the charismatic ex-President Adolfo Suárez. A large part of today's regionalists in the Canary Islands came from the regional branch of the CDS and from insular post-Franco elites, joined by former UCD members. They merged in 1992–93 with other political groups (such as the left-wing minority nationalists) to form a new party, the Canary Coalition [CC], which today receives approximately 20–25% of that region's votes and has governed the autonomous community in a coalition since 1995 (Hernández-Bravo de Laguna 1992, López-Aguilar 1996). Moreover, the regionalist position became a typical catch-all label to be adopted by any local politician in a pinch. A ridiculous example was provided by Nicolás Piñeiro, a regional parliamentarian in the Autonomous Community of Madrid, who, after leaving the PP in 1988 due to internal problems, founded a regionalist party for Madrid, claiming that Spain's capital should become a historical region with its own "personality", given the challenges it faced from other autonomous communities (Piñeiro 1991). Similar examples can be seen in other regions during the second half of the 1990s.[16]

During the 1980s and part of the 1990s, especially after the 1987 regional elections, some of the regionalist parties – such as the PAR – came into power in their respective autonomous communities in coalition with other Spanish national parties, and then succeeded in giving political content to their recently-achieved home-rule status. In this sense there is a clear imitative dynamic or "institutional mimicry", following the nationalist-ruled autonomous governments of Catalonia and the Basque Country (Genieys 1997: 244–46). Neither the PSOE nor the PP was able to avoid this, as they are constantly under pressure from their regional branches.

The "slow track" autonomous communities promoted regional consciousness among their citizens and some were even forced to "invent" new regions and new identities in order to support and legitimise the existence of current political institutions and territorial frameworks, as in the case of La Rioja, Cantabria or even Castile-Leon and Castile-La Mancha. As expressed by a Castilian politician, regional home-rule should not be justified merely on an economic basis (Cascajo-Castro 1991). Propaganda campaigns emphasising local characteristics, cultural and schooling policies; an appeal to more or less imaginary historical forerunners and invented traditions, as well as the permanent – and always useful – argument of an enduring discrimination that continually favours other regions, have all contributed to spread a sense of regional consciousness among the population. The aim of basing regional identities on history and culture and on "objective" criteria was a common feature of all the autonomous communities that had not been recognised as "nationalities", or where neo-regionalism emerged as a new political force. This tendency can be observed in regions such as Andalusia or Aragon. The latter appealed to regional "liberties" and institutions of the past that had opposed Castilian rule; in Andalusia the call was accompanied by a rather elastic interpretation of regional economic underdevelopment resulting from *internal colonialism*, in conjunction with the defence of its Arabic past (Béroud 2003). However, "rewriting history" proved to be a particular obsession in those autonomous communities in which historical foundations were the weakest, such as La Rioja or Cantabria (CEM 1978; De la Mora 1979). Similar efforts by regional intellectuals to "invent" a regional history for a new autonomous territory have been undertaken in Leon, in this case aimed at shaping a new region (Díez Llamas 1990).

From "Region" to "Nationality"; or, To What Extent can a Nation be Invented?

The dynamics of new region-building undertaken by the ruling elites of the autonomous communities have also had another effect: by making "Madrid" responsible for regional problems, increased pressure has been placed on the central government to solve almost every serious problem that directly affects the regions, such as labour conflicts or economic adjustments. The need to justify their own regional power leads new regionalists, as well as regional elites from the Spanish political parties, to demand further powers for their autonomous communities, greater decentralisation and equal treatment with the "historical nationalities" in order to avoid comparative "injustices".

Moreover, some regional governments of "slow track" autonomous communities have been pressing for the status reserved to historical nationalities. Becoming a "nationality" has been considered not only as a sign of equal treatment, but also as a label that increases the chances of receiving power transfers and resources from the Central Government, since that status would aid in accessing the category of "first class" autonomous communities (Contreras Casado 2000). This self-affirmation dynamic has even led some regionalist parties such as the Aragonese PAR to rhetorically uphold new peripheral nationalist tenets with a view to transforming their regions into a "nationality" as established by the 1978 Constitution. These claims have sometimes received a certain degree of popular support from the regional population, as seen in several mass demonstrations held in Zaragoza between 1992 and 1994. Nevertheless, in this case doctrinal coherence was of less importance than the publicity effect: according to Gómez-de las Roces (1988: 38) there was no real difference between regionalist and nationalist parties as long as secession did not become a factor. At the same time, the youth section of PAR declared itself to be nationalist, explicitly relinquishing the right to self-determination. Other leaders and members of this party insisted on prioritising socio-economic questions. The ideological blend resulting from this mix caused increasing confusion among PAR membership, to the point that during its 1996 Conference the label of "nationalist" was abandoned in order to avoid further misunderstandings among its rank-and-file members. Later on the label was reintroduced, though embodied within a longer definition: "[PAR is] a nationalist, centrist and moderate party, whose aim is to represent a majority of the Aragonese society", showing full respect for the constitutional framework while also defending "our historical rights and full-fledged autonomy". The persistence of territorial conflicts, linked to the development of the water resources of the Ebro river and water transfers to other regions, still provide an adequate framework for the PAR and other regional parties to protest, with plenty of chances to foster regional mobilisation. However, the main aim of the party continues to be the achievement of official recognition of Aragon as a "historical nationality". Although this was obtained in 1996 by means of the reform of the region's Autonomy Statute, it has not been sanctioned in practical terms by the Central Government.[17] The final goal of Aragonese regionalists continues to be the conversion of Spain into a symmetric federal state, where Aragon would enjoy equal treatment with Catalonia or the Basque Country.[18]

In the same vein, during the late 1990s the Valencian party UV attempted to adopt an entirely "nationalist" terminology and to advocate the transformation of Spain into a vaguely defined symmetrically-structured federal state, while maintaining the cause of linguistic distinctiveness (by using a "Valencian" linguistic standard that was distinct from Catalan). According to the UV's political program dated December 2000, it remains loyal to its main goals of reforming the Spanish Constitution to have the Valencian region recognised as a "historical nationality", as part of the transformation of Spain into a federal state where all units would receive comparable treatment.[19] Similarly, the Mallorcan regionalist party *Unió Mallorquina* (UM) declares that one of its political goals is to attain for the Balearic Islands the constitutional treatment reserved for the "historical nationalities", while insisting on further decentralisation within the framework of the 1978 Constitution.[20] As the ruling party in its region, the Canary Coalition has also established as its long-term political objective to be able to "define the Canary Islands as a nationality [. . .] within the framework of article 2 of the Constitution". However, the party has relinquished any inclination towards independence and emphasises the unique character of its nationalist creed, engaged "in the overall interests of the [Spanish] State". Hence it declares itself to be loyal to the Constitution but also favours a more "flexible" interpretation in all matters involving the economic interests of the Canary Islands, within the framework of the European Union. Spain should become a real federal State by means of a reform of the Spanish Senate.[21]

In some cases the new "nationalist" label gained immediate prominence, since it was functionally useful for new parties that split off from regionalist parties to define a new political identity that would differentiate them from their origins. The Navarrese UPN party, which entered a permanent coalition with the PP in 1990, split in April of 1995 due to leadership disputes and ideological clashes over its own identity as a party and the extent of self-government to be sought for Navarre. The dissident faction was headed by its former president, Juan-Cruz Alli, who founded a new party that has since advocated the existence of a Navarrese nationality. From a theoretical standpoint, Alli intended to elaborate a more

71

sophisticated ideological synthesis, a sort of defence of a deeper regional consciousness that would enable Navarre to play a prominent role in Europe (Loyer 1994).

The new regionalist creed advocated by Juan Cruz Alli is also shared to a certain extent by those who pressed for a full-fledged "territorialisation" of the political discourse of the Spanish majority parties (PP and PSOE), thus adapting their agenda to the territorial framework of the State of the Autonomous Communities. This is the case of the President of Galicia since 1990, Manuel Fraga Iribarne. Fraga's new regionalist theory – which is full of theoretical vagueness regarding the distribution of powers between the central state and the regional administrations – does not deny the existence of Spain as a single nation, but advocates a more prominent role for the sub-national units within the future borderless European Union. He supports reinforcing regional identity following the "subsidiarity principle" that enshrines decentralization as a fundamental basis for individual freedom (Fraga 1992, 1994). This "regionalisation" of the political creed of the Spanish conservatives, especially of the Galicians since the mid-1980s, has increased even more as the PP rose to state power in 1996. It subsequently sought to moderate its image, to the point of declaring itself as a party located at an ideological mid-point between the "extremes" of peripheral and Spanish nationalism. The Galician PP has since proclaimed the virtues of the so-called "self-identi-fication" doctrine, a hybrid blend of cultural and functional regionalism (Puy 1990). The entire intellectual and political tradition of Galician nationalism prior to 1936 seems to be assimilated into a new form of "Galicianism" that emphasizes the need to combine regional self-government and a strengthened subnational culture – defined in an essentialist fashion – with Spanish patriotism based on common loyalty to a Spanish Fatherland; this in turn is legitimised by the alleged existence of a common Hispanic political community since the 15th century (Rodríguez-Arana and Sampedro-Millares 1998; Rodríguez-Arana 2001).

As a result of the complex mosaic of political interactions and diverse processes of identity-building taking place in the present State of the Autonomous Communities, one can conclude that region-building in Spain at the beginning of the 21st century is still an open and evolving matter. The decentralised system established by the 1978 Constitution has proven itself to be a useful formula for peacefully integrating a majority of the peripheral nationalisms within the new Spanish democratic system. In spite of its vagueness, it has also proven to be a surprisingly flexible and robust temporary solution. But it has not yet fully and definitely incorporated the sub-state nationalisms. This lack of satisfaction period-ically rises to the fore during political debates, and is expressed in an increasingly bold fashion since 1998.

The lack of definition of political guidelines by the State of the

Autonomous Communities has also led to permanent tension between the demands of the diverse "autonomic regionalisms" seeking full equivalence of power with the "historical nationalities" on the one hand, and the peripheral nationalists desire to maintain their qualitative difference in regard to broader competencies, on the other. Peripheral nationalists consider any equality of treatment with the rest of the autonomous communities as a denial of what they perceive as the legitimate basis for their claims to self-government: their being distinct nations. For this reason they are not comfortable within the, but accept the present situation as a lesser evil. Peripheral nationalists reject proposals from the left that seek to transform the current State of the Autonomous Communities into a federal State composed of seventeen federal units based on the present autonomous communities. Instead, they propose to transform Spain into a multinational federation based on four clear "nationally defined" entities: Euskadi, Catalonia, Galicia and Castile/the rest of Spain.

However, the question is not whether the present State of the Autonomous Communities should or should not adopt a federal state structure. The real debate arises over the federal or con-federal units that would join in shaping a new Spanish state: should they be defined on an ethno-national, ethno-territorial or administrative basis, and should these "national" units receive special treatment as distinct from the rest of the regions and autonomous communities? Here a long-term disagreement emerges between those who advocate the conversion of Spain into a symmetrical federal state where Autonomous Communities would be treated just the same as "historical nationalities" (the "autonomist regionalists" and "neo-nationalists"), and peripheral "historical nationalists" who are reluctant to recognize the existence of distinct entities within any part of the Spanish state other than Catalonia, the Basque Country, or Galicia, that is, within "Spain" or "Castilian Spain".

Some Conclusions

The process of region building implies historical dynamics that, to a certain extent, are similar to nation-building ones. The identity of a region tends to be built on similar arguments (history, tradition, the people's will), which may be incorporated or defended by elites according to their interests and political motivations. The theoretical difference between region and nation, and therefore between regionalism and nationalism, lies in the notion of current collective sovereignty, which is exclusively ascribed to the nation. As a consequence, regionalist claims may provide similarities in the political game as they imitate tactics and strategies, vocabulary and images used successfully by peripheral nationalists, though the discursive narrative of those images and elements tends to be weaker than in the nationalist version. The fact that "neo-regionalist" parties do not ascribe sovereignty to their region, and that regionalist elites are aware of the risks involved in making claims that could go beyond what regional populations and voters can tolerate since voters generally share a common loyalty to both Spain and their own territories, can have at least two consequences.[22] First, opportunities to pressure the Central Government are far more limited for regionalists than for sub-state nationalists, who always question State sovereignty and challenge the State with the threat of secession. Second, in the end autonomist parties eventually become established "regional lobbies" that serve to drain resources from the Central State, or else efficient administrators that may be preferred by the citizens when electing meso-territorial governments. This can easily be seen in the fact that ideological discussions on the structure of the state are far less important for regionalists than the achievement of practical concessions in the form of investments in their territories, special competencies or resources.

However, widespread regionalist sentiments and deep-rooted autonomic identities, accompanied by a rapid consolidation of the regions as territorial networks of socioeconomic interests, also contribute to sustain the citizens' preference for regionalist parties or, at least, for "regionalised" parties. Sub-state parties are regarded as the best defenders of territorial interests in the institutional arena, as they compete for resources within the framework of the decentralised State. It is not surprising that regionalist parties survive, for even in "historical nationalities" many citizens share a dual identity (Spanish/regional) and vote for ethno-nationalist parties on pragmatic grounds (Pallarès, Montero and Llera 1998).

The Spanish case illustrates how regionalist and nationalist dynamics may converge or diverge over time. However, the existence of regional elites in need of preserving given social or economic interests may succeed in pushing a political regionalism to become a new nationalism if confidence in the previous nation-state fails or if the interests of one or more social groups require a complete change in national loyalties. In fact, it is hard to find a nationalist movement that has not emerged from a previously existing form of collective identity or ethno-territorial mobilisation. Sub-state nationalisms project a clear demonstration/imitation effect for regionalist movements. This may have a decisive influence on the level of theoretical discourse or ideology involved, but it does not contribute significantly to spread new nationalisms. Outside the Basque Country, Catalonia and Galicia, the consolidation of regional party subsystems did not result in the emergence of any new national consciousness that would exclude a sense of Spanish identity. Moreover, in many cases there has been a growing distance between the political dynamics of party elites and the evolution of regional identity sentiments, particularly in the case of neo-autonomist parties that have embarked on the adventure of proclaiming new "nationalities" and nations with almost no popular support. The evolution of feelings of regional and national identity in the Spanish autonomous communities during the 1990s manifests the reinforcement of regional identities in tandem with the consolidation of dual (Spanish/regional) identities in almost all the Spanish territories, with the sole exception of the polarised situation in the Basque Country.[23] However, the appeal of "neo-regionalisms" lies in their consolidation as party organisations during the 1980s and first half of the 1990s combined with their clever management of political-institutional cleavages within the State of the Autonomous Communities. This is manifest particularly in the peculiar dynamics of imitation and reaction that characterises the relationship between the "historical nationalisms" of the periphery and the rest of the regions, probably the most unusual element of Spanish contemporary politics.

Notes

1   For a good sampling of case studies, see Haupt, Woolf and Müller (1998), as well as Ther and Sundhaussen (2003).

2   For a description of the process of implementation of the *State of the Autonomous Communities*, see Kraus (1996), Aja (1999) and García Álvarez (2002).

3   *Constitución Española. Aprobada por las Cortes el 31 de Octubre de 1.978*, Madrid: n. ed., 1978, p. 3. My translation.

4   See del Campo, Navarro and Tezanos (1977), as well as Jiménez Blanco *et al.* (1977).

5   A good example may be found in the memoirs of José Luis Meilán Gil, a former member of the Franco Administration and later a regional leader of the regionalist faction of the UCD in Galicia. See Meilán Gil (2003, pp. 20–26).

6   A good example are the books written in the aftermath of the Dictatorship by one of the first Castilian regionalist leaders, Law History Professor Gonzalo Martínez Díaz (1976, 1977), who denounced the "unfair" practice of granting Economic Concerts to certain provinces, while the less developed territories were excluded from them.

7   Nevertheless, by 1980 the leadership of UCD and PSOE were able to impose upon their regional branches in the province of Leon, and subsequently on their Segovia branches, acceptance of the move towards integration within the newly-shaped region of Castile-Leon. The reason was the geopolitical convenience of counteracting "strong" peripheral regions such as the Basque Country and Catalonia with a territorially large and demographically numerous autonomous community in the centre, while Cantabria and particularly La Rioja were allowed to constitute separate regions by virtue of the alleged need for "transition areas" between Castile and the Basque Country.

See García Álvarez (2002, pp. 524–28) and Díez Llamas (1990, pp. 202–3 and 234–40).

8   See García Ferrando (1982), López Aranguren (1983).

9   See Garrido (1999, pp. 93–121), Serrano Lacarra (1999) and PAR (1987).

10 See Alegría Fernández (1990).

11 For instance, the various actors that backed the emergence of Castilian regionalism in the aftermath of Franco's death were mostly linked to late-Franco era provincial *Diputaciones*, while others belonged to academic circles. See González Clavero (2001).

12 See *El Partido Riojano. Ideología*, at: www.partidoriojano.es/ partido/ ideas.htm.

13 UPN, *Ponencia Política* approved by the V Party Conference held in 1997. See www.upn.org/ponencias/politica.htm.

14 See Laburu (1992), as well as V *ponencia de política general. V Congreso Ordinario de Unidad Alavesa, 16 de diciembre de 2001*, at: www.unidadalavesa.es/pgeneral.htm.

15 To give an example, the public expenditures of the Autonomous Communities tripled between 1986 and 1992, and the number of civil servants employed by regional governments increased from 44,475 in 1981 to 677,160 in 1999, while the number of civil servants dependent on the central government decreased from 1,181,820 to 887,205. See Kraus (1996, pp. 190–91), and Aja (1999, p. 236).

16 For instance, by the end of 1998 a new regionalist organisation emerged in Asturias out of a split in the regional branch of the PP, led by the former president of the Autonomous Community. The dissidents set up a new regionalist party, Union for the Renewal of Asturias [URAS], which declared itself an interclass party that intended to defend Asturias' territorial interests above any other political or social cleavages. See URAS, *Ponencia institucional. II Congreso Ordinario de Unión Renovadora Asturiana. Oviedo, 26 de enero de 2003*, at: www.uras.org.

17 See Mairal (1997), PAR (1991: 23–27, 54–57, 73–75) and PAR-Secretaría de Prensa (1992).

18 See "Saint George's Manifesto" signed by the PAR on the 22 April 2003 (available at: www.partidoaragones.es/actualidad/noticias/2003).

19 See *Un nou valencianisme per al segle XXI*, a political program approved by the 9th Party conference held in December 2000, available at: www.uniovalenciana.org/documents/nouvalen.htm.

20 See *Les Illes Balears, una nació d'Europa: Projecte de país*, Palma de Mallorca: Unió Mallorquina, 1994.

21 Coalición Canaria, *La Primera Fuerza Política de Canarias. Un programa para Canarias*, n.p.: n.ed., 1996; Coalición Canaria, *Base Programática. Aprobado en el I Congreso de CC/ Santa Cruz de Tenerife/23.01.99*. n. p.: n. ed., 1999; Román Rodríguez Rodríguez (president of the Canary Islands region), *Nacionalismo y autogobierno*, n.d. [2002], and *Resolución aprobada por el Consejo Político Nacional de Coalición Canaria*, 21 July 2001, both available at: www.coalicioncanaria.org.

22 In 1992, 89% of PAR voters admitted feeling more Spanish than Aragonese, or as Spanish as Aragonese, while 73% of UV voters held the same feeling.

That same year, 91% of PAR voters, 81% of UV voters and 85% of Canarian regionalist voters declared that their autonomous community was "a region", while only 4%, 6% and 9% respectively believed it to be "a nation". See Pallarès, Montero and Llera (1998: 221–24).

23 Compare the data presented by Moral (1998) and Díez-Nicolás (1999, pp. 15–90).

References

Abad León, Felipe. 1980. *La Rioja, provincia y región de España*. Logroño: Ochoa.

Aja, Eliseo. 1999. *El Estado Autonómico: Federalismo y hechos diferenciales*. Madrid: Alianza.

Alcántara, Manuel, and Antonia Martínez, eds. 1999. *Las elecciones autonómicas en España, 1980–1997*. Madrid: CIS.

Alegría Fernández, Manuel. 1990. *Presencia e influencia del ADIC en la historia de Cantabria*. Santander: Tantín.

Applegate, Celia. 1999. "A Europe of Regions: Reflections on the Historiography of Sub-National Places in Modern Times", *The American Historical Review* 104 (4), 1157–82.

Béroud, Sophie. 2003. "Devenir une "nationalité historique": L'usage politique du passé en Andalousie et en Aragon", *Matériaux pour l'Histoire de Notre Temps* 70, pp. 67–74.

Campo, Salustiano del; Navarro, Manuel, and Tezanos, José Félix. 1977. *La cuestión regional española*. Madrid: Edicusa/Cuadernos para el Diálogo.

Cascajo-Castro, José Luis. 1991. "El marco institucional", in J. Jiménez-Lozano et al., *La identidad regional castellano-leonesa ante la Europa comunitaria*. Madrid: Centro de Estudios Ramón Areces, pp. 31–58.

Centro de Estudios Montañeses [CEM]. 1978. *Antecedentes históricos y culturales de la provincia de Santander como region*. Santander: CEM.

Contreras Casado, Manuel. 2000. "La importancia de llamarse nacionalidad", in A. Pérez Calvo (ed.), *Estado, nación y soberanía*. Madrid: Secretaría General del Senado, pp. 128–47.

Cucó, Alfons. 1996. "Notes sobre la Transició política i la qüestió nacional al País Valencià", *L'Avenç* 201, pp. 8–19.

Díez Llamas, David. 1990. *La identidad leonesa*. León: Diputación Provincial.

Díez-Nicolás, Juan. 1999. *Identidad nacional y cultura de defensa*. Madrid: Síntesis.

Fraga Iribarne, Manuel. 1992. *Da acción ó pensamento*. Vigo: Ir Indo.

——. 1994. *Impulso autonómico*. Barcelona: Planeta.

Garrido López, Carlos. 1999. *Demanda regional y proceso autonómico. La formación de la Comunidad Autónoma de Aragón*. Madrid: Tecnos.

——. 2002. "El regionalismo 'funcional' del régimen de Franco", *Revista de Estudios Políticos* 115, pp. 111–28.

Funes Martínez, Mariano. 1984. *Las preautonomías regionales en España*. Murcia: Caja de Ahorros Provincial.

García Álvarez, Jacobo. 2002. *Provincias, regiones y comunidades autónomas. La formación del mapa político de España*. Madrid: Temas del Senado.

García Ferrando, Manuel. 1982. *Regionalismo y autonomía en España, 1976–1979*. Madrid: CIS.

Genieys, William. 1997. *Les élites espagnoles face à l'État. Changements de régimes politiques et dynamiques centre-périphéries*. Paris/Montréal: L'Harmattan.

Gillespie, Richard. 1991. *Historia del Partido Socialista Obrero Español*. Madrid: Alianza.

Gómez de las Roces, Hipólito. 1988. *El Estado del Estado de las Autonomías*. Zaragoza: Diputación General de Aragón.

González Clavero, Mariano. 2001. "Alianza Regional: Un primer intento regionalista en Castilla y León (1975–1977)", *Investigaciones Históricas* 21, pp. 319–35.

Haupt, Heinz-Gerhard, Stuart J. Woolf & Michael Müller, eds. 1998. *Regional and National Identities in Europe in the XIXth and XXth Centuries*. The Hague/London/Boston: Kluivert.

Hernández i Martí, Gil Manuel. 2002. *La festa reinventada: calendari, politica i ideologia en la València franquista*. Valencia: Universitat de València.

Heras Planells, Rafael. 1997. *Enciclopedia política y Atlas electoral de la democracia española*. Madrid: Temas de Hoy.

Hernández-Bravo de Laguna, Juan. 1992. *Historia popular de Canarias. Franquismo y Transición política*. Santa Cruz de Tenerife: CCCPC.

Jiménez Blanco, Javier, *et al*. 1977. *La cuestión regional en España*. Madrid: CIS.

Kraus, Peter A. 1996. *Nationalismus und Demokratie. Politik im spanischen Staat der Autonomen Gemeinschaften*. Wiesbaden: Deutscher Universitäts Verlag.

Laburu, Jon Gotzon. 1992. *El orgullo alavés*. San Sebastián: Sendoa.

Lamikiz Jauregiondo, Amaia. 2003. "Ambiguous 'Culture': Contrasting Interpretations of the Basque Film Ama Lur and the Relationship Between Centre and Periphery in Franco's Spain", *National Identities* 4(3), pp. 291–306.

López Aguilar, Juan Fernando. 1996. "Estado autonómico y nuevos nacionalismos: El caso de Coalición Canaria", *Claves de Razón Práctica* 65, pp. 32–39.

López Aranguren, Eduardo. 1983. *La conciencia regional en el proceso autonómico español*. Madrid: CIS.

Loyer, Barbara. 1994. "Nations, États et citoyens en Espagne", *Hérodote* 73–74, pp. 76–91.

Mairal, Gaspar. 1997. *La identidad de los aragoneses*. Zaragoza: Egido Editorial.

Martínez Díaz, Gonzalo. 1976. *Fueros sí, pero para todos. Los conciertos económicos*. Valladolid: Alce-Silos.

——. 1977. *Castilla, víctima del centralismo*. Valladolid: ARCL.

Medrano Blasco, Luis Fernando. 1984. *El partido foral necesario*. Madrid: n.ed.

Meilán Gil, José Luis. 2003. *La construcción del Estado de las Autonomías. Un testimonio personal*. A Coruña: Fundación Caixa Galicia.

Mora Villar, Manuel Felipe de la. 1979. *Cantabria histórica*. Santander: El Autor.

Moral, Félix. 1998. *Identidad regional y nacionalismo en la España de las Autonomías*. Madrid: CIS.

Moreno, Luis. 1997. *La Federalización de España*. Madrid: Siglo XXI.

Mota-Consejero, Fabiola. 1998. *Cultura Política y opinión pública en las Comunidades Autónomas: un examen del sistema político autonómico en España 1984–1996*. Barcelona: ICPS, Working Paper no. 153.

Núñez, Xosé-Manoel. 2001a. "The Region as Essence of the Fatherland: Regionalist Variants of Spanish Nationalism (1840–1936)", *European History Quarterly* 31 (4), 483–518.

——. 2001b. "What is Spanish Nationalism today? From Legitimacy Crisis to unfulfilled Renovation (1975–2000)", *Ethnic and Racial Studies* 24 (5), 719–52.

——. 2003. "A State of Many Nations: The Construction of a Plural Spanish Society since 1976", in Christiane Harzig and Danielle Juteau (eds.), *The Social Construction of Diversity: Recasting the Master Narrative of Industrial Nations*. New York/Oxford: Berghahn Books, 284–307.

Pallarès, Francesc, José-Ramón Montero and Francisco Llera., 1998). "Los partidos de ámbito no estatal en España: notas actitudinales sobre nacionalismos y regionalismos", in Robert Agranoff and Rafael Añón (eds.), *El Estado de las Autonomías. ¿Hacia un nuevo federalismo?*. Oñati: IVAP, 205–68.

PARTIDO ARAGONÉS [PAR]. 1987. *Diez años luchando por Aragón (1977–1987)*. Zaragoza: PAR.

——. 1991. *Por el progreso y la identidad de Aragón*. Zaragoza: PAR.

PAR-Secretaría de Prensa. 1992. *Hablando desde Aragón*. Zaragoza: Guara Editorial.

Petrosino, Daniele. 1991. *Stati, Nazioni, Etnie. Il pluralismo etnico e nazionale nella teoria sociologica contemporanea*. Milan: Franco Angeli.

Piñeiro, Nicolás. 1991. *Madrid. Capital y región*. Madrid : n. ed.

Puy, Francisco. 1990. *Ensaios acerca da nosa autoidentificación*. Santiago de Compostela: Fundación Alfredo Brañas.

Rodríguez-Arana Muñoz, Xaime. 2001. *Autonomías y nacionalismo*. A Coruña: Universidade da Coruña.

Rodríguez-Arana, Xaime, and Anxo Sampedro-Millares. 1998. *O galeguismo*. Santiago de Compostela: FOESGA.

San Martín-Antuña, Pablo. 2002. "La ideología nacionalista asturiana. Reflexiones sobre la nación (im)posible", Ph.D. Thesis, University of the Basque Country.

Serrano Lacarra, Carlos. 1999. "Aragonesismo entre 1972 y 1982: Cultura y práctica política", in Antonio Peiró (ed.), *Historia del aragonesismo*. Zaragoza: Rolde de Estudios Aragoneses, 131–56.

Ther, Philipp, and Holm Sundhaussen, eds. 2003. *Regionale Bewegungen und Regionalismen in europäischen Zwischenräumen seit der Mitte des 19. Jahrhunderts*. Marburg an der Lahn: Herder-Institut.

4

POLITICAL TRANSITION IN SPAIN
STATE AND BASQUE NATIONALISM

Ander Gurrutxaga Abad

In this paper I will illustrate the hypothesis that although the political transition in Spain boasts political and social success, there are certain problems when this issue is judged from the viewpoint of the Basque Country.

I will analyse the difficulties the constitution, approved in 1978, has had in attaining a comfortable political majority in the different territories. There are several reasons for these difficulties: electoral efficacy, social presence of radical nationalism that challenges the political model in the Constitution, ETA's persistent violence, problems in the relationship between the Spanish State and the nationalist majority that has ruled the Basque autonomous institutions since 1980, the difficulties the Spanish State has in ruling and politically integrating national issues.

These are the issues in Spain after over 25 years of political transition. They are neither unique nor exclusive. And they are now revealed both in Basque society and in relations between Spain and the Basque Country.

First, I propose to end all ETA violence – this would augur the beginning of a radically new period, with no place for the politics of pain – while acknowledging that many of the problems it has caused, especially those related to the victims, will not disappear immediately. Second, we need to assess correctly the internal dynamics in Basque society, based on the acceptance of a structural pluralism and with a minimum of politics. Third, we have to define a model for a stable political relationship between the Spanish State and the Basque Country. These three issues presented are the unresolved problems of the Spanish transition, despite the definition of a system of consolidated democracy with representative institutions and regulations based on the processes of democratic culture.

Political Institutionalising and Transition

It is easy to agree with the claim made by Victor Pérez Díaz (1996, 20) that Spain's transition to democracy in the 1970s is a history of success. It has produced institutions that have functioned for 25 years, so that a new generation of Spanish people has flourished in the core of a liberal democracy. In the last decade, other countries in East Europe, South America and Asia have been inspired by this transition.

It is known that the Spanish transition required democratisation of state structures and a consensus regarding their character. In other words, the reversal of Franco's movement and the consequent creation of the democratic public arena. It was also the beginning of a political process that sought to guarantee the nationalization of the state in Spain. The key to these two dilemmas was the creation of a central symbol, and the 1978 Constitution was indeed such a symbol. It united "the two Spains," both the wealthy and the poor Spain, as well as the central and the peripheral regions of the country.

Essentially, the transition period sought to solve certain dilemmas that have beset Spain for the past 150 years. My interest is in the Basque Country, where the legitimacy of the democratic framework was put to the test with the approval of the Statute of Autonomy in 1980, a direct result of the 1978 Constitution.

I defend the hypothesis that this process requires institutional support. The Basque government formalised the autonomous political framework according to state criteria, and in the belief that it was establishing the basis of the construction and institutionalisation of the Basque nation (which has been lacking for over 100 years of Basque national life).

In fact, the autonomy administration needs, on the one hand, to prove its legitimacy, which results in an overcautious institutional process. On the other hand, this perspective combines the pragmatism of democratic nationalism with the need to find legitimacy for its actions. The achievement of these objectives relates the discourse on national construction to the institutionalisation of the Autonomous Community, to the defence of the true interests of the Basque population, and to the fact that institutionalising the Basque Autonomous Community is achieved in the same way as the administrative structure of a new state is established.

During the process, the values expounded by the recently created Basque administration relied on the symbolic imagery and the ideological structure the nationalist community used to project its political aspirations. The institutional logic is a vehicle of the national construction. The four aspects of the process are: The Basque Country/ The Nationalist Community/ The Nationalist Party/ and The National Construction. The administrative structure, as the institutional projection of this imagery,

81

creates servility and paradoxes and an unending debate about the final point of competence or the instruments of political action.

If the outlined process is presented as unquestionable, we should keep in mind the meaning that the constitutional development has for the expression of nationalism. It can be asserted, without going further than what is allowed by the data, that the political objectivity expressed in the 1978 Constitution defines a process discussed in the Basque Country. Having clarified this point, I do not want to make the mistake of assuring that either the process is not taking place, or that Basque society rejected the democracy offered by the Magna Charta. It is worth pointing out that the founding moment of Basque democracy is different from other places in Spain. It is important to remember that Franco's movement was a flag-pole that dramatized the political and social perspective conditioning the answers.

It is legitimate to question why I maintain this vision of the process. I am convinced that only by keeping these factors in the forefront can we understand the immediate origins of some of the unsolved problems of the transition period and later developments.

The first aspect to consider is the discussion that politically active sectors of the Basque Community conduct on the constitutional text. In the constitutional referendum of 1978, active absenteeism and the No vote overruled the Yes supporters. This is important because many of those who defended absenteeism or the negative vote finally ended up legitimising the constitutional text. Others continue to reject the Spanish Constitution.

The same political bloc – Basque nationalists – that initially objected to the Magna Charta, were called upon to develop the legal process born of the 1978 Constitution, because they voted more in the first elections. Another reason I maintain this vision of the process is my belief in the social importance and the electoral and political efficacy of radical nation-alism that in the past rejected and continues to reject the legitimacy of the constitution. We should remember the survival of ETA and the conse-quences armed resistance has had for the Basque and Spanish civil society and for internal political projects.

The four aspects briefly listed here express and visualize a complex and problematic political map both regarding Basque society itself, and in its relations with Spain. A basic paradox becomes obvious – nationalism deals with the democratic objectivity that the Constitution represents, despite objections that some of its expressions dictate and despite perma-nent criticism of its role within the Spanish state.

The turning point of this process, as previously mentioned, is the approval of the Autonomy Statute. It is acknowledged that democratic nationalism – the radical nationalism opposed by Herri Batasuna – supported the statutory text in the 1980 referendum. Since then, this institutional nationalism (PNV followed by PNV and EA) promoted a positive understanding of the Statute and from here the nationalist account finds the legitimacy to add up to the democratic agreement that legitimates the Spanish transition.

The Statute institutionalises an accountability design that has the consensus of both the political and the social agents (nationalists or not). The accountability framework is composed of financial autonomy, an autonomous police system to control internal order and broad accountability in various other aspects (linguistic policy, education, tourism, industry, environment, etc.).

Under this ethos, social and political life is rationalized. What are the consequences of this reality? First, the naturalization of the Basque Government and the political construction of the Basque Country in record time – twenty years. Beyond the speeches and the openly expressed pretexts, and in a permanent process of vindication, the social and political configuration of Basque Autonomy sets a style that invades the social scenes and creates an imaginary society of a country organized by common institutions. This reference is transformed in the imagery that articulates the complexity and pluralism of Basque society. In summary, I think that the administrative carcass of Basque Autonomy gives new meaning to political discourse in this community.

Dilemmas of the Nationalist Narrative

Basque nationalism faces certain dilemmas and paradoxes stemming from the period of political transition. Nationalist narrative enters the twenty first century with the doctrine created at the end of the nineteenth century, when Basque nationalism first evolved. One can ask if these principles help explain the complexity of Basque society at the beginning of this century, or if a theoretical language fed not only by traditional bonds, history or adjustments in political strategy is required.

This is one of the unsolved problems in the discourse of Basque nationalism, but the latter remains frozen in its first formulation of the end of the nineteenth century. The central doctrine changes not so much in theoretical terms as in the significance and in daily life. The processes of secularisation and modernisation in Basque society open new horizons and flood the political scene with a slew of new problems. Nationalism offers a political scheme, but none of this would be comprehensible if we did not consider that being important is less relevant than the communication structure and the meaning created around it. Both nationalism and the communication structure support an ambiguous identity that allows all to enter, while at the same time appears solid enough to offer true identity and meaning. The corollary is set by the institutional construction of

the Basque Country during the transition and the creation of viable institutional, economic, and political spheres.

I do not wish to indicate that the supporting walls of the "Other" need
to fall or that the symbolic border between those who are or are not
nationalists within Basque society (the logic We – Others) must be erased.
However, Basque self-definition must gradually expand more and above
all become more diffuse, even if identification with the nationalist community is severed.

However, the questions and dilemmas remain: How can we move
forward from the definition of a nationalist community to a definition of
a society where pluralism is assumed? Currently there are probably no
reliable or final answers to these questions. The social influence of this
narrative is slowed down by the structural pluralism of Basque society. If
these are their limits, they make the nationalist community think of
Basque integrity, not in terms of something they possess and that they
transfer to the others, but as something that must be built day to day, with
others who are not nationalists, who have other identities and adhere to
other political ideologies.

Basque nationalism faces a double handicap when seeking to reach the
determined objectives. The first is to find a niche in a complex and plural
society to insert the concept of nation, a concept not self-evident for many
Basque citizens. The second is to know precisely which role to play in the
relationship with the central State and with Spain. Both handicaps are
equally significant. The following is based on the empirical data provided
by the Cabinet of Sociological Survey of the Basque Government and the
Euskobarometer of the University of the Basque Country. The first data
I want to emphasize is that between 35% to 40% of Basque population
defines itself as nationalist while between 50% to 55% declare they do
define themselves as such. The most relevant sociodemographic characteristics are: 35% are between the ages of 18 and 34, 26% are between
the ages of 35 and 50, and 39% are over the age of 50. Divided by territories, Guipúzcoa is the most "nationalist" with 46%, Bizkaia follows
with 37% and Araba, 29%. In response to whether or not it is independent, "only" between 30% to 35% of the population totally or partially
agrees, but 42% say that they totally or partially disagree.

Considering the data, it is difficult to claim that the majority of the
population shares the idea of a Basque nation. It is evident that there are
other options and the definition of a national concept is not uniform. This
data is confirmed by other issues we cannot ignore. First of all, by the electoral results that illustrate the complexity of the situation and secondly,
the objective situation of the Basque language.

I will start with the second issue mentioned. It is true that language has
a central position in the symbolic imagery of Basque nationalism. In fact,
if the remaining components of the "objective" definition of the nation

84

lose virulence in some cases and in others (the most outstanding is race), I cannot say that the same has happened with language.

The reasons for this are known to most. In the case analysed here, the results of the sociolinguistic inquiry carried out by the Basque Government present a panorama that clarifies the situation. The first aspect is that 58.5% of the population speak only Spanish. The second data to be considered is that only 24.7% of the citizens are bilingual; 16.3% know some Euskera, or are passive bilinguals and 0.6% of the population speak only Euskera.

Attitude towards the Basque language, as well as its effective possession, is an identity issue. In fact, almost all Basque speakers define themselves only as Basque (78%). On the contrary, 65% of the Spanish monolinguals claim dual identity – they consider themselves Basque and Spanish. As the sociolinguistic research suggests, greater predominance of Euskera necessarily indicates greater Basque nationalist identity. The position of the study is significant: most Basque speakers (73%) agree that to be a "real Basque" you have to know the Basque language. Thus, the language appears as the foundation of Basque identity. To speak Euskera or not, to know the language or to show interest in learning it are attitudes and/or practices that express the strict communicative function of Basque identity. It is not strange that national identity manifests itself in the language.

The electoral distribution presents a similar overview. Since 1980, nationalist parties rule the autonomic institutions. The numbers for nationalist options have always surpassed 550,000 voters beyond the total number of votes cast, while numbers for the non-nationalist electoral options have always been lower, albeit in ascending numbers if we consider the votes they won in 1980 compared to 2003. In any case, concerning electoral affinities, Basque society is very pluralistic, with over half of the population voting for nationalist parties and a little less than half voting for socialist or popular parties (the latter achieve best results in general elections to the Spanish Parliament, while the former achieve best results in autonomic and local elections).

Some data indicate two processes at work. The first is that the nationalist concept of nation does not include Basque society. The second is that national borders do not cross the societal threshold, for which we cannot presuppose the nationalist nation association is equal to Basque society. Both studies demonstrate that societal construction and national construction have followed parallel paths.

Considering these facts, we have to face a reality that I can summarize thus – construction of a national identity involves a different process than the construction of Basque identity. Historic nationalism has been unable to link the two. The question is why. I think the answer lies in the following four facts. First, the characteristics that nationalism assumes and the central axes of the nation concept. Second, the unique political history of the Spanish state. The history of contemporary Spain is full of difficulties, with too many years of anomalous politics and little opportunity to rehearse formulas that unite the different political consciences born in the territories with ardent nationalist movements. The State offers a history rife with a myriad difficulties – political and cultural centralism, ignorance (much ignorance!), and the consequences of ignoring differences as reflected in the political and social processes.

Third, the model of political action that historically results from the relationship between the State and Basque nationalism. This has been a relationship full of distrust, problems and irregularities. The consequences point to the fourth detail, the difficulties in constructing a plural civil society that is open and consolidated, with an evident socio-symbolic basis for all Basque citizens.

Basque Nationalism and State: Dilemmas of a Relationship

Another basic aspect that indicates the historic importance of this period is the relationship between the central State and Basque nationalism. The nationalist strategy was almost always imbued by a restricting character and distance from the political dynamic of the State. While that nationalist movement never exhibited much interest in joining the networks offered by the State, the State did not exhibit sufficient identity to integrate and/or dissolve nationalist pretensions.

On the other hand, the vicissitudes of Spanish history over the last hundred years provide much data on Basque nationalism. The latter, sheltered in their dissimilarity, never had to modify the perspective they offered the citizens that are identified with it. It was easier to declare a consciousness of community identity and negate the political perspective of the "Other", rather than clearly declare the position it sought within the State. The 1978 Constitution wanted to "forget" and redefine Spanish reality as democratic. To accomplish this, they venerated a new type of State. Because of its recognition of the regional autonomy, it was called State of Autonomies. According to this original definition, the State is a dual entity that superposes centralist policies with autonomist plans. In fact, there was an effort to integrate three separate self-defining units: Spain, the nationalities and the regions.

However, the text and the model presented certain inconveniences from the start. As J. Pablo Fusi has stated (1998, 163), the State of Autonomies, defined in the 1978 Constitution, bore negative elements from its inception, such as the artificiality of the definitions of some of the regions created, the grossly insufficient functionality of others and the extraordinary bureaucratic and administrative complexity of the entire group. Theoretically, the defects were insurmountable. Tomás and Valiente eventually demonstrated that the text was incomplete and deficient. Fusi (1998) detected in his analysis a basic problem and he formulates it thus: in 1978 we believed that the approval of the autonomies would end the problem of the peripheral nationalisms, time has demonstrated that this was an illusion. Fusi suggests that the real reason lay in the nature of Basque and Catalan nationalism, alien to the State structure. They did not evolve because the Spanish State was more or less centralist since the eighteeenth century. Basque and Catalan nationalism was not invented by politics, but is the result of historical realities, expressing national identities consolidated for centuries, each with a distinct personality and cultural identity.

The autonomic institutionalisation derived, in addition, from other problems. The Constitution defined certain principles and procedures to begin the territorial restructuring of the political power that could hypothetically develop into different political models. The so-called autonomic model does not appear in the Constitution because, as Fossa says (2000, 134), this would mean that the State territorial organization was, at least partially, not bound by the constitution.

As other experts point out, the limitations did not come so much from the Constitution as from its interpretation. Once again, debate is a major character in the autonomic State. In other words, the capacity to make the structures flexible, thus creating an open system, can lead to dynamic politics in the periphery.

The conditions for the basic and general consensus are raised in the following terms: they are basically those that contributed to assure a compromise between the minority and the nationalisms and the majority nationalism. The search continues for negotiated solutions to confirm the hypothesis that constitutional construction is not finalized. This does not mean that statutory logic cannot survive alongside other political aspirations, something nationalism never demanded.

For Basque nationalism, the Statute of the Autonomies defined a compromise, but it was open and subject to changes, and at no moment did it cancel or decrease the differential capacity that it had historically expressed. The statutory logic remained bound to the development of the competences and to the construction of the symbolic imagery that Basque nationalism was responsible for producing and protecting. The Statute was seen as a stepping-stone and not as the final goal in a process that would otherwise have remained inaccessible. The scene was prepared for further progress and for more advantageous adjustments towards achieving the objectives.

Nationalism based on the process of transition faces challenges. Firstly, it has demonstrated continuous electoral presence and evident plausibility structure. Both facts indicate a characteristic sociology based on a) institutional permanence b) social presence and c) the objective power of socialization mechanisms that will be developed. Secondly, it creates public opinion, brandishing aspirations of self-government. Thirdly, there is the historical trajectory of this expression. We must realize that in over a hundred years national consciousness and its imagery take root. It remains amenable, depending on the occasion, to flexible interpretations or to conclusive discourses, to pragmatic aspirations or to the most ambitious nationalist programme, but in certain cases the presence of the plausibility structure associated with a specific sociology and unquestionable political and social strength is discernible.

Hence, I do not think that the problem is the objectivity of the social and political presence of the nationalist social basis, but rather its accommodation within State structures or the fissure of the present model of State in Spain.

We have persistently asked Basque nationalism to clarify the options. And the issue is clear by the weight it grants to the following three assumptions: (1). The pragmatism of the political action and the concern about the desirable relationship with Spain.(2). The ambiguity of being a part of the State while at the same time having its own government. (3). Above all, the ultimate aspirations defined in the central doctrine. Remembering them and not concealing them is a sign of identity in the Basque national discourse. The formulae and political strategies throughout history have been developments of these three suppositions, from the social and political presence of its discourse.

The relationship not mentioned in the suppositions engages the State centre and Basque nationalist periphery in a game of politics. Thus, certain political options, autonomy or asymmetrical federalism, and others such as self-determination or independence, guarantee the definitive political vindication in the Basque Country. In one case, the manner chosen is the product of a socio-political game that does not fully satisfy the desires of the vindictive nationalism contents. In another case, the pluralism of Basque society prevents extreme solutions and probably the faithful fulfilment of the nationalist dream. One should remember, in addition to the cited matters, that others benefited from the extreme pluralism of Basque society that prevented a uniform discourse. It is not clear if the exercise in self-determination is the solution or the problem. I insist on this fact because I do not think it depends only on the casuistry of the rights or political principles, but on the social debate on creating cohesion in a pluralistic society such as the Basque, where different solutions and formulae for the same problem coexist, i.e. including the Basque in the State structures.

Basque Political Violence

The political issues mentioned raise another unsolved problem: the solution to the political violence of ETA adds much drama and compounds an already complex problem. I maintain the hypothesis that ETA's attitude towards the violent acts that it provokes and the "solution" to the consequences of the violence are factors that clearly divide Basque society and the political and social discourses. A quick look at recent history reveals that there have been different stages (A. Gurrutxaga, 1996, 2002). Without explicating all of them, it is necessary to illuminate those elements that I believe help to understand this complex phenomenon.

First, in the last twenty years the actions of ETA have lost significant support. The response, from the ranks of the armed organization, has been to create their own realm, ruled and regulated by military logic. At the same time, rejection of the actions of ETA prompted the formation of new movements whose main objective is peace and to cease the armed violence of ETA. How history will judge these groups is yet to be seen, but they all promote a peace agenda and they implement social action against ETA in an educational movement. They have found, on the other hand, a model for collective action that mobilises consciences and confronts all Basque citizens with the central role of the victim and the drama of political violence.

During this period the armed organization must remain active, although this necessarily leads to breaking the bonds with whichever political or social organization is not present in the surroundings. This has significant consequences. Firstly, ETA strategy grows more and more military. Military logic has rules that are not explained to non-members, and in the eyes of the armed organization, legitimacy is not required. Legitimacy, when sought, is internal, it is pursued within the "community of the people chosen" that view the organization as the bastion of their vindications. Its discourse abides by predefined reasons in the social space that ETA represents, but only the individuals identified with that space are required to understand. Legitimacy is sought among those "people chosen." Only they understand and the vision is of interest only to them. The opinion of those facing their own space and the armed actions of ETA is only significant for the organization because they believe that their attitudes and opinions justify the armed option, the political strategy that stems from it and the social world that is sheltered there.

Second, the activity of ETA, and of the social world that supports it, shapes the separation strategy, which I term strategy of its own space. The goal is the "adhesion" to social space in an attempt to define the territory representing the "community of the chosen ones."

The third consequence is two sided. On the one hand, it implies a fissure from any political and social community in the Basque Country and, on the other hand, it reproduces the separation between some (the inhabitants of their own space) and others. This separation provokes additional efforts to prove the legitimacy of their own space. This directs them to the psycho-morphic sight, in other words, to perceive the world and reality exclusively considering the interests of the inhabitants of their own space.

The fourth most outstanding fact is that military logic regiments the organization's thought and its own space, and takes hold of, and dissolves, the autonomy of the civil and political space of the radical world. This means that ETA acts dissolve the very political space that it helped construct. Once again, the tradition of Cain is carried out. ETA also acts as the god Saturn devouring his sons.

The devastating effect of this logic is represented in the draining of radical politics. This political world, with an impressive electoral presence, submits the socio-political dynamics to the actions of ETA. The result is that although the symbiosis between the civil front and the military front aspired to depict the submission of the civic framework to the strategy of the armed activity, which illustrated over this period that there is either no place for politics or that military logic prevails, it always involves falsehoods and an element of pain. The politics of pain negates the possibility of politics itself.

Essentially, ETA activity "dissolves" the rules of the political game. Following this conclusion, it is not a matter of there being no space for politics, rather that the game is impossible. The military logic has a tragic destiny, and it is the community logic that shelters and protects itself in "its" space, that aims for political results but instead dissolves the policy from a pain vindication that erases the same political framework, transferring it to a dimension of prepolitics. According to this model, the defence of their own space is merely an expression of the ambition to play politics when one cannot and when the social and political debate is transferred to within Basque society.

Fifth, identification with ETA generates a definition of the other not from a broad framework, but from a close social framework that defines its "own space." The limits of a symbolic border backfire in an attempt to integrate, but when the hard nucleus of the "own space" lacks influence, the group with which it identifies becomes much more coherent.

The result is the beginning of an integration process of the nucleus and the radical world. This is a very, very slow process. The data selected from multiple inquiries demonstrates that in reality, the inclination within the Basque population is to abandon and reject the violence and armed actions. The electoral results also illustrate the slow decline of the electoral base of the radical discourse.

In the past 25 years there have been several milestones in this integration strategy. First, I refer to the Agreement of Ajuria Enea, signed by all

Basque political forces, except Batasuna, in 1988. Second, we should not forget other factors such as that almost all Basque society questions the violent acts of ETA. Third, we have seen the pedagogic action of peace movements lead to the creation of a collective conscience that values the strategic importance of peace.

Fourth, the political activity of the democratic bloc that rejects any and all violence is important. Fifth, I have also observed a drop in the support of the radical political framework and the slow but continuous disengagement of the social sectors, particularly young adults that in the past supported Herri Batasuna.

Sixth, the conviction of nationalist groups that their political objectives do not correspond to the habit of violence is no less important. Seventh, nationalist groups no longer monopolize the public sphere as their own space to vindicate or frighten citizens. The achievements of over 20 years of an Autonomy Statute include the conclusion of the agonizing and victimizing image of Basque society. Finally, I should not forget the successes of police strategy and the international action of the Spanish government in "smothering" the traditional means of action of the ETA community.

The result, considering the above, is that the periphery of the radical world is enlarged and more extended, whilst the small nucleus is more coherent and results more resistant.

Another event must be considered because of its significance within this wide perspective, the agreements of Lizarra-Estella. An ideological, political and mediating confrontation has been erupted this agreement. The agreement is difficult to evaluate under conditions other than Basque political and social life in the present.

The Agreement was initially presented as the need to illustrate the truce with ETA, but according to those who signed it, it also points to a new political phase, where, above all, chaos is the initial stage, followed by a process of adjustment between the political forces involved.

Lizarra's first objective was to give a political guarantee to the 1999 ETA truce, disregarding its many secret causes. In words of its architects, it was the beginning of a political process that aspired to attract the radical nationalist world to institutionalised positions. In reality, the political arrangement of that time was implemented under conditions comparable to a long-distance marathon runner entering the race at the speed of a 100 metre sprinter.

I am under the impression that this agreement was affected by a political formula shaped by four facts. First, the need to demonstrate to ETA that we can achieve more than originally stated in the political framework designed within the Statute. Second, the meaning and consequences of the "final point" of the Statute are not explained to Basque citizenship – perhaps because they are unknown, perhaps because it is neither a true nor attainable goal. Third, theoretical formulae are improvised, and precarious analytical baggage is incorporated, brought from other historical experiences (mainly Ireland and Quebec) by the social engineers of the negotiations, obviating the confrontation of the models that they proposed with Basque empiric reality (its complexity and extreme pluralism, the pluralism of the nationalist discourse, the political processes in Europe and the changes in the definition of the future for Basque society).

Thus, analysing and drawing conclusions from the tendencies in Basque society and from the plausibility structure of its discourses to support the consequences that such a process puts into motion would be avoided.

I find it unreasonable to disregard the difficulties implied in a political change such as the one announced. Certainly, many internal as well as external difficulties exist. First, as previously mentioned, there is the political fragmentation and the pluralism of Basque society, and the non independent character of political and social sectors traditionally identified with political nationalism, as well as the unequal approval of the nationalist discourse in different Basque territories (nationalism has great electoral presence in Bizkaia and Guipúzcoa, but not Araba, and its presence is minor in Navarre and almost irrelevant in the Basque territory that is part of France). Likewise, it is divided into two Autonomous Communities within the Spanish State and in two countries (Spain and France).

The discussion and revision of the political principles venerated in modern European history, such as territoriality, sovereignty or the present connotation of the nineteenth century state, all relate to this fact. It is also important to remember that processes such as those mentioned – the case of Quebec is a good analogy from which to draw conclusions – provoke uncertainty and restlessness among many citizens because of the dynamics they unleash and the pressures other political forces exercise, etc.

I cannot ignore in this debate certain outside factors such as the simplistic interpretation of autonomy that the central state, Spain, defines as a tendency to uniformity in what in reality is significant pluralism in the state territory. The role that the reason of State plays is also a key factor in the constitutional defence of what we want Spain to be.

One cannot lose sight of the revival of the identity of Spain that, ideologically, is unquestionably a cohesive factor for many social sectors. Thus, for example, the revived identity of the Partido Popular is nothing more than reinvented neo-nationalism that moulds its discourse, involving peripheral nationalisms (particularly Basque and Catalan), and positions itself as an anti-peripheral discourse.

Not surprisingly, Lizarra opens a serious debate in which we are still anchored. The questions of who will finally pay the bill, who should explain the accumulated debts, and above all, what has been the purpose of this effort, are not foreign to this debate.

I do think, for example, that it can be said that institutional nationalism has paid a high price. I am indeed certain that political relations were subjected to a game of mirrors and non-definitions, a game where the art of simulation etched the scenery that wanted to be created there. Several elements have not been taken into consideration: The observations of others (the connection between Basque Autonomy Community and the government of Madrid); the part that central government should play in ending ETA; the prominent role of the mediating strategy that the media enforced, thus negating any potential the Lizarra agreement held and eliminating the possibility of any arrangement or negotiation with the armed organization to disband; Batasuna's lack of political maturity and, above all, what ETA thought and wanted.

However, the Spanish transition has not answered the question of whether it is even possible that ETA can cease to exist. My answer is no. Why am I pessimistic? Because the basic conditions have not been fulfilled. The Spanish State does not seem ready to face the problem, nor is the internal Basque political agreement to end armed organization feasible. ETA does not appear willing to consider disbandment, nor does it seem that the mediating strategies will be modified or that the State wants to get involved in such problematic work. However, it must be tackled. The problem, as always, is where to begin, particularly in a situation such as the present where nobody foots the bill for ETA to continue – excuse me! someone does pay: the victims and all those threatened. But currently the survival of ETA has no electoral cost for the political parties that control the institutions in any government. There are no economic nor excessive social costs – the Basque Country continues to develop at a reasonable rate. It is as if the attempts to disband ETA have been abandoned. It is sad to say, but I am convinced that ETA survives not so much because of its technical, political or military capacity, but because its actions do not generate a significant price for those who define the strategies from the institutional powers. Does anyone think that if voter support depended on ETA or if economic progress and citizen welfare would be jeopardised by the actions of the organization, it would continue? We are facing an example where the lack of impact of the actions' effects allows the survival of the organization. While this can maintain ETA, it cannot make it disappear. Who is going to fight for it? It is as if everybody trusted police pressure to demobilize the organization or that the democratic call for political consensus will put a stop to the violent actions.

Another possible scenario, however, is to reduce the organization's military capacity so that the activity comes closer to what is termed low intensity violence. Four mechanisms are used to achieve this: police action, international pressure concerning the armed organization's logistics, avoiding militant duplication of ETA, and preventing political representation. I think that this is the most efficient way to reach minimal influence on the organization.

In any case, it is obvious that the capacity to intimidate and its symbolism continue to yield ETA substantial benefits. This explains the discrepancy between the almost non-existent activity in recent years and ETA's continued power to intimidate, however altered. Political and social life continues much the same as when the organization had greater military capacity. Today, as never before, ETA, wields political influence by its mere presence, through intense exploitation of its symbolism. It divides and frightens, despite notoriously inferior military capacity, and shapes political life more than at any given time in its long history.

Conclusions

Castoriadis said that the crisis of the Western world lies precisely in its not questioning itself. Such questioning is the deepest secret in many of the astonishing searches by man.

The 25 years of democracy in Spain is a long enough period to draw conclusions on the subject/object of this article.

1. Empiric reality indicates that Basque society is well developed, and enjoys a high degree of economic growth and material welfare, cultural sophistication and political competence as never before. The people express high regard for the autonomy administration and the many services it creates, deals and administers. Institutional stability has been a reality and an unquestionable fact for almost 25 years.

2. At this point, one has to admit to a paradox: we face a society with economic development and social modernisation similar to that of any Western society in the region, a society that enjoys vast political competence and impressive managerial ability. This contrasts with the image sometimes projected of a anxious society, turned inwards due to the precariousness of the social and political cohesion mechanisms that the armed action of ETA provokes. One fact is conclusive – Basque society is a dynamic society that faces a situation that questions both its foundations and its cohesion as a society. These data provoke some evident questions. For example, what issues must be addressed in the Basque country: assure the standard of living, societal cohesion, peace, national construction, institutional stability or allow the Basque to deal with their own matters? Are these elements compatible or do we have to select one or the other?

The debate within nationalism has little to do with the dream of a most ambitious programme, and quite a lot with the stubbornness of the empiric referents and the moderation that corresponds to societies with these structural characteristics. Thus, I do not think, for example, that the vindication of independence formulated in a traditional way, following the political tradition of the nineteenth century, is needed in the political debate to support one's aims. Neither do I think it is worth opening the proverbial Pandora's box to discover – on behalf of Basque nationalism – what happened with the sovereignty that was never realized. Nor is it worth pulling Ariadna's thread to find the territory that never was, or does someone think historic restoration of the past can stop the paralysing changes imposed by globalisation?

3. Nationalism has three basic resources to survey the present. First, the structure of the opportunities connected to the internal social and political compromises and to a new concept of hegemony. One can ask on what are these principles founded. I think that Basque society, and institutional nationalism, have known the answer all along: principles of welfare, identity and the plausibility structure. Second, the political, institutional and administrative resources available due to the development of the Statute of Autonomy – the competence, or in other words, the political capacity to accomplish what is necessary. But competence is the instrument founded on plausible objectives and on empirically defined goals. The third resource available consists of both formally and materially assuming the role that the political and social scene fills, the interdependence. The challenge is not in negating it, but in finding the gap and filling it.

4. The debate for the present and the near future should not be about what is negated, but rather about what is stated. In other words, the debate should be about how to adjust to the political scene without becoming dependent on political conceptualising or on the habit of resistance, which has proved so fruitful in the past. There are some basic tasks that can describe this future. One is the radical assumption of the pluralism of the Basque country. This has the most significant and essential reference with clear consequences. The first consequence is the inability to perceive the references to the nationalist discourse from the idea and praxis of hegemony. The pluralism of Basque society indicates that it is composed of a mosaic of social and political spheres: interdependent, some more dominant than others, but without a single sphere with the capacity to construct or represent the entire Basque society. Pluralist societies do not depend on a single metaphysical unit or conclusively defined principle for their cohesion, for what is valid for some is not necessarily valid for others. Aspiring to cohesion without being attentive to the difficult issues is inviting failure. Thus, the expressions of Basque society should not be thought of as "hegemonic ideas" but as the basic ambitions shared by most of the population.

5. The concept that defines the nation is not alien to this situation. If

we accept Basque society as a radically pluralistic framework, there is no sense in defending a concept deemed unidentifiable by many citizens, even if the nationalist definition of nation recognizes the symbolic representation of the group. But this neither defines nor includes all the political and social activities of the Basque citizens. This implies a problem of great magnitude, even if the traditional definition of nationalism has social strength, electoral presence and a powerful structure of plausibility. But if this is so, what can be done so that those citizens who do not share the concept of nation proposed by the nationalist community, or who do not share some of the distinctive signs derived from it, are satisfied and identify with the idea of nation aimed at? Is this possible?

There are three resources available to hasten the aim of national identity. One is the citizens' reconciliation with the institutions of self-government and political autonomy, results of the institutionalisation of the Basque Autonomy Statute, as well as with the symbols of identification that have been created in recent history. In addition, the identification circumstances of the Basque citizens are produced independently of the electoral structure and of any political affinities or ideologically inspired positions they defend.

The identification that allows the citizen to interact with the institutions and the social and institutional emblems, without demanding loyalty to a specific culture or political perspective, is another resource. This implies that rather than manipulate society as the representation of this specific culture, the citizen perceives social life as integrating an elastic and flexible network interlaced by multiple identities. Thus, the individuals choose with whom to identify, when and how. The third resource is citizenship, founded on the accumulation of the individual's fundamental rights resulting from one living in this society.

After detailing these three resources, I think that a concept of nation that equates nation to society can be recreated. Currently, nation, for a complex and radically pluralistic society such as the Basque, can only represent all of its citizens if its definition presumes the basic ambitions. The remainder is recreating a strong concept, integrating for some, but scarcely operative when facing the issue of nationalist community cohesion, but more importantly the construction of the framework for all Basque society in its radical plurality. I have already intimated that the definitions must be neither intense nor strong but rather faint and integrating, viewing reality from the intersection of the multiple social and political meetings.

6. In the Basque Country, no structural reality is more evident than the pluralism of ideas, geographical origins, political attachments, electoral resources, etc. Thus, Basque society need not reinvent pluralism, but merely coexist with this most unquestionable fact of its modern history. The problem of Basque pluralism lies in the political sphere (noting that

we do not know of cultural crashes nor attempts at coexistence between, for example, immigrants and natives, if such concepts are still valid), particularly in the tactics and strategies of the political forces. One can argue, with or without reason, that the best formula to represent the basic pluralism is when no one can claim exclusive representation nor transform one voice to represent a single faction, but the political game, while rarely accepting nuances, does indeed tolerate rebellion on many occasions, sufficiently to convey the rhythm of social pluralism to the political sphere.

7. Another issue is the future relationship between the Basque nation and the Spanish State. For years, the relationship has been tumultuous, often distrustful, nourished by mutual accusations. Such accusations include the Spanish State's non-compliance with the Statute. In reality the autonomic model provided in the Constitutional Charter ended up as something termed "coffee for everybody," adulterating the original model and homogenizing the pluralistic Spanish reality. This does not express the political aspirations of nationalism because the State considers that the maximum degree of political development in Spain has been reached with the present statutory model. Such discourses nourish the relationship. The result of this never-ending discourse is the inability to secure a loyalty agreement.

8. On behalf of the Spanish State, the nationalism that governs the Autonomous Community is "required" to accept the Statute as its final political trajectory, to bury the dream of its most ambitious programme, or to renew it within the limits of the statutory solution provide by the State.

This requires nationalism to convert itself into a statutory political force. This modification in the very essence of nationalism cannot be assumed, for it would mean casting aside the political project and negating the very nature of nationalism. At the same time, nationalism conceptualises the political time of the Statute as historical time, and not as the final point in vindication on the road to realizing its most ambitious programme.

But if this is the conclusion reached by nationalism and the State, what on some occasions becomes apparent in fact entails serious problems. The present proposal of lendakari (president) Ibarretxe demonstrates what I argue here. There are problems of the precise definition of what is wanted and what exists in reality; there are problems of social integration to explain, and those who still insist on fighting for the nationalist goals in their entirety must be convinced to reconcile with the accomplishments secured. There are also problems related to the uncertainty that such processes generate, such as a sufficient critical mass to conduct post statutory strategies and the need to engineer, in the hope of achieving additional aspects of the most ambitious nationalist programme in the future.

We should not lose sight of something that I have already suggested – that the traditional political instruments (classic State-nation, sovereignty and territory) have significantly suffered throughout the entire Western hemisphere in recent years. The State has changed considerably, as has the concept of sovereignty, and the relationship to territory. It is difficult to answer questions regarding the sense of political independence in the twenty-first century, what is the adequate expression for the State, or what role can nationalism, such as the Basque, ascribe in the twenty-first century. It is not easy to escape these problems and to seek shelter in the ecosystem or in the accepted, prosaic, common answers.

I sense that a new statutory agreement founded on these premises is foreseeable on the immediate horizon. This can come only from an open model incorporating new abilities particularly adapted to address Basque presence in Europe. Perhaps then, the existence of an open Statute (without possible political closing), Basque presence in Europe, the signing of a new statutory agreement based on diffuse sovereignties and the development of new abilities will help to free the present relationship model.

9. Almost nothing that I say makes sense if peace continues to evade the region. Four decades of life in the shadow of ETA have trapped three generations of Basque people. In many cases, ETA has defined the political socialization of these people, their social definitions, the personal drama and the death of too many of them!

Much has been written about the significance of ETA violence, and I do not wish to expand on this subject. However, there are two observations I would like to raise. The first is that the Basque Country (and with it institutional nationalism) has no future with ETA. The second is that I have the impression that the time for negotiation with ETA has passed and that at this point in time the key question is how ETA wants to admit failure, and who is going to deal with it. However, I would rather not refer too much to the price that the answers to these questions raise. Can Basque society pay any more than it has already paid and continues to pay?

Other data should be considered as they relate to these affirmations. First, previous attempts to approach the world of ETA have always been rejected by the armed organization, most times with conclusive and unfortunate results. Second, failure has generated significant costs for all involved. Third, the mythology of the negotiations with ETA shatters the legitimacy of the political system and submits those that impugn it to very high costs without considering the positive effects sought. Fourth, the reasons given to maintain the relationship with ETA have not enjoyed popular legalization. Fifth, the violence employed by the armed organization has converted the means into an end. Perceiving it any other way leads to a dead-end. Sixth, the autonomy of the violent discourse engages all those who think they contribute to a successful relationship. And seventh, Basque civil society lives in a state of crisis lacerated by violence. There is no legitimate justification to shelter the illusions of radical nationalism.

The integration strategy is really affecting the universe of ETA. This means a more moderate radical world, in the sense that many of those who at one time had confidence in a radical approach have abandoned this view, and many others, once situated in the nucleus, have moved to the periphery.

10. Although the political transition in Spain has been a success, there are still unanswered questions in the Basque Country. The twenty-first century is presented as full of light and myriad shades. The democratic nationalism and the Spanish State need to reread the future, considering the historic change which encloses us. Neither globalisation, nor the reconfiguration of political power transpiring throughout the Western world, nor the new networks being developed in Europe, leave them much time to probe the issue. The important instruments in their possession allow them, on the contrary, to pose incisive questions regarding the process we have analysed. For example, rethinking the idea of nation that Basque nationalism has upheld during its century of existence, and finding a way to solve the political tension created by the structural pluralism of Basque society. It also needs to discover its role in the State and its unique relationship with the discourse it has designed about the nature of the future State. But the basic issue is violence. This is particularly true when searching for a strategy that combines the integration process with its consequences and with the governance of Basque institutions.

The capacity of the Spanish State to contain the differential pluralism of the territory that governs and deals and rereads its role in this century should not be omitted. Nor should appeals by elements in the centre of Spain to quell nationalisms, nor the negation of the peripheries, nor the reality of what the future holds. The reconfiguration of the political power in complex societies, with the game rules no longer controlled by traditional, national agents of power, may be the second transition awaiting Spain, particularly should it refuse to be reinvented.

Twenty-first century politics cannot escape inventing political power, and traditional instruments used to invent the present during the last two centuries are no longer relevant. This is another problem, perhaps the object of a new transition, where we should all speak differently because our political references and the social supports "of all life" are no longer where they should be.

References

Fossas, Enric. *Asimetría y Plurinacionalidad en el Estado Autonómico*. Ed. Trotta. Madrid. 1999.

Fusi, Juan Pablo. *España. La Evolución de la Identidad Nacional*. Ed. Temas de Hoy. Madrid. 2000.

Gurrutxaga Abad, Ander. *La Transformación del Nacionalismo Vasco*. Ed. Haramburu. San Sebastián. 1996.

Gurrutxaga Abad, Ander. *La Mirada Difusa*. Ed. Alberdania. San Sebastián. 2002.

Pérez – Díaz, Víctor, *España puesta a prueba*. Ed. Alianza. Madrid. 1996.

5

DEMOCRACY AND TERRORISM IN SPAIN

Juan Avilés

When General Franco died in 1975, few observers expected Spain to experience a fast and consensual transition to democracy. Franco's dictatorship that arose after a cruel Civil War, had lasted four decades and had completely excluded all democratic political movements from legal life. Yet the transition was initiated by a king who had been chosen by Franco as his heir, and by politicians molded in the dictatorial regime. In 1977, socialists and communists, the defeated parties of the Spanish Civil War, took part in free elections, and a democratic Constitution was approved by a huge consensus in 1978. Furthermore, the Constitution substituted the dictatorship's centralist system for a decentralised one that recognises the right to autonomy to the "nationalities and regions", which according to the constitutional text compose Spain. The Spanish territory was divided into 17 autonomous communities endowed with great powers, thus satisfying at least the immediate aspirations of the mainstream national parties from Catalonia and the Basque country. After some years of a centrist rule, the Socialist Party won the elections of 1982, a date that can be considered as the end of the transition. During the long period of the Felipe González socialist rule (1982–1996), Spain became as *The Economist* stated, "a fairly normal European country".

Nevertheless, not everything took place under consensus in the Spanish transition. On some occasions, it seemed that terrorist action could cause an authoritarian regression. One of these occasions was the "Black Week" of January 1977, in which the extreme left terrorist organisation, GRAPO, kidnapped a lieutenant general and killed four members of the security forces, whilst extreme right killers shot dead one student in a demonstration and five people at a labour lawyers' office linked to the Communist Party. Paradoxically, these extremist attacks strengthened the

Spaniards' resolve to consensus, and in June 1977 the firsts democratic elections since 1936 were called.

The threat of ETA's nationalist terrorism was even graver for the newborn Spanish democracy. Although by the end of 1977 all jailed ETA militants were released, and although the new Basque autonomous institutions became operational in 1980, these were the toughest years of ETA terrorism that resulted in 234 people killed between 1978 and 1980. Many of the ETA victims were members of the army and security forces, and this contributed to create a tense atmosphere that to some people looked auspicious for a military coup. Nonetheless, the failure of the February 1981 coup attempt furthered the consolidation of democracy and the socialist victory in the 1982 elections.

Both the democratic transition and the terrorist wave in Spain followed international patterns. The Spanish transition was drawn by a great democratising wave that originated in Portugal in 1974, and successively spread in Mediterranean Europe, Latin America, East Asia and East and Central Europe (Huntington 1991). Spanish terrorism emerged in the context of an international wave that affected several developed countries, such as North Ireland, Italy and Israel (Moniquet 2002). The critical year was 1969, when terrorism reappeared in North Ireland and began in Italy, and the first Palestinian attacks outside Israel's borders took place. A year earlier, in 1968, ETA had committed its first assassination. This terrorist wave basically had a revolutionary socialist objective, similar to that of the Latin American guerrillas, which in its first stage peaked between 1956 and 1970 (Wickam-Crowley 1991). However, the most influential terrorist groups, such as the IRA, ETA and the Palestinian organisations had a strong nationalist component.

Spanish experience with terrorism differs from the Italian and is more akin to the Irish or the Israeli due to the long period of time that the terrorist phenomenon has persisted. Both extreme left and extreme right terrorism practically disappeared with the consolidation of democracy, but ETA has kept killing for more than thirty years and, though fairly debilitated, it is Europe's oldest operative terrorist organisation today.

Some remarks on terrorism

As Raymond Aron wrote long ago, definitions are neither true nor false, but rather more or less useful. When considering terrorism, it is necessary to explain what is meant by this sometimes controversial term. According to its common definition, terrorism is a type of violence committed clandestinely against non-combatant people in order to terrorise a population or to coerce a government's resolve in order to achieve a political purpose. It is not to be confused with insurrection, which is an open struggle, nor with guerrilla, which implies armed confrontations between combatants (Ganor 2002; Merari 1993).

Neither should it be confused with other kinds of political terror. Types of massive terror, those that claim the most victims, are usually exerted by a State through its official agents in order to terrorise its own population or a specific group of it. This type of openly exerted terror contrasts with the clandestine ways of what we usually consider terrorism. In this sense, Franco's regime exerted extensive terror, particularly in its first years, but that was not terrorism as such. However, it is appropriate to include in the concept of terrorism the political violence exerted by a State through clandestine agents, that is to say through the same procedures used by terrorist organisations.

There are two main schools in the interpretation of terrorism. One upholds the theory of rational choice and asserts that terrorism can be considered as an option taken by an organisation according to a rational consideration of benefits and costs. The lack of balance between the resources available to a terrorist organisation and those of its enemies is thus a key element, since terrorism embodies a mechanism that compensates for its weakness. According to this interpretation, several factors encourage the terrorist option: ideological extremism that makes it difficult to obtain the wide popular support that is needed for other strategies; the minority nature of the social group which the terrorist organisation presumes to represent, as sometimes occurs with religious or ethnic based organisations; the authoritarian nature of the State, which thwarts pacific opposition; or simply the resolve to adopt a strategy that is faster than those requiring a major popular mobilisation (Crenshaw 1990).

The second interpretation is founded on the psychological reasons that may incite terrorist violence. On the whole, terrorists do not present significant psychopathological attitudes, and they do not match an archetypical psychological profile. Nevertheless, they usually are aggressive people, directed to action, and looking for exciting experiences. Frequently, they also exhibit psychological mechanisms of split personality and externalising nature, a trait of psychologically disturbed people, who hero-worship their ego and split and project onto others the aspects of their own personality that they reject. Therefore, they need to ascribe their inner difficulties to an external enemy, and at the same time they consolidate their identity and get a sense of belonging when adhering to a tightly knitted group. The terrorists are such a kind of group and present specific dynamics characterised by the tendencies to reinforce cohesion and erase internal discrepancy; to take decisions riskier than any member could ever have taken on his own; and to reject any intermediate solution, which would imply halting the struggle, while the final aims permit the continuation of the struggle (Post 1990).

Both interpretations are useful to understand terrorist phenomena, even

103

though the sources at the historian's disposal hinder him to inquire into the role played by certain psychological impulses. Instead it is possible to examine the spread of certain ideas, myths and images that incite to terrorism, applying the theory that anthropologist Dan Sperber labelled epidemiology of mental representations (Sperber 1996). In brief, it is convenient to identify the diffusion of those ideologies that make some individuals eager to kill and even to die.

A glance at the history of terrorism shows that those ideologies emerge at the juncture between religion and politics. In some cases, they arise from a political ideology that has some features of a religious faith, in others from the politicisation of religion. The latter is dominant at present, as terrorism looks for its vindication in religion (Benjamin and Simon 2002). On the other hand, the terrorist movements that emerged in the secularised Western societies in the late 19th and the 20th centuries had their origin in what some authors call "political religions". A political religion is a type of political ideology that consecrates the primacy of a secular collective entity, such as Nation, Race or Class, forces the individual to yield to ethical and social imperatives based on it and construes its political action in messianic terms (Gentile 2001).

The concept of political religion is certainly useful to understand totalitarian parties, but can also be applied to terrorist organisations, which often have totalitarian tendencies. Several terrorist movements have used secular messianic ideas about Nation and Social Revolution as a source of inspiration and stimulus. The terrorist movements that emerged in Europe in the seventies and eighties of the 20th century, fascist, communist or nationalist tendencies. But it should be noted that by then Fascism was already a discredited ideology that was able to incite vigilante terrorism, but it was not a genuine political religion able to raise faith and hope, as it used to be during the inter-war period. Communism had also lost its messianic component in the Soviet Union and throughout Europe, although it retained this element in other parts of the world. The enthusiasm shown by some Europeans youths for Mao, Ho Chi Minh or Che Guevara did not last long. Nevertheless, the messianic faith in the communist revolution became the ideological template for terrorist movements such as the Red Brigades in Italy. In contrast, the idea of Nation retained a strong appeal, with the peculiarity that in Spain, Spanish nationalism was discredited due to its usage by the Francoist regime, whilst other nationalist movements, such as the Catalonian and Basque, which the dictator had tried to expunge, flourished.

This ideological panorama explains to some extent the distinctive fate of the terrorist movements in Spain during those years. Extreme right terrorism decreased to occasional actions, which did not seem to be driven by a coherent strategy. Marxism- Leninism inspired GRAPO, a terrorist organisation quite active during the transition years, but which never had significant support and soon was relegated to a marginal role. On the other hand ETA, whose ideology is based on a combination of Basque nationalism and revolutionary socialism, became one of the bloodiest terrorist organisations in Europe. In the past thirty years, ETA has killed more than 800 people.

Extreme left and extreme right

The extreme left terrorism that emerged in Europe in the late seventies did not surface in Spain until the last months of Franco's regime, and never developed significantly. Like in other countries, its origin stems from the repudiation of the pact strategy adopted by the orthodox communist parties. Since 1956, the Spanish Communist Party (PCE in its Spanish abbreviation) had adopted a national reconciliation policy that encouraged Spaniards to overcome their differences caused by the civil war, and fostered a pacific and democratic path towards socialism. This was a political line that those who were still supporters of the Leninist principles considered as a "revisionist" betrayal and an effective renunciation of the revolution. On the other hand, the examples of Mao Zedong and Fidel Castro showed that the violent revolutionary path was still valid. Consequently, several groups and subgroups from the new Spanish left that emerged in the seventies added to their blame of the PCE's revisionism an emphatic defence of violence as a revolutionary duty, although in most cases, this defence remained theoretical. Besides attempts that were quickly frustrated by police action, only two organisations succeeded in setting a terrorist strategy, FRAP and GRAPO. Both emerged from exile and adopted the Maoist line (Castro 2002).

FRAP began its terrorist activity in the summer of 1975, but the consequent repression, culminating with the execution of three of its members in September 1975, shortly before Franco's death, practically put an end to the organisation, which was dissolved in 1977.

GRAPO's first terrorist attacks took place in late 1975. This organisation maintained a significant activity during the whole period of the transition, and kept operating sporadically afterwards. Although they barely reached two hundred militant members and about a thousand active sympathisers, GRAPO's history confirms the thesis that a terrorist group may have an impact on public opinion completely out of proportion to its social support, as occurred in Germany with the Red Army Fraction. The incidence of GRAPO was higher since its action was concentrated during the politically difficult years of the transition in which ETA was also most active. Of approximately eighty people killed by GRAPO, more than half were killed between 1977 and 1979. On the other hand, its tendency to reply with weapons to any attempt at arrest

105

resulted in the death of almost thirty of its members in confrontations with security forces. The bloodiest year was 1979, when 31 people were assassinated, but throughout that year detentions continued, and the organisation was practically dismantled. Although a group of fanatics has preserved the organisation until today, the truth is that its operative capacity has been ineffective since the mid-eighties.

During those years, there were also several extreme right attacks, thus causing an increase of the tension that emerged from the inherent difficulties of the democratic transition and from the attacks by ETA and GRAPO. The open question is whether these were single actions, fostered by groups with scarce cohesion between them and without a clear political purpose, or if on the contrary, there really existed a "tension strategy". This probably occurred in Italy during these years. Yet in the Spanish case it may have been designed in order to make the transition to democracy unattainable (Rodríguez Jiménez 1994).

Without further research, which would be really difficult indeed because of the lack of handy sources, that question cannot be answered with absolute certainty, but the available data points to the first option: there was not a strategic terrorist plot from the extreme right, but rather single crimes (Casals 1998). Nevertheless, such crimes had a heavy political impact in the first months of 1977.

The rise of ETA

There are several regions in Western Europe in which nationalist movements have emerged, but in very rare occasions this led to the arising of terrorism. It would be interesting to consider why terrorism did not strike in Scotland nor in Flanders, why it had so little relevance in Brittany, Corsica, Catalonia or Galicia, and why it became so significant in Ulster and Euskadi (Basque Country).

ETA's terrorist activity began in the final stage of Franco's dictatorship, reached its highest intensity in the first years of democracy, kept a high level during the whole decade of the eighties, and lessened considerably since 1992. Ninety five percent of ETA's victims were killed after Franco's death and it is relevant that the highest number of assassinations took place in 1978, the year in which was approved the Spanish democratic Constitution; in 1979, the year in which was approved the Basque autonomy status; and in 1980, the year in which were established the first Basque parliament and government. It seems that ETA considered the democratic transition as the best opportunity to impose through weapons its project of a socialist and independent Basque Country, and foresaw that the establishment of Spanish democracy and of Basque autonomy would put an end to that opportunity.

Founded in 1958 by a group of young nationalists, ETA developed its ideological identity in the decade of the sixties. It operated a fusion between the doctrine of Sabino Arana, the founder of Basque nationalism, who died in 1903, and the revolutionary tendencies of the sixties. Arana's nationalism was based on Catholic fundamentalism, on the affirmation of Basque race, on anti-Spanishness and on anti-liberalism (Corcuera 2001; Elorza 2001). The founders of ETA were no longer Catholic fundamentalists nor racists, but they inherited from Arana the messianic belief in the Basque Nation. And under the spur of the Chinese and Cuban revolutions and of the wars in Vietnam and Algeria, they came around to believe that a national liberation war was possible, in which the Maoist or Castroist guerrilla strategy would be implemented in the Basque mountains.

The nucleus of ETA's initial strategy, which was based on the action-repression-action concept, was defined by the terrorist organisation itself in a report entitled *Theoretical Basis of the Revolutionary War*, approved in 1965. Its main thesis was the following:

> Let us consider a situation in which an organised minority assails materially and psychologically the State administration, thus forcing it to respond to the aggression with violence. Let us consider that the minority manages to avoid repression and makes it fall over the popular masses. Let us consider, finally, that this minority succeeds in generating rebellion among the population instead of panic, so that the population helps and shelters the minority from the State, and so the action–repression cycle is ready to repeat itself over and over again, becoming each time more intense. (Garmendía 1996, p. 242)

This strategy did not work in the sense that ETA could not manage to "avoid repression", but with regard to making the repression fall "over popular masses" the strategy worked quite well. The indiscriminate repression and Franco's regime hostility to any expression of Basque distinctiveness generated a wave of sympathy towards the organisation that directly opposed dictatorship on behalf of the Basque nation. Consequently, when in late 1975 ETA was almost dismantled, it had support that would enable it to recruit a large number of militant members after Franco's death and to plan a great terrorist offensive starting in 1978, just after the imprisoned ETA members were released by the 1977 amnesty. The delegitimization of the State as a result of the Francoist repression became evident in a 1980 survey, according to which 47% of Basques agreed that State violence was graver than terrorist attacks, against 18% who disagreed with that statement (Llera 1994). The tragic paradox was that ETA was legitimised by a large sector of the Basque population due to its struggle against dictatorship, then benefited from the efforts of the rising Spanish democracy to end the conflict through concessions and nevertheless considered democracy its greater enemy.

During the sixties and early seventies intense ideological debates took place inside ETA, which resulted in several expulsions and divisions. The most nationalistic factions always took the lead, whilst the defeated were accused of "Spanishness", considered the gravest heresy in nationalist eyes. The so-called "Spanishists" were, in fact, those who stressed the significance of the revolutionary socialist objective, and therefore the involvement in the working-class movements. This involvement had acquired greater weight in the Basque industrial areas since 1967, implying a more positive attitude towards the immigrated population and Spanish extreme left organisations (Jáuregui 2000).

The real question was how to combine the different fields of struggle, which initially were assigned to different branches of ETA, called fronts, and more particularly how to combine terrorist action, "military" in its terminology, with socio-political action. This led to a disagreement in 1974. On one side were those who stood for abolishing the division into fronts, which in their opinion was leading to the predominance of the military front, and to turn ETA into an organisation able to combine military action with popular mobilisation and organisation. On the other were those who stood for an ETA that would exclusively dedicate itself to armed struggle and to the diffusion of its political positions, letting the popular and working-class groups in favour of independence organise themselves outside ETA, thus enabling them to act more freely without endangering the strict underground of the armed organisation. The first group would form the politico-military ETA (ETApm), and the second group the military ETA (ETAm).

After Franco's death, ETApm weighed its strategy in the seventh assembly, held in September 1976, when it resolved to create a political party, EIA. EIA ran in the 1977 elections under the Euskadiko Eskerra coalition, which was backed by ETApm. Likewise, supporter groups of ETAm began to run in the elections with the creation of the Herri Batasuna coalition in 1978. Nevertheless, hopes that radical Basque nationalism would give up guns and integrate into the democratic polity were thwarted. In 1982, a sector from ETApm forsook the armed struggle and dissolved, but some of its militants joined ETAm, which thereafter would be the sole ETA.

The structure designed by ETAm turned to be quite effective. Instead of being an organisation composed of several underground fronts, ETA became an organisation that only kept its deadly commandos in absolute underground, whilst a large part of its political and logistical sectors operated openly and even benefited from official support, particularly from the Basque government. Herri Batasuna and other organisations belonging to ETA could operate for years without any restrictions, whilst they kept their underground connections with the terrorist band.

Counter-terrorist Terrorism

Successive Spanish governments made different mistakes in the struggle against ETA. During the dictatorship and in the first years of the transition, Spain lacked security forces trained for the tough struggle against terrorism. A common recourse was to arrest indiscriminately people linked to ETA, and subsequently release them. The benefits of this measure in terms of information were lower than the negative effect it produced in terms of radicalisation of the arrested people and their relatives and friends, especially in cases involving mistreatments (Reinares 2001, pp. 126–145). Subsequently, the development of efficient information services led to a reduction in the amount of detentions, which were then focused on real accountable terrorists, a measure that obviously weakened ETA.

Another mistake, which has not been rectified until very recently, was the belief that ETA only comprised gunmen. This allowed ETA's political and logistic sectors very often to act without restrictions. The origin of this position was the assumption that if radical nationalism had legal action opportunities, ETA would put an end to terrorism. But the results were very different: ETA's fellow organisations operated openly in society, thus contributing to increase the intimidating effects of terrorist attacks and inflicting on the Basque country a climate of fear. The change of attitude took place in 1998, when magistrate Baltasar Garzón stated for the first time that ETA was not only an armed organisation, but a whole movement in which different elements acted in a coordinated way.

The severest moral and political mistake was the one committed by those who thought that it was convenient to fight ETA with its own weapons, that is, through counter-terrorist terrorism promoted by sectors in the State administration. It became a "dirty war", promoted against a terrorist organisation that seemed too difficult to eradicate by other methods, since it had a safe rearguard refuge in French territory. Most of the counter-terrorist attacks took place in French-Basque territory that was used by ETA as a base of operations (Woodsworth 2001).

In the "dirty war" against ETA, it is necessary to distinguish two periods, which are not equally known . In the first period, which lasted from 1975 to 1981 and in which the so-called BVE (Spanish Basque Battalion) claimed responsibility for most of the attacks, there are only hints about the connections between the perpetrators of the attacks and sectors of the administration. During the second period, between 1983 and 1987 the Antiterrorist Liberation Group (or GAL, in its Spanish abbreviation) claimed the terrorist attacks, and the implication of the then leaders of the Interior Ministry has been proven in court.

It seems that the main objective of GAL was to coerce the French government to adopt a firmer attitude against ETA terrorists that planned in France the attacks they were to commit in Spain. The French government changed its attitude in 1986, but it is difficult to estimate if the Gal's offensive influenced their decision. One thing that is certain is the negative consequences of the "dirty war". Due to the GAL attacks, a sector of the Basque population would not accept the reality of democratisation and the government's moral standing was harmed when in 1994 people became aware of what happened. However, the "dirty war", which started in 1975, ended definitively in 1987.

The slow decline of ETA

The successive periods in the strategic evolution of ETA (Domínguez Iribarren 1998, Sánchez-Cuenca 2001) can be designated as a period of revolutionary war, a period of wearing-down strategy and a period of nationalist front. During the period of revolutionary war, that lasted approximately from 1968, the year of its first terrorist actions, to 1978, the year of the approval of the Constitution, ETA's strategy was inspired by the Third World revolutionary wars. At that time, ETA considered its terrorist actions as the detonator of an armed insurrection that would lead the Basque people towards its independence from the Spanish State.

After the consolidation of democracy and the establishment of the Basque Autonomous Community, a popular insurrection was no longer conceivable, not even for the most fanatic ideologists, and ETA had to switch to another strategy. The new strategy of attrition was based on the assumption that terrorist pressure would succeed in inducing the State to renounce its principles and to yield to ETA's pretensions. In this strategy, terrorism no longer represented a stage of the struggle that would succeed in generating a massive insurrection, but instead constituted the key element that would lead directly to victory.

A key element of the "wearing-down" strategy was negotiation with the Spanish State. By offering negotiations, ETA achieved a propaganda success, since it seemed disposed to dialogue. If the government agreed to dialoguing, ETA would achieve a second propaganda success, since it would prove that the State admitted its power. But negotiations came to naught, since ETA was not likely to renounce its main objective. Therefore, the successive negotiation attempts promoted by Spanish governments, which culminated with the Algiers talks that took place between 1987 and 1989, were self-defeating, since they indicated to ETA that it was on the right track (Sánchez-Cuenca 2001, pp. 109–142).

However, ETA itself was wearing-down, due to both political and operative factors. From the political point of view, the consolidation of the Basque autonomy was very important, since those who assumed that

110

armed struggle was the only mechanism that would achieve the main objectives of nationalism had their arguments curtailed. Since 1981, Euskadi has its own parliament and its own government, both with great powers, and the president of the government has always been a member of the Basque Nationalist Party (PNV), the party that Sabino Arana founded. But, according to the well known tendency of terrorist organisations to justify their permanence by rejecting any compromise solution, ETA and their spokespersons keep saying that the autonomous Euskadi still lacks sovereignty and also that it does not include the remaining traditional Basque territories, that is Navarre, which had opted for its own autonomous status, and the French Basque region.

Throughout the years ETA's political thesis, although not its criminal activism, has retained the support of a significant minority of the Euskadi population. In the elections to the Basque parliament, votes for Herri Batasuna have kept around 10% of the electorate, reaching its highest score in 1998, when ETA had declared a truce, and its lowest score in 2001, when the truce came to an end. The electorate of Herri Batasuna presents, according to a 1990 survey, a high percentage of Basque language speakers (62% against an average of 36% in all the electorate) and of people whose two parents are Basque (64% against an average of 44%). Nevertheless, the trait that represents the majority of this group is the extremely low percentage of practising Catholics (18% against an average of 46%). This reveals how much radical nationalism has switched over from Sabino Arana's Catholic fundamentalism. By comparison, 68% of PNV electors were practising Catholics (Llera 1994).

Nevertheless, although Herri Batasuna's retained the votes, there was a marked loss of support for ETA itself. According to surveys carried out by the Politics Department of the University of the Basque Country, the percentage of those who support or justify ETA decreased from 12% in 1981 to 8% in 1989 and to 5% in 1998, dropping to less than 1% in 2003.

Support has been greater among young people. A 1990 survey revealed that 27% of Basque youth considered that terrorism was justified under certain circumstances. The percentage rose to 46% among those who did not consider themselves Spaniards but only Basques, and to 61% among those who usually smoke cannabis, which reveals both the nationalist and the anti-establishment components of youth sectors that support ETA (Elzo 1990). Moreover, adhering to ETA offers a field for Basque identification for youths from non-Basque families, since the struggle for the independence of Euskadi is considered by the radicals as the real proof of being truly Basque (Mata 1993). Among ETA's militants, many are immigrants, as shown in a recent study on the imprisoned terrorists, which revealed that almost a quarter of them have neither paternal nor maternal Basque surnames (Reinares 2001, p.198).

Political evolution has curtailed ETA's arguments, but the increasing efficacy of security forces has had an important role in the decline. As mentioned, the indiscriminate arrests of the late seventies and early eighties, when lots of people were arrested and then released without charges, gave way to an intensive intelligence work leading to more selective detentions (Domínguez 1998b).

The beginning of effective French anti-terrorist cooperation has also been very helpful. The French attitude changed in the mid-eighties, when Spain joined the European Community. Since then, the partnership between both countries increased, irrespective of the political stance of the successive governments in Paris and Madrid (Morán 2002). The detention of ETA's leading members in the French locality of Bidart in 1992 is particularly noteworthy. Since then, the number of attacks decreased significantly.

Despite all this, ETA has managed to last for decades. This is due to the fact that ETA, as already seen, consists of a great number of clandestine and legal organisations that are loosely connected. The central nucleus is ETA itself, and the ensemble is connected in a network that from 1975 to 1998 was called "Koodinadora Abertzale Sozialista" (KAS). Furthermore, several radical organisations connected to ETA benefited until very recently from great freedom of action and even from some support of Basque institutions governed by democratic nationalists.

The relationships between the radical nationalist conglomerate led by ETA and the democratic nationalism of the PNV and EA parties that rule Euskadi are complex. On the one hand, the success of democratic nationalism in constraining ETA's support is unquestionable, since it proved that it was possible to preserve the distinct Basque identity inside an increasingly decentralised Spanish State. On the other hand, by defining Euskadi as a completely different nation from Spain, despite their obvious and very ancient ties, democratic nationalism tended to reinforce the ideology that nourishes ETA. In addition, the PNV has not forsaken its main objective, i.e., independence.

Consequently, there is certain ambiguity in the PNV regarding ETA. This was clearly shown in a secret interview that took place in March 1991 between a delegation of the PNV, headed by its charismatic leader Xabier Arzalluz, and a delegation of radical nationalists, one of whom wrote a report about it that later on was discovered by the police. In that interview Arzalluz made three fundamental statements: that ETA's defeat would not benefit Euskadi, that the Spanish government did not trust them because it perceived that the final objective was the same both for the PNV and ETA, and that no nation had ever reached its freedom without having a group of people shaking the tree and another picking up the fallen nuts (Gurruchaga and San Sebastián 2000). The meaning of this metaphor is pretty obvious: ETA, whose role is to fight the Spanish government, complemented the PNV, whose role is to reach an agreement for independence.

ETA's attrition, evident from 1992, and the ambiguity of democratic nationalism led to a new strategy in the mid-nineties: the nationalist front (Domínguez 2002). This strategy did not propound direct negotiations between ETA and the State, as the Algiers talks aimed to, but rather suggested that the State should accept the Basque country self-determination and the integration of Navarre. In order to achieve these ends, ETA intended a union of all nationalist forces, including the democratic parties PNV and EA. Since this was no longer a matter of forcing the State to capitulate, but rather to reach independence by an agreement of the Basques themselves, the non-nationalist Basques, representing half the population of the Basque Autonomous Community, became the main enemy. Moreover, a new factor in the Basque policy emerged in the nineties: humanitarian mobilisations of those rejecting terrorism. ETA answered this challenge with increasing pressure against non-nationalist Basque politicians, members of the Popular Party or of the Socialist Party, and against intellectuals and journalists who stood against terrorism. Some of them were assassinated, others suffered different kinds of harassment, such as insults, menaces, aggressions, and incendiary attacks on their dwellings, on their belongings or on their party headquarters. The kidnapping and assassination in July 1997 of a young Basque councillor, Miguel Ángel Blanco, member of the Popular Party, generated anti-terrorist demonstrations in the Basque country as well as throughout Spain, which were unprecedented in their massive nature. This worried the Basque Nationalist Party, which ruled in Euskadi since 1981 and saw the nationalist hegemony endangered.

From then on, democratic nationalists considered that it was necessary to reach an agreement with ETA which should forsake terrorism and integrate itself in a nationalist union that would endeavour to reach independence in a short time. The new strategy materialised in a secret agreement between the PNV, EA and ETA, that took place in July 1998, which was followed by the announcement of an ETA truce. The agreement envisioned a partnership between the three organisations to create a sovereign and unique political entity that would include the current Basque Autonomous Community, Navarre and the Basque territories in France. The agreement did not last long, due to reasons usual in the dynamics of terrorist groups. Since the agreement opted for a peaceful way to independence, the political circumstances would impose slower progress, and the effective leadership would transfer to democratic parties, while ETA, by stopping the killing, would become irrelevant. Terrorist attacks had become ETA's guarantee for permanence. After realising that both the PNV and the EA were against an untimely unilateral proclamation of independence, ETA broke the truce and re-initiated its terrorist attacks in 2000. Apparently, the attrition strategy was coming back. But the loss of support, the international anti-terrorist cooperation and the efficacy of police have indeed curtailed the operative capacity of ETA. A radicalised PNV has gained a significant part of the electorate that supported ETA's political wing, now called Batasuna, which was declared illegal in 2002. Other organisations linked to ETA suffered the same fate. All this suggests that ETA has arrived at the last stage of its definitive decline.

Conclusions

Benjamin Franklin once warned that a country that curtails its freedom in order to obtain more security ends up losing both its freedom and its security. Spain has not committed that mistake. For a quarter of a century Spanish democracy has maintained the struggle against ETA, one of the deadliest terrorist organisations in the history of Europe, without sacrificing any citizen freedoms. Regrettably, the brutal action of ETA and its milieu has curtailed significantly the liberties of many Basque citizens, particularly of the non-nationalist half part of the population.

There have been mistakes in this long struggle, during which, on behalf of a presumed efficacy, the principles of Constitutional State were abandoned, either by the "dirty war" or by granting immunity to ETA's collaborators. Nevertheless, the "dirty war" came to an end fifteen years ago, and recently a decisive step has been made towards ending impunity, by outlawing Batasuna and other organisations.

The Spanish experience reveals that once a terrorist movement has taken root, the only way a democratic State may defeat it is through a resolute and prolonged effort, in which any departure from democratic principles is counter-productive.

References

Benjamin, D. and Simon, S. 2002. *The age of sacred terror.* New York: Random House.

Casals, Xavier. 1998. *La tentación neofascista en España.* Barcelona: Plaza y Janés.

Castro, Lorenzo. 2002. "La izquierda armada: FRAP y GRAPO". In: González Calleja, E., ed., *Políticas del miedo: un balance del terrorismo en Europa.* Madrid: Biblioteca Nueva.

Corcuera, José Luis. 2001. *La patria de los vascos: orígenes, ideología y organización del nacionalismo vasco.* Madrid: Taurus.

Crenshaw, Martha. 1999. "The logic of terrorism: terrorist behaviour as a product of strategic choice". In: Reich, W., ed., *Origins of terrorism.* Washington: Woodrow Wilson Centre.

Domínguez, Florencio. 1998. *ETA: estrategia organizativa y actuaciones, 1978–1992.* Bilbao: Universidad del País Vasco.

——. 1998b. *De la negociación a la tregua: el fin de ETA.* Madrid: Taurus.

——. 2002. "La ulsterización de Euskadi". In: González Calleja, E., ed., *Políticas del miedo: un balance del terrorismo en Europa.* Madrid: Biblioteca Nueva.

Elorza, Antonio. 2001. *Un pueblo escogido: génesis, definición y desarrollo del nacionalismo vasco.* Barcelona: Crítica.

Elzo, Javier. 1990. *Jóvenes vascos 1990.* Vitoria-Gasteiz: Gobierno Vasco.

Ganor, Boaz. 2002. "Defining terrorism: is one man's terrorist another man's freedom fighter?" *ICT Papers on terrorism.* Jerusalem: Ahva Press.

Garmendía, José María. 1996. *Historia de ETA.* San Sebastián: Haramburu.

Gentile, Emilio. 2001. *Le religioni della politica.* Roma-Bari: Laterza.

Gurruchaga, Carmen y San Sebastián, Isabel. 2000. *El árbol y las nueces: la relación secreta entre ETA y PNV.* Madrid: Temas de Hoy.

Jáuregui, Gurutz. 2000. "ETA: orígenes y evolución ideológica y política". In: Elorza, A., ed., *La historia de ETA.* Barcelona: Planeta.

Llera, Francisco J. 1994. *Los vascos y la política: el proceso político vasco, elecciones, partidos, opinión pública y legitimación en el País Vasco, 1977–1992.* Bilbao: Universidad del País Vasco.

Mata López, J.M. 1993. *El nacionalismo vasco radical: discurso, organización y expresiones.* Bilbao: Universidad del País Vasco.

Merari, Ariel. 1993. "Terrorism as a strategy of insurgence". *Terrorism and Political Violence,* 5 (4).

Moniquet, Claude. 2002. *La guerre sans visage: de Waddi Haddad à Oussama Ben Laden: les réseaux de la peur, 1970–2002.* Neuilly-sur-Seine: Michel Lafon.

Morán, Sagrario. 2002. "La colaboración antiterrorista: el eje Madrid-París". In: González Calleja, E., ed., *Políticas del miedo: un balance del terrorismo en Europa.* Madrid: Biblioteca Nueva.

Post, Jerrold. 1999. "Terrorist psycho-logic: terrorist behavior as a product of psychological forces". In: Reich, W., ed., *Origins of terrorism.* Washington: Woodrow Wilson Center.

Reinares, Fernando. 2001. *Patriotas de la muerte: quiénes han militado en ETA y por qué.* Madrid, Taurus.

Rodríguez Jiménez, José Luis. 1994. *Reaccionarios y golpistas: la extrema derecha en España, 1967–1982.* Madrid: CSIC.

Sánchez-Cuenca, Ignacio. 2001. *ETA contra el Estado: las estrategias del terrorismo.* Barcelona: Tusquets.

Sperber, Dan. 1996. *Explaining culture: a naturalistic approach.* Oxford: Blackwell.

Wickham-Crowley, Timothy P. 1991. *Guerrillas and revolution in Latin America: a comparative study of insurgents and regimes since 1956.* Princeton, NJ: Princeton University Press.

Woodsworth, Paddy. 2001. *Dirty war, clean hands: ETA, the GAL and Spanish democracy.* Cork: Cork University Press.

Links

www.mir.es
   Spain: Interior Ministry.
www1.euskadi.net/estudios_sociologicos/sociometros_c.apl
   Basque Government: Gabinete de Prospección Sociológica.
www.ehu.es/cpvweb/pags_directas/euskobarometroFR.html
   Universidad del País Vasco: Euskobarómetro.

6

BETWEEN PAST AND FUTURE
CHILDREN AND THE CONTEST OVER CULTURAL AND POLITICAL IDENTITY DURING THE SPANISH TRANSITION TO DEMOCRACY (SALAMANCA 1977–1979)

Tamar Groves

Children represent the future. In times of change, their socialization is especially important. Education thus, becomes a very crucial topic in countries experiencing political transformation. During the Spanish transition to democracy educational issues remained at the center of public debate. A combination of the regime's preoccupation with the education system and the emergence of an active teachers' movement, ensured that education grew to be central in Spain even before Franco's death.

There is as yet not enough historical research on the regime's educational policies in the seventies or on the teachers' movement.[1] This article will touch on them only briefly. It will concentrate on an even more neglected topic – the pupils who were affected by both. Dealing with children is not common in political analysis because they do not seem important enough and it is difficult to find relevant sources. Nevertheless, as I will try to demonstrate, examining children can not only enhance our understanding of how educational policies and the projects of the teachers' movement were translated into everyday practice, but can also illuminate new aspects of this crucial period of transition.

The Spanish educational system went through a continuous process of change. But in the sixties it was still far from being able to fulfill the expectations for modernization invested in it. National Catholicism and religious dogma, which were the guiding principles of the education system founded during the civil war, were still omnipresent three decades later. Combined with the inertia that usually characterizes educational systems, they limited attempts to modernize the curriculum. Furthermore,

117

even though some effort was made to gradually expand state educational services, this was hampered by the limited resources allotted to education.[2]

Consequently, by the late sixties, both for economic and social reasons, the regime perceived educational needs as pressing. The educational institution headed by Villar Palasí initiated an ambitious plan designed to modernize and amplify the system. The plan culminated with the "Ley General de Educación" enacted in 1970 that was to be implemented during the following decade.[3] The transition to democracy, therefore, coincided with the most ambitious reform in educational matters in Spain since the mid 19th century.

Evaluating the "Ley General de Educación" is difficult because it included contradictory elements and also because of the immense difficulties involved in implementing it. Some researchers argue that the reform program consisted of totalitarian ideals and technocratic elements mixed with democratic values. Others maintain that the law merged technocratic modernization projects and Spanish conservatism typical of the beginning of the century, which aimed to reform society from above without democratic participation.[4]

The law was complex because of the delicate stage at which the Franco regime found itself at the end of the sixties. The economic boom that was accompanied by a certain cultural liberalization and relaxation of the strict means of control, brought about social and political dissent unknown in authoritarian Spain. The reaction of the regime was a retreat to the old methods of subjugation alternated with apparently liberal initiatives. Indeed a well known interpretation of the law of 1970 is that it was one of the grand projects of the dictatorship to adopt a liberal image while conserving the old structure of power. By stressing values such as equal educational opportunities and free and compulsory schooling, the law gave an impression of progress and liberalization unprecedented in Franco's Spain. However, the aim of the regime was to provide the false notion that the inequality characterizing Spanish society stemmed from the shortcomings of the educational system and was not inherent to the nature of the regime. Educational reform would thus ameliorate this situation and open the way for the establishment of a new and just society without threatening the stability of the regime.[5]

Irrespective of whether one fully adopts this thesis, its observation of the regime's plan to promote education in public discourse is important for the understanding of education's significance in Spain of the seventies. Before the passing of the law the educational administration published a report known as the "Libro Blanco".[6] The report gave for the first time in years, a relatively honest account of the educational services and referred openly not only to their anachronistic state, but also to their elitist characteristics which were a direct outcome of the regime's educational policy for many years.

The report was published by the educational institution and was distributed among several educational organizations. Although only official institutions were allowed to participate in this notionally democratic process, the report also circulated among opposition groups of teachers. In fact the debate about the educational initiatives of the regime stimulated the expansion of the semi-clandestine groups of teachers who were in their first stages of organizing at that time. [7]

The new educational discourse of the regime as it manifested itself in the "Libro Blanco" and in the law that followed it, emphasized the role of teachers in the educational process and the importance of their preparation and guidance as well as the need to raise their social status. Consequently, the establishment's policies such as improving salaries, integrating teachers' seminars in the universities and changing primary teachers' name from "maestros" to "profesores" (hence equating them with their colleagues in higher education), were driven by the aim to replace the "Apostolic Teacher", central to the project of the National Catholicism, with a new specialized professional, responsible for reform.

Nevertheless, owing to its progressive appearance, the law did not receive the support of Franco's reactionary parliament and the regulations proposed to finance it were never approved. Thus, although the law passed, its implementation was limited by lack of funds. Teachers' hopes for both the improvement of their salaries and the establishment of a better public educational system were hence frustrated. This development encouraged teachers to assume direct responsibility for modernizing and liberalizing the educational system and acted as a catalyst for the consolidation of the teachers' movement that had begun in the previous decade. Moreover, by placing education at the forefront of its policies the Franco institution itself endowed teachers with a status they used in their struggle against it. If at first they tried to force the government to keep the promises implicit in the law, their subsequent confrontation with the regime led them to mistrust its legitimacy. [8]

All this coincided with unprecedented social and political unrest, which encouraged teachers and gave them models for collective action, thus fomenting the emergence of a wide and active teachers' movement. The teachers, like other white-collar workers, joined the battle for democratization headed by the workers, hence strengthening the anti-Franco mobilization, which characterized the years of the transition.

Although 70 percent of Spanish teachers took part in the strikes held during the seventies and more than 24,000 participated in alternative pedagogical initiatives throughout the transition, their movement is a relatively neglected aspect of the social unrest experienced by Spanish society during the crucial years of the transition. [9] The struggle to form a free professional union and to improve working conditions brought teachers into a frontal clash with the authorities; but this struggle was never violent enough to draw the attention of researchers.. Likewise, the teachers' pedagogical struggle to change Spanish society through the transformation of the school mostly took place in classrooms, so although ambitious and directed at their young pupils, it was low profile.

Nearly all published evidence dealing with the period of the transition directly relates to the political arena. A few specialized books dedicated to education include sources regarding the government's educational policies and even the alternative programs offered by teachers.[10] But, the children whose education and future stood at the center of this debate are absent altogether, similar to most discussions dealing with political processes. Testimonies like the following, written by an eight year old pupil attending a small rural school, might seem insignificant, but as I will try to demonstrate, can illuminate interesting phenomena related to the nature of the transition.

> A mí antes no me gustaba la escuela porque tenía papeles de la "política" y había maestras muy malas porque nos daban en las uñas con las barras nos mandaban leer tres veces a la semana el testamento de Franco. Ahora me gusta porque han quitado los papeles de la "política" y han puesto papeles de la constitución de España y niños y posteres de Unicef y trabajos manuales nuestros.[11]

To observe the children who formed the object of the opposition pedagogical movements we have to move from the national to the local level. Salamanca was chosen for a closer observation of this phenomenon because the province experienced the emergence of an active teachers' mobilization, but the group in Salamanca was not part of the leadership of the movement, which was to be found in Barcelona and Madrid. Thus, studying Salamanca permits the evaluation of the practice of one of the many groups forming the movement and of what actually happened in the classrooms as opposed to a mere analysis of the discourse of a handful of leaders.

Another reason that makes Salamanca interesting and instructive is that although its capital was a religious and academic center (a fact that certainly contributed to the emergence of the teachers' movement) the province is agricultural and conservative and thus permits studying the work of the teachers' movement in a rural environment outside the large urban centers. Since teachers cut across all levels of society, unlike many other opposition movements, their mobilization was characterized by the fact that it reached the most rural areas of Spain such as Jaén, León, La Rioja and Extremadura.

Teachers, children and parents are the three crucial elements in the contest over cultural-political identity, which I wish to illustrate. Ambitious projects of teachers to change society through the school have a long and known history in general and in Spain in particular. Before going on to talk about the children who constitute the heart of this article

120

I must dedicate few words to the specific pedagogical ideas held by the local teachers' movement in Salamanca.

An important source of inspiration for the "Salamantinian" teachers was the Spanish branch of the international movement of teachers practicing the methods of the French educator Célestin Freinet.[12] Freinet worked during the first half of the twentieth century in poor rural Provence and sought to use education to promote the rural population. His ideas were popular in Spain during the second republic (1931–1936) and at the end of the sixties as part of the emergence of opposition groups of teachers, cells of teachers inspired by Freinet were also reestablished all over Spain.[13]

The Franco regime abolished the pedagogical innovative tradition that existed in Spain and succeeded in enforcing rigid norms in the schools. Only in Cataluña, where the pedagogical initiatives were connected to the struggle to preserve local identity, a certain level of activity was maintained despite the limitation imposed by the regime. The alternative educational activity in Cataluña reached its peak in 1965 with the establishment of "Instituto Rosa Sensate" which served as an independent center for shaping teachers. The Instituto's ideas were inspired by the "new school movement" that placed the child at the center of the educative process, and wanted to ameliorate the authoritarian relationship characterizing traditional education.[14]

The teachers practicing Freinet's pedagogy took part in distributing innovative pedagogical ideas outside Barcelona. In 1973, after nearly a decade of activity they established their own independent legal organization named ACIES (Asociación para la Correspondancia y la Imprenta Escolar). Because of the need to conceal the organization's political tendencies, its name referred to the technical aspects of its activities. Nevertheless, the aim of the organization was to form citizens for a democratic transformation of Spain and it was inspired by Marxist and Anarchist convictions (Freinet was a member of the French communist party and belonged to a forum of anarchist educators).

According to Freinet's pedagogical vision the teacher should not be an authoritarian figure but a partner in a common voyage of learning. He should be a part of the social group of the class whose life is based on equality and cooperation. The school, maintained Freinet, is an integral element of the social reality in which it is situated, and should be used as a platform for the struggle of the popular classes.

Freinet's ideas provided his Spanish followers with a variety of techniques enabling them to change immediately the ambience of their classes. The most important technique they adopted was the printing of school newspapers. Such a school newspaper distributed in February 1979 among the residence of three small estates from the area of Ledesma will enable me to present this technique. In the paper called "Campo de

Ledesma" the readers came across the following editorial written by the teacher in the name of his pupils:

> Más de uno preguntará el por qué de unas hojas y dibujos con textos, todo ello del mismo color, que los niños llaman PERIODICO ESCOLAR. Tenemos conciencia de estar viviendo y de pertenecer a una zona rural que como la mayor parte del campo salmantino, se encuentra cada día más muerta, abandonada, aislada y envejecida . . . Por qué el Periódico Escolar? Porque no queremos seguir aislados. Queremos comunicarnos con otros niños y otras escuelas. Queremos comunicarnos con los padres y con la gente que aún queda en las fincas.[15]

According to Freinet's theory, the process of publishing the newspaper in which the children use home made methods of printing in order to duplicate their own texts is valuable because it allows them to be engaged in a common action that blurs the distinction between physical and intellectual activity. Distributing the newspaper among the members of their community and exchanging it with other schools, is essential for the establishment of brotherhood and solidarity.

The cited text, coming from the school, illustrates very clearly the influence of Freinet's ideas and more important, reveals the nature of the cultural and political project the children encountered in their school. Curiously enough the efforts to communicate with the farmers did not go unnoticed but the reaction was not of the expected nature as can be clearly deduced from the following apology published in the next edition:

> Sabemos que ha habido gente a la cual no le ha caído bien lo que se decía en el periódico. Nuestra intención no ha sido herir a nadie en concreto, sino narrar una situación real . . . .Entendemos que la escuela no son las cuatro paredes del edificio, los niños y el maestro. Debe existir una mayor relación, participación y colaboración de los padres-madres en la escuela. Comprendemos la dificultad del trabajo y la distancia en Kms entre unas familias y otras. A pesar de todo, merece la pena ganar un día y dedicar una asamblea para hablar sobre la educación de los hijos. Vayamos pensando en ello.[16]

The text reflects the tension between the children (led by their teacher) and the rest of the community. The call for a public meeting made in the text indicates that the teacher's aspirations did not stop at the school gates, and he was actually using the children and their newspaper to mobilize the farmers. His initiative is an attempt to import to the rural villages, the urban model of neighbors' organizations emerging in the seventies as part of the anti-Franco social movement. This incident shows the way in which the children served as connectors between the projects of democratization practiced in their class and their homes.

This school paper did not circulate only in the village but was sent to other rural schools. One of the villages which received it on a regular basis was "Valdelosa del Vicente" whose children sent in return a paper they published in collaboration with children from two other rural schools, that of the village of "Castellanos de Villiquera" and the village of "Valdunciel". Their paper was called "Las Armuñas" and its third edition provides us with a text written by a 15 year old girl from "Castellanos de Villiquera" summing up her experiences in the school:

> Para mi este año la escuela ha cambiado incluso me ha cambiado . . . Me gusta mucho el periódico, por la razón de que lo hacemos en sociedad y podemos *esplicar* a los mayores lo que pensamos y sentimos, ellos siempre piensan que somos niños y que solo servimos para jugar pero nosotros con el periódico tenemos que hacerles comprender que también pensamos y nos gusta hacer las cosas que ellos hacen, vivir la vida como niños pero que sepan comprendernos. También me gusta hacer obras de teatro por la razón de que con ellas se nos va la verguenza y el temor yo antes no me atreví hablar de un tema concreto con otras personas con el temor de que a esa persona no le guste. Me gusta la poesía y el texto libre porque es libre no como antes que nos ponían un tema y teníamos que escribir sobre ese tema nos decían dibuja una casa y teníamos que dibujarla. Tambien quiero seguir haciendo entrevistas porque el primer día yo tenía miedo por si las personas me respondían bien o mal pero cuando la hice y salió bien quise seguir haciendolas . . . Bueno esta libertad de la escuela me ha cambiado . . . [17]

Unlike the previous text written by the teacher, this piece, written by one of the pupils, supplies information not only regarding the variety of techniques used in the class and the ideology behind them, but also demonstrates their effect on the pupils. Possibly the presence of the teacher influenced the way the pupil decided to describe her experiences. Nor can we discount the possibility that the teacher actually revised the text with her before he integrated it into the paper. However, even if the teacher did influence his pupil, this makes an authentic case of socialization.

Like in the case of "Campo de Ledesma", "Las Armuñas" provides us with evidence of the discrepancy between the pedagogical project held in the school and the educational ideas common in the village. The school paper brings the results of an investigation regarding education carried out in the village of "Castellanos de Villiquera". The children present the answers they gathered in the following way: "La gente mayor opina que hay demasiada libertad y sinverguencería, ya que no dan ha respetar los maestros y ya que se les tutea, tampoco se respeta a los personas mayores, hay mucho hijo-puta suelto. Los chabales estudian poco y gamberrean mucho." And the children add: "esta respuesta esta sin razonar y creemos que sin pensar."[18]

The critical spirit of the children evident in this text exemplifies a phenomenon characterizing the school papers I read. A more significant case can actually be found at the end of the description written by the previous pupil. It is interesting that she decides to end her school experience with a clear reproach to the head of the village for his attitude to the school: "El señor alcalde hace lo que puede por el pueblo, ¿pero por nosotros qué hace? Nada la escuela es vieja y aun que vieja la podía pintar, un encerado nuevo, persianas para ver mejor las filminas incluso me gustaría que pusieran un laboratorio para que nosotros pudieramos estudiar mejor."[19]

Forming an opinion regarding social reality means taking an active part in the community. It is obvious that children were encouraged to do so by their teachers and sometimes they clearly quoted them without really assimilating their ideas. This of course did not damage, even if it did not enhance their function in communicating the social and political values they received at school to their parents and community.

The children were not only encouraged to observe their school in a critical manner, but also the society in which they were living. The following text which appeared in a school paper in one of the villages of the mountain area in Salamanca was also published in May 1977 in the local newspaper of Salamanca "el Adelanto" under the title "Nuestro Pueblo":

En mi pueblo siempre ha habido autoritarismo. Nunca ha habido participación del pueblo, siempre lo ha hecho el Ayuntamiento y el alcalde. De las cosas que proponían nunca han consultado al pueblo, han hecho todo a propia y santa voluntad . . . Aquí, en el pueblo, el que más tierras tenía era el que mandaba. El rico imponía unas rentas mayores a las que se sacaban de las tierras y el pobre labrador se tenía que aguantar, y el que no quisiera se tenía quedar sin comer . . . El Ayuntamiento es el centro donde se hacen toda clase de reuniones. Las gentes no quieren cambiar sus costumbres. Están acostumbrados a vivir como antiguamente aceptando un poco la vida de ahora, pero lo aceptan muy lentamente . . .

After analyzing the situation the children continue making a series of suggestions:

Organización administrativa: Propondríamos: que el mismo pueblo propusiera unas asambleas para discutir estos mismos problemas que le surgen al pueblo, como pueden ser: el alquitrán de la carretera, el agua etc. El ayuntamiento tenía que ser el que menos mandara sobre los problemas del pueblo sino que era el mismo pueblo el que tenía que tratar de resolver esos problemas. El alcalde y el ayuntamiento no deberían ser elegidos por personas de fuera, sino por las mismas personas del pueblo. Por voto secreto, etc.[20]

Based on their experiences in the school, the children criticized the village people for their submissiveness and conservatism. More importantly they offered an alternative political system for the village. This text, which was written two years before local democratic elections were held in Spain, illustrates how teachers mobilized the children to take an active role in the struggle for democracy in their country.

Although in this case, like in the previous ones, it is difficult to delineate the boundaries between the pupils and the teachers, it is clear that the children found themselves torn between two contrary sets of values: that of the school and that of the village and the home. Moreover, they themselves were pushed to take an active part in the confrontation not only as channels of information but also as social agents establishing opinions and offering alternatives.

The generation gap causing tensions between parents and children is a common phenomenon. Children always constitute the connecting link between past and future. In the cases I studied this gap was intensified not only by the general political situation, but more importantly because the teachers were engaged in ambitious projects designed to transform the political and social environment in which they were working. The opportunity to be in contact with impressionable young people at such a crucial stage of their life gave the initiatives of the teachers' movement a unique social resonance. The psychological development of children makes them simplify reality and adopt a relatively extreme version of the values to which they are exposed. Thus the message they deliver will be sharp and clear.

To complete our understanding of the capacity of the teachers to mobilize the children we also have to take into account their working conditions in the rural areas. Although the "Ley General de Educación" made an effort to abolish small rural schools, as late as 1981 more then 61 percent of the schools in the province of Salamanca did not have the 8 grades required by law.[21] Thus many teachers worked alone or in small groups that hardly interrelated with each other. The inspectors, who served as the single official link between the rural school and the administration rarely visited it and were interested mainly in bureaucratic issues. The rural teacher thus was relatively independent in his work. Moreover the law of 1970, with its aim to improve quality and its progressive and liberal aspirations, gave teachers a high level of pedagogical freedom. This state of things allowed the practice of original teaching techniques including ones inspired by opposition political and social ideas. Furthermore, the rural teacher not only enjoyed considerable freedom in his work but also a special status. He was among a small group of officials set apart from village society. He was therefore respected and even if his pupils returned home with unusual ideas, neither the parents nor the rest of the village tended to interfere in his work.

I would like to conclude with a hypothesis stemming from my research, which still awaits proof. I believe that the trend in the province of Salamanca I have tried to describe is an example of a wider phenomenon. Because of the rapid expansion of the public education system in the seventies, teaching was a young profession. A high percentage of teachers came from rural background and obtained their professional preparation in urban centers where they were exposed to anti-Franco movements. The young teachers were mostly sent to rural schools while veterans were promoted to the cities. Thus the young teachers, experiencing the social and political unrest of the seventies found themselves working in conservative, rural Spain. Many teachers were not active members of the teachers' movement but they were exposed to its ideas and probably returned to the villages not only with a more democratic and progressive mentality but with a broader vision of their work as teachers.

In their classrooms these teachers disseminated a stream of ideas, which naturally influenced their pupils, whose school experience put them at the heart of the confrontation lived by their country during these critical years. On the one hand they were exposed to the young teacher who experienced the vigorous atmosphere that characterized Spain's urban centers in the seventies, and on the other hand they belonged to the areas least touched by the social and political transformation. They thus had to deal with contradictory messages, which they naturally passed on from the school to the home and vice versa. In the contest between the future and the past of their country, the children became active mediators between an authoritarian history and democratic prospects.

Notes

1   Most of the research being done about the regime's educational policies is from an educational perspective. For an historical evaluation and a bibliographical essay see: *Revista de Educación* n. extraordinario (1992). The following articles refer to the importance of the teachers' movement and the lack of research dedicated to it: J. Bonafe Martínez, 'Diez años de renovación pedagógica organizada: invitación a una etnografía política' en J. Paniagua y A. San Martín eds., *Diez años de educación en España (1978–1988)* (Valencia, 1989), pp. 337–349; A. Espinosa, 'Algunos materiales para el análisis de la conflicividad docente (1978–1988)' en Paniagua y San Martín eds., *Diez años de educación en España (1978–1988)*, pp. 363–391; Jaume Carbonell, 'De la ley general de educación a la alternativa de escuela pública – Algunas notas introductorias sobre los movimientos sociales en el sector de la enseñanza', *Revista de Educación*, n. exraordinario (1992), 237–255.

2   On the slow process of modernizing the Spanish Education System see: Puelles Benítez, *Educación e ideología en la España contemporánea* (Madrid, 1999); Agustín Escolano Benito, 'Los comienzos de la modernización pedagógica en el franquismo (1951–1964)', *Revista Española de Pedagogía*, mayo–agosto (1992), 289–310.

3   Ley 14/1970, de 4 de agosto, General de Educación y Financiamiento de la reforma Educativa. *Boletín Oficial del Estado* 6–8–1970.

4   For different interpretations of the law see for example: Manuel de Puelles Benítez, 'Tecnocracia y política en la reforma educativa de 1970', *Revista de Educación n. extraordinario* (1992), 13–29; Carlos París, 'Realizaciones y frustraciones de la reforma educativa', *Documentación Social*, 23 (1976), 5–24; Manuel Salguero,'Valores dominantes y lo que permanece de la Ley General de Educación de 1970', *Revista de Ciencias de la Educación*, 174 (1998), pp. 217–235.

5　For this critical view of the reform see: Félix Ortega, 'Las Ideologías de la reforma educativa de 1970', *Revista de Educación* n. extraordinario (1992), 31–46.

6　Ministerio de Educación y Ciencia, *La educación en España. Bases para una política educativa* (Madrid, 1969).

7　Pamela O'Malley, 'Education as resistance: the 'Alternativa" in Oliver Boyd Barrett and Pamela O'Malley eds., *Education Reform in Democratic Spain* (London and New York, 1995), pp. 32–40.

8　Marta Jiménez Jaén, *La ley general de educación y el movimiento de enseñantes* (1970–1976) (La Laguna, 2000).

9　The evaluation of the percentage of teachers participating in strikes is taken from: Espinosa, 'Algunos materiales para el análisis de la conflicividad docente (1978–1988)', pp. 363–391. The estimation of the number of teachers involved in pedagogical initiatives is based on an evaluation of the number of teachers who participated in "Summer Schools" organized by the teachers' movements. Not all the members of pedagogical movements participated in this initiative, so it is logical to assume that the number is actually higher. Regarding the "Summer Schools" see: C. Elejabeitia, *et al.*, *El maestro. Análisis de las escuelas de verano* (Madrid,1983), pp. 278–309.

10　Sources regarding educational policies can be found in numerous publications of the ministry of education. Few publications reproduce documents published by the teachers' movement. See for example: V. Bozal, *Una alternativa para la enseñanza* (Madrid, 1977).

11　The main written sources regarding the practice of the teachers used for this paper are texts written by children from about a dozen villages of the province in the years 1977–1979. These written testimonies were complimented by interviews held by the writer with ex-pupils from five other villages from the province. Referring to the school news papers I will mention their name and the date in which they were published. Campo de Ledesma no. 1 (21-2-1979). Some of the texts contain spelling mistakes. I have reproduced them to maintain their authenticity.

12　For an English publication about Freniet see: Victor Acker, *Célestin Freinet* (Westport, CT, 2000).

13　For the influence of Freinet in Spain see: Fernando Jiménez Mier y Terán,' La revista "Colaboración" – Órgano del movimiento Freinet en España', *Historia de Educación*, XIV–XV (1995–1996), 541–557; Movimiento Cooperativo de Escuela Popular, *La escuela moderna en España* (Madrid, 1979); idem, *Freinet en España* (Barcelona, 1996); Agustín Escolano Benito,'Discurso ideológico, modernización técnica y pedagogía crítica durante el franquismo', *Historia de la Educación*, enero–diciembre (1989), p. 26.

14　There is relatively little published about 'Instituto Rosa Sensat'. For example see: Ramón Moragas, 'La Escola d'Estiu de Barcelona en la escuela de Cataluña', *Cuadernos de Pedagogía*, 6 (1975), document no. 750609 in the journal's CD.

15　Campo de Ledesma, no. 1 (21-2-1979).

16　Campo de Ledesma, no. 1 (21-2-1979).

17　Las Armuñas, no. 3 (23-2-1979).

18 Las Armuñas, no. 1 (19–1–1979).
19 Las Armuñas, no. 3 (23–2–1979).
20 'Nuestro Pueblo', *El Adelanto* (6–5–1977).
21 For an analysis of the structure of the education system in Salamanca in the seventies see: Miguel, Grande Rodríguez, *La escuela rural* (Granada, 1981).

PART II

INSTITUTIONAL AND CULTURAL DIMENSIONS OF THE LATIN AMERICAN TRANSITIONS

7

REPRESENTATIVE DEMOCRACY AND EFFECTIVE INSTITUTIONS
DEMOCRATIC PRACTICE IN CONTEMPORARY LATIN AMERICA

Luis Roniger

There are many models and traditions of representative democracy, which vary from republicanism to procedural models and from elitist to participatory models based upon civil society. This article aims to go beyond a mere discussion of the formal principles and ideal models of representative democracy. It deals with the working of democratic institutions, with political practices and with new modes of articulation of politics and markets, which have affected the level of trust placed in public institutions. It identifies the importance of institutional efficacy and at the same time the centrality of mechanisms of participation and open configuration of public spheres, inherent in democratic practice. Finally, it suggests some ways of effecting possible changes in the working of democratic institutions and the representative dynamics of democracy in the region.

An operative balance

Assessments of the political and economic performance of Latin American countries indicate a decrease in public trust in the last decade. From the public opinion surveys published by Latinobarómetro for the year 2002 (Latinobarómetro 2003), for example, it appears that even though most of the citizens interviewed supported democracy, preferring it over other forms of government, the rates of support decreased since 1996 in 13 out of 17 countries covered by the survey, with 5 nations showing a very low percentage, ranging from 37 to 45 percent. In 2002 Colombia, Brazil, El Salvador, Paraguay and Guatemala were in this range.[1]

The level of support for authoritarianism had increased in 8 countries between 1996 and 2002. A persistent increase in the popular demand for hard line policies against criminals and marginal people was also traced, even in countries in which the population was strongly in favor of democracy after long periods of authoritarian and military governments, such as the Southern Cone countries. In parallel, in 11 out of 17 countries surveyed between 1996 and 2002, the level of dissatisfaction and disenchantment with the functioning of the democratic system was higher than 50 percent.

These figures indicated a significant lack of confidence in the system, despite its formal acceptance. Paraguay and Argentina were extreme cases, with over 90 percent of dissatisfaction in 2002. Mexico was another case of great discontent with the democratic system: over 80 percent, in a country that started an innovative process of transfer of government after a decade-long period of single-party rule, corporatism and clientele politics. In Colombia, Brazil, Chile, Bolivia, Peru, and Ecuador, the level of disenchantment with the democratic system was between 60 and 80 percent of the representative samples. Regarding economic policy, public opinion tended also to tilt towards a negative evaluation of its performance (Latinobarometro 2003).

What is the implication of such disappointment? Is it an expression of immaturity and failing democratic consolidation, or is it just the opposite, reflecting a trend found elsewhere in mature democracies, which by definition are pluralistic and open to criticism and civilian control?

In order to evaluate the significance of these trends, it may be useful to take two parallel lines of analysis: one comparative and the other, diachronic. Applying the comparative line, it is necessary to keep in mind that in the postwar democracies of the so-called "trilateral" countries – the USA, Europe and Japan – there has been a constant concern with the 'crises of democracy,' at least since the 1970s. Diverse indicators reflected a deep disappointment with representative democracy, as it was shown already in the seminal report of Crozier, Huntington, and Watanuki (1975). The more recent work on the deterioration of public trust by Susan Pharr and Robert Puntam (2000) indicates that this is more than an ephemeral trend in these democracies. From a Latin American perspective, these democracies are considered to be mature and consolidated, and to have admirable achievements. And, yet, their citizens express low levels of public trust towards politicians and the ruling class. So, perhaps public distrust may not necessarily be a sign of institutional immaturity.

As one evaluates the performance of democracies it is equally important to follow a diachronic perspective, which takes into account accomplishments *vis-à-vis* expectation. This perspective enables a contextualization of the current disappointment expressed toward democracy. The survey results mentioned must be analyzed by taking into account the high expectations that democratization and the shift of economic policy raised in the 1980s and '90s. At the end of the Cold War democracy was perceived as 'the only game in town', transforming the political game into more open and consensual and less polarized than before, however not less but rather more subject to the criticisms of the citizenry. That is perhaps why, despite the hailed establishment of representative democracy in the '80s, after the long series of systemic breakdowns and authoritarian governments, the high expectations rapidly changed to disappointment.

In addition, despite some innovative trends of democracy in the region – which include the adoption of discourses of empowerment of civil society and human rights, and mechanisms of decentralization and civil participation in some of the countries of the area – the old political and administrative culture remained resilient. It is important to take into consideration that the latter continues to affect the parameters of operation of democracy and the policies of economic liberalization in the region. The Presidential system and the fragility of checks and balances in politics, low institutional credibility, corruption, the lack of public accountability, the persistence of authoritarian enclaves and the emergence of neo-clientelism, are all mechanisms and traits recreated against a background of deep socio-economic gaps and continuing poverty. These trends limit participation and merge with other institutional tendencies inherited by the Latin American political systems to create an institutional complexity of partial or limited democracy (Sznajder 1996, Waisman 1998, Sznajder and Roniger 2003).

In this kind of democracy it is typical for large sectors to be sidelined, with little autonomous access to goods and services, and lacking a capacity to fully participate in the public spheres due to their placement at the margins of society, economy, and politics. In parallel, other sectors continue to have mediated access to markets of goods and services and to use the clientele networks to connect to the political system and the public administration. The performance of the political system and the economic markets has generated widespread disenchantment, loss of confidence in institutions and a cynical approach toward the supposedly public commitment of elites. Often, the process of privatization has been carried out by neglecting regulation and competition, and by opening serious problems of costs for large sectors of the population. Decentralization and administrative reform did not produce a democratic political and administrative culture reaching down to the entire society. The constitutional reforms had various results, depending on the effectiveness with which they managed to reformulate the distributive policies and to establish rules of government that in Norberto Bobbio's terms could combine the normative principles of democracy with its substantive aspects.

Institutional fragility and violence

Every democracy is fragile. Some of the Latin American democracies became especially fragile, particularly during the later phases of the Cold War, but even during the so-called third wave of democratization such fragility was reenacted, even in an internationally propitious framework. To mention just three cases: At the end of the 20th century Argentina was about to sink, the severance of the political system led to a decline and economic disarray; in Venezuela Chavez began a process of acute polarization, making the country lose its political stability, and in Colombia the high rates of violence are a blemish which over-determines the problematic operation of democracy.

The Colombian case is perhaps paradigmatic of other democracies in the region, for it shows both a systemic persistence as well as the fragility of the rule. The most remarkable thing about the Colombian case is the capacity of the democratic political system to persist and renovate itself, despite the pressures that are put on this nation by the guerrillas, the paramilitaries, the drug traffickers, the repressive violence and the criminal and social violence. According to local observers, the patterns and traditions of violence are recorded "by fire" in the flesh and memory of generations of Colombians. This encoding of violence has been defined by Myriam Jimeno (1998) as one of the most persistent traits of Colombian identity. Against such background, one feels respect towards the capacity of that political system to stand by democracy and the firm political will of great parts of its elites, which try to develop institutional mechanisms designated to improve the democratic capacities of the polity and the public administration.

The persistence of representative democracy in the third wave of democratization in the region corresponds to a few paradoxes present especially in those countries that pulled out of authoritarian governments and regimes in the 1980s. As one considers cases as varied in other respects as Guatemala, the Southern Cone and Brazil, it is precisely under democracy that people in these settings have raised questions and expressed their doubts concerning the representative character of their political system. It is also under democracy that criminal and social violence – and in the case of Guatemala in the 1980s also state violence – increased, closely following the liberalization of the public sphere. No wonder that many citizens have asked whether the institutional channels are functioning effectively, whether they are broad enough, too limited or perhaps too wide with regard to their early expectations.

The solution, of course, is neither a return to previous authoritarian rule nor the curtailment of civil rights and free public spheres. However, there is no doubt that due to the conditions generated under democracy, considerable parts of the population expect the security forces to act severely against sectors thought to be threatening the social order, be they criminals or marginal individuals. While this demand for harsh measures follows its own logic within the context of social deterioration and economic decline, it constitutes a problem for the newly established democracies as far as civil and political rights are concerned, even if the current systems have condemned the use of repression as carried out by previous *de facto* governments.

As violence persists under democracy, this has crucial implications for the system's institutional viability. Whether related to the political system as in Colombia, where violence crystallized very early, fuelled by party identities; or in countries such as Brazil, where social and criminal violence has proliferated even though relatively disconnected from the political system, violence generates a process of amalgamation of identities. In this connection, both anthropological research and cultural studies have emphasized that violence cuts off the ties of shared identity between strangers, replacing them with the illusion of finding security and stability through the construction of an image of the "other" as an enemy. This process of reconstruction of identity predicates exclusion and the adjournment of dialogue (Bowman 2001, Feitlowitz 1998, Rojas de Ferro 1998, Roniger 2003). When such restrictive sense of identity is forged, individuals cling to distrust and exclusion towards the members of other classes, social groups or ethnicities. This is even more pronounced if occurring together with a deterioration of traditional norms and forms of reciprocity replaced by high residential mobility, the weakening of ties of locality and agrarian connections, the perception of authoritative figures as arbitrary and unexpected, and the perception of the public sphere with suspicion and lack of confidence.[2]

There is a second aspect that results in institutional fragility through social complexity and above all the images of uncertainty and despair that this generates. Supposedly, the more complex a society is, the higher the levels of uncertainty and risk, as analyzed *inter alia* by Ulrich Beck (1992) and Zigmunt Bauman (2000). This exacerbates a general trend according to which, whenever the codes of sociability are disrespected, every interaction carries the risk of turning into violence.

Often, under such conditions, the social system is perceived as influenced by sheer power, reinforcing the predictions of violence and fuelling a vicious circle of 'self fulfilling prophecy' which ensconces fear in the public space and disarticulates social solidarity, tilting the odds towards force and violence (Rotker 2002). The line between victims and victimizers is then often blurred. As Antanas Mockus and Jimmy Corzo (2003) analyze on the basis of the situation in Bogotá, suffering from violence and acting violently tend to be associated with a kind of behavior that characterizes especially those who perceive their surroundings as colored by social irregularity, hindering the co-existence in internally diversified spaces and locales.

It should be stressed that mass society is not "naturally" created around emergent models of reciprocity. The key issue here is whether democratic institutions can thrive by becoming the vectors of a sense of a community and polity committed to collective life rather than entering into a spiral of recurrent fear, suspicion and violence. The latter is precluded once the political leadership and the public administration succeed in creating a common vision, which will include the protection of civilians as part of a package deal of "public goods", the absence of which may turn social life into a nightmare. Institutional efficacy is thus essential for guaranteeing public security, access to public services and quality control of goods and services. Furthermore, while the control of product quality can be entrusted to market self-regulation, in the case of generalized violence the operative balance of institutional mechanisms has an immediate effect on the image of institutional capability, and consequentially on the capacity of attracting capital, investments and on the maintenance of a 'strong' population in the country.

The "Global Competitiveness Report" published by the World Economic Forum provides some indications of the difficulties faced by the Latin American democracies in this connection. Among the countries in the region only Chile appeared in the 1998 report among the first 20 countries in terms of competitiveness (18th place), followed by Mexico (32), Argentina (36, before the crisis), Peru (37), Venezuela (45, before the crisis), Brazil (46) and Colombia (47). In the 2001–2 Latin American Competitiveness Report, among the 75 countries included in the global competitiveness index, Chile was placed in the 27th place, Mexico declined to the 42nd place, followed by Brazil (44), Argentina (46), Uruguay (49), the Dominican Republic (50), Panama (53), El Salvador (58), and finally Colombia in the 65th place.

The wide-ranging lack of institutional guarantees and the impact this has on the institutional image also implies that influential sectors of the society might opt for leaving their country of origin, escaping from the vortex of violence and lack of institutional security. Since the 19th century two basic forms of escape have crystallized. One is the political exile of political oppositions, magnified in the 20th century by the mass phenomenon of refugee flight. The second form, differing only slightly from the previous, is the escape of professionals, intellectuals and individuals of all social classes, which are distinguished from the previously mentioned by their lack of confidence in the future of their country of origin.

Under democratic systems, about 500,000 individuals have departed annually from Latin America, trying to settle in other countries. Between 2000 and 2003 a million and a half persons emigrated from Ecuador. Almost 2 millions left Brazil, and about 600,000 left Peru 160,000 annually emigrated from Argentina; approximately 1,360,000 people left Colombia during the five years between 1996 and 2001. Although it is impossible to discern which category corresponds to all the millions of inhabitants that have left Latin American countries and at a certain moment are living abroad, this phenomenon reflects, most likely, the loss of vitality of those nations, which instead of being a focus of attraction, are becoming, at least in the short and intermediate terms, centers of expulsion of part of their own population. The fundamental problem has its roots in the institutional fragility, which brings us to rethink the basic boundaries and the operative dilemmas of democracy, analyzing them beyond the formal plane.

Returning to basics

No matter what definition we follow – whether Robert Dahl's concept of polyarchy or Ralf Dahrendorf's "pacific regulation of socio-economic conflicts"– the core of democracy refers to its systemic and normative regulation of competition for power, built upon a shared commitment not to stop the ever renewed competition following short term political triumphs over adversaries. The comparative advantage of the democratic political system *vis-à-vis* its late alternatives (namely, Fascism, Nazism, and Communism), has been its built-in flexibility for incorporating new demands and interests by groups and political movements. One of the most basic conditions for such perpetuation is the existence of channels of open representation.

Democracy cannot survive without ensuring institutional channels of representation and participation, whether through political parties or alternative channels. In other words, the expression of different interests must be articulated normatively, since otherwise democracy will be drained. The question is how to implement those norms – predicated constitutionally and legally – without reducing the flexibility of the democratic system to renew itself by incorporating new demands and interests.

In every democracy the pluralism at the basis of representation is in tension with the constitutional elements that express certain common vision of common goals and interests, well beyond the specific interests of particular social sectors. Thus even those individuals and groups that in the short-term may gain from policies benefiting their particular interests can be unsatisfied with the overall performance of the system. Two parallel aspects are crucial for evaluating the systemic capabilities of democracy. One, the general obligation to abide by the normative framework of democracy; and two, the balance between interests and the sense of confidence, and the will to live in that society, especially in an era of open frontiers and global horizons.

These aspects are articulated in the public sphere, through the expressed confidence in the institutional channels and guarantees for the regulation of services and markets, the possibility of access to public education and healthcare, or the provision of security, running water and pollution control as public goods. Furthermore, Latin American societies are highly stratified societies in which social classes are separated by life styles and differentiated by their future horizons. This, combined with rising expectations of participation, becomes a problematic area through which the willingness of citizens to see themselves as part of society is assessed. A fundamental aspect of this sense of belonging, which affects institutions and participation, is increasingly connected to the new modes of articulation between the political-administrative sphere and the markets of goods and services, particularly those considered public services.

Institutional efficacy

Individuals evaluate institutions by their performance, i.e. by their actions, efficacy, style, and more than anything else by their concrete results. The quality of the air we breathe and the state of personal security in the public realm, are examples of generalized goods that we cherish and that affect our perception of institutional efficacy. Due to their generalized character, once in existence they cannot be denied to those entitled to them, or otherwise, once they deteriorate, no one can escape from their corroding effects, independently of the contributions individuals have made towards financing their production, as indicated by Albert Hirschman decades ago (1970:101). These are complemented by other goods accessed through the markets or consumed in the private sphere, which require public intervention in the form of regulation or the setting of non-market criteria for their differential provision to various groups or individuals. Examples can be found in areas such as education, healthcare quality, electricity, and water consumption.

Ever since the crisis of the developmental capitalist model related to the protectionist and/or populist state, the Latin-American countries have endorsed in different degrees neo-liberal capitalist models. Although we are used to thinking that the shift occurred due to the international demonstration effect of the Thatcher and Reagan policies and the pressures put by organizations connected to the so called Washington consensus, we should keep in mind that in Latin America this was preceded by the implementation of the Plan Ladrillo in 1975 by the government of General Augusto Pinochet in Chile (Fontaine Aldunte 1988; Delano and Traslavina 1989).[3]

Whatever the details of this transformation, we must realize that a profound change has taken place in the collective image of the role of the

138

state and its relations with the markets. First, the state is now perceived as part of the problem of lack of development and not as a part of the solution to the problem. Although states continue to perform many roles, by the end of the 20th century and the beginning of the current one, in the social imagination the idea of the withdrawal of the state and the self-regulation of the markets, prevails. Partly, this reflects the collapse of the model of autarchic capitalism and the ISI as hegemonic ideas of development. In part, this process has been legitimized through the opening of the media in Latin America. As these countries were connected for centuries to international ideas and models of institutional organization (Roniger and Waisman 2002), the respectability of the idea of free markets on a global level reinforced internal tendencies in that direction. This is how various processes were triggered in the region, parallel to similar developments elsewhere:

(a) The diffusion of the market and consumption as social practices, which are generalized or at least become part of peoples' desiderata; and the massifiction of life styles. Even though there is no equality in the access to consumption nor to the political channels of decisions related to the economy, the idea of the market as a self regulating mechanism takes hold;

(b) The diffusion of the idea of the withdrawal of the state, although actually the state reforms and preserves many of its functions. So there are various models of intervention by the states when regulating basic aspects of the economy, such as the exchange markets, the protection of property and the formulation of the legal frameworks, so important for the operation of firms and corporations (See Roniger 1995: 259–285).

(c) The emergence of a new political culture (NPC). The new political culture takes on forms in Latin America that differ from the ones configured in the developed countries. In the USA, Canada, Japan and Western Europe, a research by Terry N. Clark, Vincent Hoffman-Martinot and Ronald Inglehart, identified the NPC based on a series of characteristics, among them the increasing distinction between fiscal and social themes, the emphasis on individualism, and the growing importance of public debate replacing old loyalty to political parties. The NPC is supported especially by the youth, the better educated sectors with higher purchasing power, which demand efficiency in services and lower taxes. In parallel, these social sectors tend towards "post-materialist" values (Inglehart 1990). Although these issues are not absent in Latin America, in this case the NPC became dominant in societies with restored democracies, limited public spheres and societies with significant social gaps. For that reason, the NPC is distorted by the constant concern of major parts of the population to survive, to overcome marginality and unemployment, and to stand by institutional opacity and lack of public confidence.

This has various consequences for the provision of public services and goods. There are consequences related to state responsibility, and others that are related to the changing relation of the population with the political system and with the public spheres. In a certain way, whatever occurs in one of these realms affects the others. The idea that the state abandoned the central role it played in the era of protectionism and populism, affects primarily the state responsibility to guarantee the quality of public goods and intervene in cases of market failure. In many cases, consumers have been unable to appeal to institutional channels as they encountered widespread problems when relying on market mechanisms. For example, in Argentina in the 1990s there were numerous incidents of indigestion, caused by the consumption of unhealthy products in bars or supermarkets that resulted in the hospitalization of hundreds of patients. In countries with normative codes and appropriated institutional channels of appeal, like the USA or Western Europe, such incidents would generate judicial prosecution and a demand for monetary compensation. In Latin America, at most, those involved lamented the case, and in other cases even that would not happen, but just end with a generous smile. The institutional frameworks often failed to sustain the bond of trust between customer and vendor that once disavowed could be taken to superior instances for adjudication. If such effective protection of customers would exist, the affected party could opt to bring the claim into relief, which beyond the specific merits of the case would have wider implications in terms of fiduciary trust. That would have the effect of repairing the damage if the case warranted it. What is even more important for the constitution of a public sphere, an ethics of market responsibility is sustained whenever consumers realize that their expectations of market fairness are not deceived.

Whenever this is not possible, expectations of impunity are consolidated. In brilliant essays, the late Argentinean sociologist Carlos Nino and the Colombian analyst John Sudarsky have analyzed the devastating consequences of this for the public confidence in both markets and institutions supposedly charged with regulating such cases of malfunction of mercantile and associative transactions (Nino 1992, Sudarsky 1988). The problem is not confined to the national borders, but has international implications as well. States cannot ignore their duty to guarantee the control of quality of products and services used by their population without running the risk of losing credibility and the capacity of their firms to enter markets abroad.

The issue of protecting the public goods – maintaining their quality, or at least, compensating for their faults – is thus transformed into a central problem that affects the political and social agenda of the analyzed countries. In Brazil, the issue of water quality or the interrupted supply of electricity became an extensive issue in the 1990s. In some of the major metropolitan areas, e.g. in Caracas or Rio, the issue of public security has reached alarming aspects. Although a long existing problem, the growing social gaps have deepened the problem, especially as parts of the middle class and the lower-middle class suffered considerable downward mobility and some of the Latin American cities have become battlefields of crime and survival (Rotker 2002).

The problem is even more acute when the ethics of impunity are projected into the ranks-and-file of the public security forces. This is happening in sectors of the Argentinean and Mexican police, many of whose members have been involved in abuses, extortions of bribes and extra-legal payments, wrong use of their power and an "easy trigger" tendency, violating civil rights as much as the application of the law. The methods of action used by the forces of order under civil governments have contributed to their general distrust among large sectors of the population.

The impact of the change is even more conspicuous in the privatized companies and their provision of what were formerly conceived as public services. Privatization was intended to deal with fiscal problems and the external debt, and to gather funds for the public tasks, halting the pressure of the public debt and thus obtain refinancing (Ramamurti 1992, Mosley 1988, Glade 1995:96–98). Once privatization was carried out, the gap between the expectations of public benefit and the opaque and sometimes-ineffective way in which many privatizations were executed created public discontent. Sociologist Oscar Oszlak closely observed this process in Argentina, his country:

> In the first period, the privatizations had a very high support. The right climate was created; there were talks about all types of corruption in the public companies, from people who took bribes for any repair to the entire system of purchase and supply of the companies. Supported by things that indeed happened, the campaign that was initiated in those years had an enormous public consent. Nowadays the surveys show a high level of dissatisfaction among the customers of the services, due to the high tariffs, problems in the scope of services. Surveys show more than 50 percent of dissatisfaction with the results of privatization . . . On the other hand, there has been indeed transference of profits from consumers to the companies . . . According to a research financed by the World Bank, the additional price on the tariffs was estimated in a media of 16% and in 20% for the less favored sectors of the population. The additional cost means that the consumers paid about 1000 million dollars more to the companies. All the indicators show that the companies that made the highest profits were the most attractive companies, the leading companies, something that was expected and was not an

unintended consequence of the change. And in addition, the process of concen-
tration of capital has created optional conditions for negotiating and renegotiating
terms of contracts, etc., in order to maintain their privileged status. (Oszlak 2000)

Every process of privatization implies aspects concerning accountability, the regulation and consequences of the economic decisions. The
speed and manner in which privatization was carried out in Argentina led
to some serious faults in the subsequent regulation of the functioning and
supply of the privatized services. In this respect the early privatizations,
were done irrespective of procedures and creating what many saw as
conditions for corruption and scandals that reached top government
officials, their associates and families.

The preceding also affects the issue of equality and access to services
and goods related to the so called "third generation rights", e.g. healthcare and education. Peter Knapp and his associates, among others, have
indicated the importance of these realms, stating that there is a level of
inequality beyond which the ideals of basic equal opportunities, social
equality and inclusive community are transformed into a vacuous claim
(Knapp *et al.* 1996:202. and see also Chalmers *et al.* 1997 and Klihsberg
2000).

Using this perspective, we can identify several problematic aspects in
the operation of the privatized public services and in the nature of public
goods, connected with economic restructuring and with important consequences for institutional trust under democracy.

1. The weakness of the institutional channels of appeal in face of failure
    in the delivery and quality of public services.
2. Problems of accountability and effective regulation in the operation
    of public services.
3. The separation between investments in routine operation of the
    public services and those investments needed for maintenance of the
    services.
4. Considering the socioeconomic context of deep inequalities, how to
    establish differential prices for different sectors of the population, in
    order to guarantee the widest possible access to those services.
5. The problem of regulating tariffs and the quality of services.
6. The possibility of renegotiating contract conditions that pledged
    elevated profits to the concessionaires, especially in situations of a
    quasi-monopolist provision of services.
7. The relative weakness of the organizational entities charged with
    regulation.

Dealing with these aspects of malfunctioning is crucial for the reinforcement of public trust, and is central to the public perception of an

effective functioning of institutions and the formation of a view of the political and administrative leadership committed to the collective well being of the population in an effective manner.

Politics and Representation

The changes in the articulation of states and markets analyzed above are related to parallel transformations in the conception of the role and weight of politics in contemporary life. In fact, the change initiated in the last few decades has raised the possibility of de-politization of the economic realm, even though the new view is no less ideological than the former, since it prioritizes the realm of economics almost as a matter of faith, i.e. as part of the projection of some worldview that I would define as "market fundamentalism". In contrast to the past, and differing between countries, it may now be possible in the near future, to address specific issues as discrete problems that are not politicized immediately, as was the case in the past. The negative side of this trend is that economic decisions can be isolated, to be treated by experts, and not perceived as being open to public debate. This can imply, as mentioned above, the political difficulty of delineating alternatives and debating them publicly. According to Martin Hoppenhayn from the CEPAL,

> The good thing is not letting any specific problem to spread . . . [But] a relationship between politics and economy is created, in which the economy is so powerful, so structural and so rooted, that it is not merely an ideology transmitted by discourse, but it has been incorporated in daily behaviors. It is an 'incarnated ideology'. Therefore, politics and politicians or at least some of them have to make a tremendous effort in order to stop the tendency to make politics merely instrumental and technocratic. This is an effort that in some way is meant to fail, but on the other hand it must be done in order to generate a certain resistance against the total technocratization. (Hoppenhayn 2000)

On the other hand, there is some disenchantment with the politicians and with their current way of doing politics, which remains opaque and little committed to the public interest. Even in Colombia, where compared to other countries in Latin America, party identification was very strong and volatility in the behavior of politicians was smaller than say in Brazil, in the 1990s one could perceive a slight increase in electoral absenteeism, reflecting the public apathy towards its representative institutions.

Representation is one of democracy's *sine qua non*. Nevertheless, the weakest point of democracy in the Latin American nations seems to be the relationship between governance and public accountability. In accountability I would like to stress its element of inner motivation to keep a public mission rather than merely the administrative review of conduct or the rhetoric of the public good. The essential thing in this respect is to generate the personal motivation – and generalize it- towards the public wellbeing. This view does not imply a search for a communitarian vision, nor subordination to an authoritarian will, but the building of public goodwill and governance. Without governance, the public commitment cannot be generated and the personal interests become prioritized to public concerns, without being balanced by a certain vision – of course, pluralistic – of the common will. The combination of representation with governance and public commitment in terms of some shared vision of the public good is important. Venezuela seems to have lost this shared vision in the last few years and has witnessed political crises and urban and economic deterioration as a result. In contrast, after being exhausted by violence, Colombia seems to have reached the point of recovery, based on initiatives made by its most dynamic elites, which have a profound vision of democratic public co-existence, as shown in the last three administrations of the capital of Bogotá.

How to improve institutions and representation

Many of the studies concerning representation emphasize the aspect of formal structure of the electoral systems, expecting representation by political parties to express social pluralism. They also conceive that the parliamentary organs are those charged with holding serious and informed debates over the actual and future alternatives, as part of policy formation process. According to these views, power-holders are supposed to make decisions in a balanced way, being fully informed and able to assess information rationally, combining special interests with the common well-being. To what extent do Latin American systems function according to design and model expectations?

The elections seem to function well in the region. However, the disenchantment with the politicians is wide, both in settings where the clientelism remains widespread and in those less prone to be pervaded by it. The problem seems to be rooted in the disenchantment with the basic role of the politicians, which is to seek power. In this connection, we recognize a series of problems in the functioning of the Latin American democracies in the third wave of democratization.

One of the main problems of these democracies is that they maintain the gap between the formal and rhetorical level, and the practical level of operation of politics. Ever since their establishment as independent states, it is possible to note the gap between those principles aimed at generating systemic legitimacy –for example, the division of powers, parliamentary representation, constitutionalism, and embedded legalism – and the mechanisms, such as the presidential executive rule, authoritarianism and clientelism, aimed to ensure the aggregation of interests and the elaboration of consensus. The public confidence in democracy and the transformative efficacy of democratic institutions depend mainly on reducing this gap.

Let us observe the case of the clientele system, that I call clientelism and its renewed upsurge in the region. Under the transition towards economic changes and despite poverty in which 200 out of the 516 million inhabitants of the region are living, clientelism reappears, despite the predictions of modernization theories that forecast its decline. Scholars have presented diverse explanations for this trend, ranging from cultural explanations to structural considerations (see. Roniger 2001, 2004). In most cases of clientelism, despite the differences between them, it is possible to trace, in one way or another, the genesis of reliance on such networks to solve the problem discussed here, of disjuncture between principles and practice in the political level. When it exists, clientelism reinforces this gap, i.e. (a) it prevents the empowerment of the state despite its institutional enlargement; (b) it generates incentives for fragmentation, which damage the political parties; and (c) it creates a distance between the official politics and its personal and party derivatives. Institutional stability is achieved in an inflationary way, by elevating the operational costs, while the image of the state is weakened and remains open to an extra-parliamentary de-structuring and to the propagation of violence (On Colombian clientelism see Leal Buitrago and Guevara 1991; Losada Lora 1984, Martz 1997, Escobar 2000).

A parallel phenomenon of *disjuncture* concerns the introduction of the discourse and practice of respect for human rights. Let me address it from the perspective of the Southern Cone societies, which I researched with political scientist Mario Sznajder (Roniger and Sznajder 1999). Once democracy was reestablished in Argentina, Chile and Uruguay, human rights were introduced as part of the programs of civic education, but their study remained separate from the study and discussion of the recent experiences of violations of human rights under the military governments, which was relegated to the field of history. The formality, with which the principles and legal provisions for the protection of human rights were taught, hindered a process of learning from the concrete experiences of political polarization and repression of the last decades. A gap between principles and the practical endorsement of those principles was thus recreated in the socialization of the young generations, in spite of declarations and rhetoric to the contrary. Vanguard initiatives, for example the elaboration of teaching manuals like the successful book written by Bustamante and González (1992) in the framework of the Servicio de Paz y Justicia (SERPAJ) in Uruguay, did not have the impact they deserved. Of the 1000 copies published only 300 were sold. In a similar way, the Argentinean state accepted the supra-constitutional status of the international treaties on human rights. But, once the Center of Legal and Social Studies (CELS) and other NGOs presented judicial claims in the mid-1990s demanding recognition of the right of mourning and the clarification of the individual fate of the disappeared, relying on the international treaties, the Secretary of Human Rights rejected the argument, resorting to the old principle of national sovereignty.

Disjuncture also occurred in the economic area, where many privatizations were predicated in terms of improving efficacy. Yet they were used – in addition to repayment of the national debt and the interests – as a means for creating profitable conditions for private sectors under conditions of quasi-monopoly instead of opening competition, which would have been the only way of reducing costs in the public services.

Another area in which reform is necessary refers to the capacity of regulating the institutional apparatus. As indicated above, the public evaluates institutions in terms of their efficacy. It is foreseeable that faults and deficiencies appear in the operation of markets. The question is then how should they be dealt with. The inefficiency in this area creates impunity and generates frustration and institutional distrust. The global environment forces improvements in this area. With the collapse of the Soviet Union and due to the decrease of regional threats, we should expect democracies to be more responsive to criticisms and civilians to be more critical of performance. Meanwhile, personal factors of leadership may continue to draw great attention, as they are amplified by the mass media. In parallel, it is obvious that the issues that caused the deterioration of institutional confidence will remain. The regulation of the economic framework (see the negative example of Argentina), the control of foreign policy in order to avoid diplomatic adventures, and the supervision of normative implementation in the public administration, in order to avoid the recurrence of corruption. The emphasis put here on institutional performance is reinforced by recent research in the area of institutional trust. This research rejects older views relying on psychological and personal variability models, which stressed differences in education, gender, age, and other personal characteristics as effecting variance in trust. Instead, the new studies emphasize the importance of public efficacy, commitment and loyalty in generating or eroding public confidence (Newton and Norris 2000, Uslander 2003).

Civic participation is another area for institutional reform. What is the reason for turning to the citizens when the public agenda becomes more complicated and thus requires the intervention of experts? Democratic theory emphasizes the importance of doing so, whatever the analytical view followed. Both from the perspective of republicanism as from procedural approaches there are reasons for this initiative. From a republican perspective, the political community perceives itself as auto-governable, which in complex and pluralistic societies forces negotiations over public programs and shared normative frameworks. From the perspective of procedural democracy, participation is also fundamental, facilitating the structuring of deliberative models, be they those of Jürgen Habermas, built upon rational and legal procedures of deliberation and formation of public opinion, or a model such as John Dewey's social cooperation and the practical establishment of reflexive and autonomous initiatives, in the tradition of civil society.

Various macro-sociological factors have led to a deep change in that direction: the erosion of the centralizing models of the authoritarian and communist countries, the diffusion of the participatory model of civil society in the tradition identified by Alexis De Tocqueville in the USA; and the erosion of the idea of the nation-state in its homogenizing and dominative character. All have contributed to generate the conditions for the legitimacy of a new participatory pluralism. In this new format, citizens are perceived as able to disagree democratically, to develop public will and to acquire skills that once were limited to the traditional political and administrative elites. In some cases, this has shaped the rise to the centers of power of politicians coming from relatively lower class and limited educational background. In parallel, the G-7 societies have been able to maintain high levels of voluntary participation of civil society in local politics and organizations. Sydney Tarrow has traced some of the characteristics of this profound transformation:

> It brings activists further into the realms of tolerated and prescribed politics and makes possible relations of working trust with public officials. It has produced hybrid forms of behavior that cross the boundaries of the polity and link grass-root activists to public interest groups, parties, and public officials. On the one hand, these new forms of activism are unlikely to sustain high levels of confidence in government, and they may discourage public trust by demonstrating the inadequacy of governmental performance. On the other hand, they do not create enduring negative subcultures. Their variable form and shifting organizations, their tendency to produce rapid and rapidly liquidated coalitions, and their focus on issues of short- and medium-term issues rather than fully fledged ideologies do not produce enduring membership commitments or deeply held loyalties outside the polity. (Tarrow 2000: 289)

In Latin America there is a wide tradition of parallel attempts, in the past mostly futile yet recently crowned with success. Practices such as the electoral control in Mexico or the model of participatory budgeting – in Brazilian cities such as Porto Alegre and Belo Horizonte – are exemplary. In Brazil, following the reform of the Constitution, there has been a process of institutional innovation based upon a tripartite structure that involved public administrators, professionals and local delegates representing civil society. It concerned the process of provision of public services, in which macro policies are translated into the every day practice of decision making regarding the nature of services, their costs and the quality of their supply. The analysis of the recent experiences by Boaventura de Santos (1998) and Leonardo Avritzer (2002), suggests an alternative to the elitist theories of democracy. According to the elitist theories, democracy will exist wherever there is a fair political game of recurring competition for power, structured through electoral decisions. This view, identified among others with Robert Dahl and his concept of polyarchy, is widely accepted in political science, sociology and international relations as satisfactory for a political system to qualify as democratic. As such, while it focuses on the political level, it is widely accepted for Latin America, by scholars, policy actors and citizens.

The origins of such minimalist definition – focusing on the selection of political leadership and the election of government – can be traced to the inter-war period in Europe, when wide mass mobilizations disrupted the political systems of the first wave of democratization. Something similar occurred at the end of Cold War, when the violence on the right and the left disarticulated many of the democratic systems of the Third World, through the wave of protests, demonstrations and mass mobilizations. In the case of Latin American countries, this led ultimately to the emergence of guerrilla warfare, para-military and state violence. The legacy of such collective experience had its political impact in the form of the wide acceptance of theories that, like Dahl's, looked for the minimal parameters of operation and survival of democracy.

In contrast, authors such as Avitzer (2002), Adriana Delgado (2003) and Chantall Mouffe (2003), suggested recently that the Latin American experience of the last decades should prompt a wider view of the relations between democracy and the formation of a public space in which citizens participate as equals and public decisions are taken through the open discussion of political projects. This alternative democratic theory puts emphasis on the practices taking shape in the public sphere, where rulers and citizens meet and have a mutual influence on each other. It suggests viewing democracy as a series of social practices, which try to be institutionalized in order to acquire stability and permanence. While in the first and second wave of democratization there was a contradiction between mobilization and institutionalization, in the current stage in which we are living, democracy may be consolidated through citizenship participation.

These trends seem to indicate that a key in the changing character of democracy in Latin America derives from the capacity of institutionalizing successfully the participatory practices. Practices such as the electoral control in Mexico and the participatory budgeting in Brazil demonstrate that mobilization does not necessarily hamper or threaten democracy. On the contrary, when it leads to deliberation, citizen participation seems to be the only way for strengthening democracy, especially in those societies in which there are strong pressures for participation and, on the other hand, remnants of elitism and distrust, especially among the popular classes. Avritzer suggests transferring the democratic potential arising from civil society into the political sphere, through the mechanisms of participation and deliberative public spaces.

The target would be to generate public concern and involvement from the bottom-up in order to develop the effective capacities of implementing democratic changes and improving the public conduct of civil servants. The third wave of democratization in Latin America seems to encourage such public engagement by citizens, in ways perhaps less prone to be manipulated as in the past. We should recognize, however, that we do not know yet how to move successfully in this area of deepening effective democracy in different domains. It seems much more difficult to institutionalize participatory mechanisms in the field of human rights than in the area of public services.

Latin American democracies have not found yet the way of combining personal and public security with the respect for human rights. Similarly, deliberation practices have greater chances of success when they are structured to resist damaging practices than when they are proposed in terms of innovation. The challenge would be to combine both lines. For example, it is possible to suggest consolidating the normative transference and use of public budgets between the different administrative levels through citizen participation, while restricting the use of ad-hoc monies that the politicians, supposedly the representatives of regional and local interests, have been granted to use at their discretion. The advance setting of universal criteria for budget transference, aimed at reducing the misuse of public monies, could be combined with subsidiary criteria contemplating the differential needs of the various regions, provinces and states, in the federal countries of the region.

These initiatives could overturn the tendency of erosion of public confidence evident in both the affluent and the poorer Latin American strata, parallel to the declared triumph of democracy over the alternative political systems.

Conclusions: political determination and dynamic leadership as keys to change

The axiom that democracy requires open channels of representation, governance and some public commitment is correct. The problem, however, is not the mere transition from traditional into modern societies. Although basically correct in a broad sense, we should avoiding turning these into essentials and forgetting that much depends on the dynamic process of transformation, the agents that can accelerate or delay it, as well as the timing of the process.

New historical studies by scholars such as Thomas Ertman (1997), Simona Piattoni (2001) and Nico Raanderad and Wolffman (2001) show that the combination between an effective political-administrative center and a politically mobilized – and not only controlled politically – local sphere seems to have been a broad formula that allowed for reforms and the modernizing transformation of different Western societies. The case of the Netherlands is significant, for the above combination precluded the oligarchization of local government, and sustained the emergence of a non-violent and mobilized society. Other studies such as Frank O'Gorman's, demonstrated that such a highly clientele society as the English could transform itself in the 18th century through an incremental and progressive process of change. In the first stage it initiated a political reform triggered by the indignation and charges of corruption, which the loss of the American colonies in the 1770s projected back home. Determined to maintain public confidence, elites initiated a process of reforms in the administration, which continued in the 19th and 20th centuries with the extension of franchise, the mobilization of mass parties, the modernization of the central and local administration, and finally the introduction of a system of meritocracy in the nomination and promotion of public officials (O'Gorman 2001).

A few additional points, addressed elsewhere must be briefly mentioned here. One, crises, such as the crisis of public confidence, constitute key opportunities to initiate intense transformations in the political and administrative system. Another is adjusting the timing of the hoped-for changes, which often determines their failure or success. Also, much depends on the leadership of those performing the change, as a fundamental part of the process of institutional transformation. A dynamic leadership, socially oriented and not merely drawn by the will to retain power is essential for benefiting from global openings (Sznajder and Roniger 2003). Finally, I believe that this analysis has revealed the importance of rethinking the public domain in the widest possible terms, as a focus for the recreation of sociability, the forging of collective identity and the building of a shared sense of future.

In conclusion, I wish to indicate certain interpretative hindrances that, for decades and maybe centuries, have impaired analysis of the Latin American countries. Maybe the most important has been to assume that there is an ideal institutional format, which once unveiled, could bring a once-and-for-all solution to the problems of governance and public commitment. It has been customary to look for such model in the advanced and most successful societies of the West. Since the times of the conquest and colonization, Latin American elites conceived their societies as part of Western civilization. Observers have recognized and criticized this propensity in the region to incorporate the models, ideas, techniques and institutions elaborated in the core countries of the West. For example, the Brazilian critic Roberto Schwartz's characterization (1992) of Latin America as dealing with "ideas out of place"; or political scientist Laurence Whitehead's definition of Latin America as a mausoleum of modernities, full of the material and intellectual scrap deposited throughout the centuries and lacking the ability to infer the institutional effects of the derivative models in an integral way (Whitehead 2002).

By thinking themselves as part of the civilized world, by visiting or following attentively the centers of diffusion of new ideas and styles, as either exiles, students or tourists and facing the enormous task of creating new states and nations since the 19th century, it was almost natural to be tuned to the universal, as reflected by the gaze of locality (Roniger 2002). The tragedy is that even though today we are conscious of the fact that there is not one but multiple models of modernity, we still tend intuitively to look for the ideal institutional format which will be the definitive solution for the problems of democracy in the region. Similarly, political marketing has become fashionable, directing the use of media strategies as political weapons for identifying preferences, orienting public opinion and capturing votes. Even if one recognizes their importance, the emphasis on the ways we do politics cannot obviate dealing with deficiencies in the efficacy of public institutions.

The search after the ideal model has induced us to think, for example, that some democracies are successful due to their electoral system, which seems to be better than others, or that the issue of optimal representation can be formally resolved by an intelligent use of the mass media or a referendum. We should remember that the problem of development of representative democracy cannot be dissociated from nourishing shared ideas regarding the public good, elaborated democratically, and from the creation of social capital vital for institutional transformations, as illustrated by the case of Colombia presented by John Sudarsky (2001). I do not believe that political marketing or media strategies would be enough to maintain representative democracy. In parallel , work has to be done to improve public performance and efficacy, and to reinforce the equation of growth-redistribution-and-inclusion instead of the inverse equation of stagnation-(recession or decline)-widening socioeconomic gaps-exclusion. I suggest that the democratic institutions could be improved, and that this is a task that must go beyond the mere formal format of institutions.

Notes

These ideas were first expressed in the international colloquium on "Transitions from Dictatorship to Democracy: The Cases of Spain and Latin America", organized by the Institute of Latin American History and Culture of the University of Tel Aviv (May 2003) and were elaborated in the international seminar on "Bogotá, Colombia, América Latina: sistema político y cultura política", organized by the Pontificia Universidad Javeriana and the municipality of Bogotá, in July 2003. I would like to thank the Truman Research Institute for the Advancement of Peace in Jerusalem for its support of this research, and Pnina Wein for her assistance in the completion of the typescript.

1   Even if aware of the limitations of public opinion polls, we should recognize they are highly indicative of trends and changes, especially when taken over relatively long time periods and following consistent criteria of data collection.

2   In the last decade, other processes have contributed to a fragmentary point of view, among them a decline of old political commitments and the weakening of trade unions (Clark, Lipset and Rempel 1993).

3   Experiences cannot be reproduced, even in countries with similar institutional dynamics. The local anchoring of change is crucial. In Chile a highly authoritarian and repressive government adopted the change of policy. In spite of the social price demanded, Pinochet's government was able to overcome the crisis of the early 1980s and managed to transfer its institutional model during the transition to democracy. In Argentina, in a formal democratic framework, many of the changes were introduced by presidential decree, against a background of disarticulation of the opposition and the widespread fears of the population about the perils of hyperinflation, as experienced in the late 1980s.

References

Avritzer, Leonardo (2002) *Democracy and the Public Space in Latin America*. Princeton: Princeton University Press.

Bauman, Zygmunt (2000). *Liquid Modernity*. Cambridge: Polity Press.

Beck, Ulrich (1992). *Risk Society. Towards a New Modernity*. London: Sage.

Bowman, Glenn (2001). The Violence in Identity", in Bettina E Schmidt and Ingo W Schroder eds. *Anthropology of Violence and Conflict* London: Routledge, pp. 25–46.

Bobbio, Norberto (1987). *The Future of Democracy*. Oxford: Polity Press.

Bustamante, Francisco y María Luisa González (1992). *Derechos humanos en el aula. Cuadernos para docentes: reflexiones y experiencias*. Montevideo: Servicio de Paz y Justicia.

Chalmers, Douglas *et al.* (1997). *The New Politics of Inequality in Latin America*. Oxford: Oxford University Press.

Clark, Terry Nichols and Vincent Hoffman-Martinot (1998). Eds. *The New Political Culture* New York: Westview.

Clark, Terry Nichols, Syemour Lipset and M. Rempel (1993). "The Declining Political Significance of Social Class". *International Sociology*, 8: 293–316.

Crozier, Michel; Samuel Huntington and Joji Watanuki (1975). *The Crisis of Democracy*. New York: New York University Press.

Delano, Manuel y Hugo Traslavina (1989). *Laherencia de los Chicago Boys*. Santiago: Ornitorrinco.

Delgado Gutiérrez, Adriana (2003). "Expansión de ciudadanía y construcción democrática", en *Inclusión social y nuevas ciudadanías*. Bogotá: Pontificia Universidad Javeriana, 195–208.

Ertman, Thomas (1997). *Birth of the Leviatán: Building Status and Regimes in Medieval and Early Modern Europe.* Cambridge: Cambridge University Press.

Escobar, Cristina (2000). "Bullfighting Fiestas, Clientelism and Political Identities in Northern Colombia", in Luis Roniger and Tamar Herzog eds. *The Collective and the Public in Latin America.* Brighton & Portland: Sussex Academic Press, 174–191.

Feitlowitz, Marguerite (1998). *A Lexicon of Terror. Argentina and the Legacies of Torture.* Oxford: Oxford University Press.

Fontaine Aldunate, Arturo (1988*). Los economistas y el presidente Pinochet.* Santiago: Zig-Zag.

Glade, William (1995). *Privatization of Public Enterprises in Latin America,* San Francisco: ICS Press.

Hirschman, Albert (1970). *Exit, Voice and Loyalty.* Cambridge: Harvard University Press.

Hoppenhayn, Martin (2000). Interview in Santiago de Chile, 23 August.

Inglehart, Ronald (1990). *Culture Shift.* Princeton: Princeton University Press.

Jimeno, Myriam (1998). "Identidad y experiencias cotidianas de violencia", en Gabriel Restrepo, Jaime Eduardo Jaramillo y Luz Gabriela Arango, eds. *Cultura, política y modernidad.* Bogotá: CES/Universidad Nacional, 247–275.

Kliksberg, Bernardo (2000). *La lucha contra la pobreza en América Latina.* BID y Fondo de Cultura Económica.

Knapp, Peter *et al.* (1996). *The Assault on Equality.* New York: Praeger.

Latinobarómetro 2003 [http:// www.latinobarometro.org]

Leal Buitrago, Francisco y Andrés Dávila Ladrón de Guevara (1991). *Clientelismo: el sistema político y su expresión regional* Bogotá: Tercer Mundo.

Losada Lora, Rodrigo (1984). *Clientelismo y elecciones* Bogotá: Pontificia Universidad Javeriana.

Martz, John D. (1997*) The Politics of Clientelism. Democracy and the State in Colombia* New Brunswick: Transaction Publishers.

Mockus, Antanas y Jimmy Corzo (2003). "Dos caras de la convivencia: cumplir acuerdos y normas y no usar ni sufrir violencia". Unpublished manuscript.

Mosley, P. (1988). "Privatisation, Policy-Based Lending and World Bank Behavior", in Cook and Kirpatrick (eds*) Privatization in Less Developed Countries,* Brighton: Wheatsheaf Books, pp.125–140.

Mouffe, Chantall (2003). "Participación ciudadana en los asuntos públicos de las ciudades". Seminario internacional "Bogotá, sistema politico y cultura democrática". Bogota, 29–31 de Julio.

Newton, Kenneth and Pippa Norris (2000). "Confidence in Public Institutions: Faith, Culture or Performance?"in Pharr and Putnam, eds. *Disaffected Democracies,* pp. 52–73.

Nino, Carlos (1992). *Un país al margen de la ley.* Buenos Aires: Emecé.

O'Donnell, Guillermo (1997). *Contrapuntos. Ensayos escogidos sobre autoritarismo y democratización.* Buenos Aires: Paidós.

O'Gorman, Frank (2001). "Patronage and the Reform of the State in England, 1700–1860", in Piattoni, *Clientelism,* pp. 54–76.

Oszlak, Oscar (2000). Interview in Buenos Aires, 5 September.

Pharr, Susan J. and Robert D. Putnam (2000). Eds. *Disaffected Democracies.*

What's Troubling the Trilateral Countries? Princeton: Princeton University Press.

Piattoni, Simona (2001). "Clientelism, Interests and Democratic Representation", in idem, ed. *Clientelism, Interests and Democratic Representation* Cambridge: Cambridge University Press, 2001, pp. 193–212.

Randeraad, Nico y Dirk Jan Wolffram (2001). "Constrains on Clientelism: The Dutch Path to Modern Politics, 1848–1917", in Piattoni, *Clientelism*, 101–121.

Ramamurti, R. (1992) "Privatization and the Latin American Debt Problem", in Grosse (ed.), *Private Sector Solutions to the Latin American Debt Problem*, Miami, Transaction Publishers, pp.153–176.

Rojas de Ferro, María Cristina (1998). "Civilización y violencia: la lucha por la representación durante el siglo XIX en Colombia", en Gabriel Restrepo, Jaime Eduardo Jaramillo y Luz Gabriela Arango, eds. *Cultura, política y modernidad.* Bogotá: CES/Universidad Nacional, pp. 217–246.

Roniger, Luis (1995). "Globalization as Cultural Vision". *Canadian Review of Sociology and Anthropology,* 32 (3): 259–285.

—— (2001). "Patron-Client Relations", in Neil Smelser and Paul Baltes, eds. *The International Encyclopedia of the Social and Behavioral Sciences.* London, Elsevier, vol. 16, pp. 11118–11120.

—— (2002). "Global Immersion: Latin America and its Mutiple Modernities", en Luis Roniger and Carlos Waisman eds. *Globality and Multiple Modernities: Comparative North American and Latin American Perspectives.* Brighton & Portland: Sussex Academic Press, pp. 79–105.

—— (2003). "Identidades individuais, incertezas coletivas." *Revista 18* (São Paulo), 2: 16–17.

—— (2004). "Political Clientelism, Democracy and Market Economy". Forthcoming in *Comparative Politics,* vol. 36.

Roniger, Luis and Mario Sznajder, *The Legacy of the Human-Rights Violations in the Southern Cone.* Oxford: Oxford University Press, 1999.

Rotker, Susana (2002) Ed. *Citizens of Fear. Urban Violence in Latin America.* New Brunswick: Rutgers University Press.

Santos, Boaventura de (1998). "Participatory Budgeting in Porto Alegre: Towards a Redistributive Justice". *Politics and Society,* 26 (4): 461–51.

Scheper-Hughes, Nancy (1992). *Death without Weeping,* Berkeley, University of California Press.

Schwarz, Roberto (1992). *Misplaced Ideas: Essays on Brazilian Culture.* London: Verso.

Sudarsky, John (1988). *Clientelismo y desarrollo social. El caso de las cooperativas* Bogotá: Tercer Mundo Editores.

—— (2001). *El capital social de Colombia* Bogotá: Departamento Nacional de Planeación.

Sznajder, Mario (1996) "Transition in South America: Models of Limited Democracy." *Democratization,* 3, pp. 360–370.

Sznajder, Mario and Luis Roniger (2003). Trends and Constrains of Partial Democracy in Latin America". *Cambridge Review of International Affairs,* 16 (2): 323–341.

Tarrow, Sydney (2000). "Maid Cows and Social Activists: Contentious Politics in the Trilateral Democracies", in Pharr and Putnam, eds. *Disaffected Democracies*, pp. 270–290.

Uslaner, Eric M. (2003). "Trust, Democracy and Governance: Can Government Policies Influence Generalized Trust?". Unpublished manuscript.

Waisman, Carlos (1998). "Civil Society, State Capacity, and the Conflicting Logics of Economic and Political Change", in Philip Oxhorn and Pamela Starr eds. *Market or Democracy?* Boulder: Lynne Rienner.

Whitehead, Laurence (2002). "Latin America as a Mausoleum of Modernities", in Roniger y Waisman, *Globality and Multiple Modernities*. Brighton & Portland: Sussex Academic Press, pp. 29–65.

World Economic Forum (2002). "Global Competitivess Report" [http://www/weforum.org].

8

THE "SLOW, GRADUAL AND SECURE TRANSITION" TO DEMOCRACY IN BRAZIL

Background

According to J. C. Zorzenon Costa, "the economic crisis that occurred in Brazil in the early 1960s is considered an important factor in the aggravation of the political crises under way since the start of the previous decade, resulting in regime change and the establishment of a new economic development model starting with the military coup" (Costa, 2002).

At the climax of a turbulent process that culminated in the overthrow of President João Goulart the military seized power on March 31, 1964. The military coup was supported by the United States and by conservative forces in Brazil. Within the context of the cold war, US support for the coup was motivated primarily by fears that the Cuban Revolution would trigger a domino effect throughout the region. Cuba's revolutionary regime then enjoyed significant international prestige and segments of the Brazilian left were turning to thoughts of armed struggle as a solution for their own country. Even though the Partido Comunista Brasileiro (Brazilian Communist Party – PCB) was by far the largest party on the left and had recently reaffirmed its faith in a peaceful and democratic road to revolution at its 1962 national conference, other groups were trying to organize a guerrilla war. The growing support for armed struggle came into evidence when, in 1962, a Cuban diplomatic pouch with reports of Francisco Julião's movement was found on a plane that had crashed in Lima, Peru (Gaspari, 2002a).

In Brazil support for the coup came primarily from powerful traditional elites, who, despite of having survived the 1930 bourgeois revolution (thanks to a pact that preserved the structure of land tenure) felt threatened by land reform and other "grassroots" redistributive measures raised by social movements and adopted by Goulart in his "Reformas de Base" program. The urban middle class also fell in behind the forces that favored a coup. Led by the Catholic Church, who feared the "unforeseeable subversion of democratic values", they assumed a key role in garnering support (Gaspari, 2002a). Also supporting the coup were intellectuals linked to IPES (Instituto de Pesquisas e Estudos Sociais). IPES was a government think-tank that had been working on modernization projects that sought to boost Brazil's productive capacity and align it with international capitalist economic interests. In this sense the 1964 military coup was not simply a putsch or a military movement with civilian support but rather a broad-based, elite driven social coalition (Dreyfuss, 1981).

By the end of 1963 the mounting economic crisis was evident. The annual inflation rate reached 79.9% (the highest ever experienced in Brazil until then) and a Gross Domestic Product (GDP) growth rate of only 0.6%, the lowest since 1947, when calculation was first used. As a result of this Brazil was left with a Treasury deficit of approximately Cr$500 billion (Gaspari, 2002a).

Brazilian political life in 1962 was not much better. While election results showed Goulart's Partido Trabalhista Brasileiro (Brazilian Labor Party – PTB) in the lead, the conservative right had achieved significant gains, winning gubernatorial elections in many important states. At the same time, even though the PCB was banned, a large number of the party's candidates won seats in the Congressional election, running on the PTB line. The Supreme Electoral Court, however, only allowed Marco Antônio Tavares Coelho to assume his mandate, arguing that the other elected candidates were "notorious Communists" (Coelho, 2000). The courts decision was an indicator of the growing conservative encroachment into all areas of the Brazilian state.

The year 1963 was both a year of political advances and retreats for Brazilian democracy. In January presidential regime was restored as a result of a plebiscite and strengthened Goulart's administration,[1] however, the same month also witnessed the founding of Comando de Caça aos Comunistas (CCC). This was a paramilitary group that promoted McCarthyite witch hunts and was not averse to street violence. Strikes were a daily occurrence. By mid 1963 it was obvious that conservative political forces were preparing a coup and in September Carlos Lacerda, Governor of Guanabara, publicly advocated Goulart's removal by the armed forces. In response to the mounting pressure Goulart tried to declare a state of emergency but given its weak support was forced to back down. The rightwing began organizing openly against the Government. The Instituto Brasileiro de Ação Democrática (Brazilian Institute for Democratic action – IBAD), originally an independent think-tank had been co-opted by the CIA and large corporations. Their strategy

157

included working their way into the leadership position of several mass organizations after which they supplied financial resources to various rightwing politicians.

The initial months of 1964 saw even greater political conflict. On one side, supporting Goulart and the Government were nationalist and left-wing groups and in the opposing camp the rightwing political forces led by the União Democrática Nacional (National Democratic Union – UDN), Lacerda's party. In the past the UDN had been at the center of several institutional crises and had attempted a coup in the 1950s. The climate steadily deteriorated and tensions were further exacerbated by an institutional military crisis due to growing acts of insubordination by non-commissioned officers and the conflict between Goulart's supporters and Congress over questions regarding changes in the process of presidential succession, such as the re-election of the president.

It was in this context that on March 31, 1964, the military seized power, with very little resistance from pro-government forces in the military or by popular movements. The following day, April 1, the new leaders were in full control of the country, promising a revolution to save the nation from communism and corruption.[2]

Consolidating the New Regime

By early April ex-President João Goulart was forced into exile and Marshal Castello Branco was appointed the new president. As its first major political act the new regime promulgated Institutional Act no. 1. The Act empowered the military to immediately remove 40 politicians from Congress. In June the Government organized the National Intelligence Service (SNI) under the command of General Golbery do Couto e Silva and now acquiescent Congress extended Castello Branco's term in office until March 1967. At the end of the year the first reports of torture begin to emerge and approximately 4,500 people had been punished under Institutional Act no. 1; of these 2,750 were members of the armed forces.

While still in power Goulart had commissioned a three-year economic plan from then Minister Celso Furtado and was in the midst of implementing the plan when the military seized control. The plan had many limitations, making major concessions to the International Monetary Fund (IMF) and Brazilian bourgeoisie; however it also contained progressive elements inasmuch as it sought to accelerate the modernization process of the national economy. After the coup many aspects of the three-year plan were put into practice as part of a project geared to accelerate the economic modernization process at an even faster pace. The military's goal was to transform Brazil into a "great power."

To spearhead this project the military regime appointed two of the most eminent and conservative economists, Otávio Goofier de Bulhões and Roberto Campos, to the positions of minister of finance and minister of planning respectively. Not surprisingly only three months after the coup Brazil succeeded in renegotiating its US$3.8 billion dollars in foreign debt. Some of the first economic decisions of the new Government included the creation of a Central Bank; a severe general wage reduction (the largest Brazil had ever experienced) with the use of new mechanisms for calculating wages and a total ban on strikes (Frederico, 1990). At the same time the government submitted to Congress a national economic action plan to combat inflation, organized the Banco Nacional de Habitação (National Housing Bank – BNH) to finance public housing and introduced regulatory measures for "monetary correction" (this linked prices and contracts to the inflation rate), and passed a new law which facilitated the remittance of capital gains by foreign investors.

The political conflict that was radically reshaping Brazilian political life was not an isolated event. The international political spectrum was similarly complex, as left-wing guerrilla movements emerged over much of Latin America, China tested its first atomic bomb; in the Soviet Union Nikita Khrushchev was deposed and replaced with a neo-Stalinist troika headed by Leonid Brezhnev, while President Lyndon Johnson intensified U.S. intervention in Vietnam and invaded the Dominican Republic with the participation of Brazilian troops.

The Authoritarian Regime and the Opposition

In October 1965 (a year and a half after the coup), the military leaders allowed the elections for governor to be held. Negrão de Lima and Israel Pinheiro were elected in Guanabara and Minas Gerais respectively, two of the most important states in Brazil. Both were members of the opposition with ties to the deposed Goulart regime. In response to their electoral defeat, the Castello Branco government signed into law Institutional Act no. 2. This law dissolved all political parties and guaranteed that the presidential successor would be appointed rather than elected. Just as important, the new act introduced the concept of political crimes into law in a system where political dissidents would be tried by military tribunals. Castello Branco, however, had been forced to sign this Act by military hard-liners. The passage of the second institutional act proved to be politically damaging for the regime and led to the decline of civilian support, especially from UDN leaders such as Milton Campos. Responding to the pressure from forces that had once supported the military regime the government promulgated Supplementary Act no. 4. This measure reformulated the electoral system and set the ground rules for the creation of new political parties. Supporters of the military regime founded the Aliança Renovadora Nacional (Alliance for National Renewal – ARENA) and those opposed to the military regime organized the Movimento Democrático Brasileiro (Brazilian Democratic Movement – MDB).

Meanwhile, a fierce battle was being fought on the left. The pro-Soviet PCB was divided. On one hand there were those who argued that leftist adventurism had opened the door to the rightwing forces. On the other hand the opposing group condemned the party leadership for collaborating with Goulart government and subsequently failing to prepare the Brazilian people to resist the coup. This debate also reflected how the different groups viewed the future struggle against the dictatorship. The first group advocated the formation of a broad political front while the second group believed the only way to defeat the dictatorship was through armed struggle. In the midst of a tense internal struggle and the mounting political repression, in December 1967 the PCB held its Sixth Congress clandestinely. The winning thesis at the congress was " . . . mobilize, unite and organize the working class and other patriotic and democratic forces for the struggle against the dictatorial regime, for its defeat and for the conquest of democratic freedoms . . . " (Carneiro Pessoa, 1980). The PCB argued that the creation of a broad political front would ultimately isolate the dictatorship and weaken the support it enjoyed among various sectors of Brazilian society.

Even though victorious at the congress, large sectors of the party refused to accept the decision and left the PCB to alternative left organizations, such as, the Aliança Libertadora Nacional (National Liberation Alliance – ALN), the Partido Comunista Brasileiro Revolucionário (Revolutionary Brazilian Communist Party – PCBR) and the Movimento Revolucionário 8 de Outubro (October 8 Revolutionary Movement – MR-8). Also other organizations emerged on the left giving rise to innumerable small groups, all of which were dazzled by the idea of urban guerilla warfare and the Cuban Revolution. Former non-commissioned officers who had been expelled from the Army and stripped of their political rights organized the Vanguarda Popular Revolucionária (Revolutionary Popular Vanguard – VPR). Their first action was to send militants to Cuba for training in guerrilla warfare. They were soon robbing banks and armored cars to provide resources for the movement. The exception was the Partido Comunista do Brasil (Communist Party of Brazil – PCdoB). As a left alternative that resulted from the Sino-Soviet split they advocated a strategy similar to the Chinese Communist Party and the development of rural guerilla war. In this way they began preparing the infrastructure for armed struggle in the Araguaia region, a vast area in the heart of the Amazon forest where land disputes were endemic.

The mounting political conflict was not peculiar to Brazil. Rather it was

160

the expression of the Tricontinental Conference held in Havana, Cuba, in January 1966. This meeting of the Latin American left gave rise to the Latin American Solidarity Organization (Organización Latino Americana de Solidaridad – OLAS). As a result guerrilla groups backed by Ernesto "Che" Guevara and Regis Debray, the author of a famous book on *foco* theory (Debray, 1967) sprang in much of Latin America (Castañeda, 1993). It is important to note that Brazil's pro-Soviet PCB was unique in advocating a "peaceful and democratic road" in an adverse international context. Algeria had recently won independence by using armed struggle; China and Cuba were calling for revolutionary armed struggle; the Soviet Union had deposed Khrushchev and halted his reforms; Warsaw Pact tanks had put an end to "socialism with a human face" in Czechoslovakia. All this, plus the ongoing Vietnam War, indicated the primacy of violence was fundamental in shaping revolutionary politics on the continent (Almeida, 2002).

Notwithstanding the actions of the armed left, banned politicians, ex-governors and ex-presidents began organizing the Broad Front (Frente Ampla). Carlos Lacerda, ex-Governor of Guanabara and a leader of the UDN, contacted two of his archenemies, former Presidents João Goulart (PTB) and Juscelino Kubitschek (PSD), for talks on a return to civilian government in Brazil. On April 5, 1968, however Minister of Justice Gama e Silva declared the Front illegal in yet another victory for the hard-liners within the military regime.

It was in this context that the confrontation between regime and opposition continued to escalate. By 1968 armed guerrilla actions became a daily occurrence. In spite of the strike ban and strike control of trade unions, metal workers organized strikes in Osasco (metropolitan region of São Paulo) and Contagem (Minas Gerais) as intellectuals and students mounted public protests against dictatorship (Pöerner, 1968). The resurgence of the oppositionist movement in Brazil reflected in part the political climate in other parts of the world, such as the student-led uprisings, from the Latin Quarter of Paris and Berkeley, California, to Prague University and Mexico City (Hobsbawm, 1994). The slogans echoed Guevara's call for "two, three, many Vietnams" to defeat imperialism, and Guevara himself disappeared into the Bolivian jungle in an attempt to initiate the armed struggle in Latin America. The Brazilian armed forces responded to the upsurge of political activism with the violent repression of all protests, whether they took the form of strikes, marches, songs or other cultural manifestations. The army quickly routed Brizola's guerilla from the Serra do Caparaó and set up a counter insurgency unit (Centro de Informação do Exército – CIE). In one single event almost 1,000 students were arrested when they attempted to hold a national conference of the União Nacional dos Estudantes (National Student Union – UNE). Expressing the desire of military hardliners to end the mounting political resistance General Emílio Garrastazu Médici (commanding officer of the Third Army), demanded that a state of siege to be declared. Responding to the governments' demands MDB Congressman Márcio Moreira Alves asked his fellow-congressmen: "When will the Army cease to be a sanctuary for torturers?" On December 12, 1968, when the lower house of Congress refused to grant the Government permission to prosecute Alves for his remarks the military responded by issuing Institutional Act no. 5 (AI-5). As a result of the Act congress was shut down, strict censorship of the press imposed and hundreds of people arrested, tortured or stripped of their political rights. With the introduction of the measure the regime had suffered a qualitative transformation; it assumed the characteristics of a fascist dictatorship. In 1969, then President General Costa e Silva became incapacitated by a stroke. The command of the armed forces appointed a military junta who took power for a short period. The appointment of Costa e Silva's successor mirrored in large part the ongoing dispute between moderate and hard line military leaders. In the dispute for the presidency, between Generals Albuquerque Lima and Garrastazu Médici (representing the hardliners), the latter was chosen president. Despite the continuing political turmoil the year ended with an annual inflation rate of 25.5% and economic growth had reached almost 10%, as a result of the 15% expansion of Brazil's industry and exports.

In October 1969 the Government issued a new Constitution incorporating AI-5, thus incorporating the repressive measures into the country's legal framework, after which Congress was reopened. Médici's presidency was characterized by torture and the physical elimination of the armed opposition, an "out-and-out dictatorship". As Gaspari wrote: "Torture was the extreme instrument of coercion and extermination, the last resort of political repression released by AI-5 from the fetters of legality. The bashful dictatorship was replaced by a regime that was at once anarchical in the barracks and violent in the prisons. Those were the years of lead." (Gaspari, 2002b) Total terror reigned. One after another, all of the left organizations were dismantled and many of their militants physically liquidated, including many members of the PCB, even though the party was against armed struggle. In a final desperate attempt to save lives, armed groups kidnapped the ambassadors of Germany, the United States, Switzerland and Japan. The hostages were eventually exchanged for a few dozen militants who were subsequently exiled by the regime. By the end of 1973 the government had liquidated the Araguaia guerrilla movement, the last armed group still operating.

As the economy boomed, the middle class, frightened by the upsurge of "terrorist" activity reiterated their support to the military regime. Moreover, the "economic miracle" which coincided with the period of hard-line military dictatorship reflected a gross domestic product of approximately 10% per year. In contrast with Argentina, where the military regime destroyed the nation's industry, Brazil enjoyed a period of accelerated capitalist accumulation and became an exporter of many manufactured goods. The First National Development Plan, introduced in 1970 under the slogan "Brazil: a Great Power", called for state investment in basic industries, such as mining, metals manufacturing, petrochemical, agricultural and cattle raising projects, with the expansion of the production of electric power as a top priority. As a corollary of this process the state was able to invest heavily in the development of nuclear technology, satisfying those who since the 1940s had advocated this new energy source as an option for Brazil. The Plan promised to accelerate the modernization process of the Brazilian economy and its integration with the broader global economy by developing its basic industry. Its framers believed Brazil would become a "great power". In the context of the cold war this entailed an alliance between Brazilian and international capitalism and the military. The regime was perverse and repressive, yet from the standpoint of material growth and the development of the nation's productive forces it laid the foundations for a new economic model driven by exports instead of import substitution. During the period of the "economic miracle" the GDP grew 14% in a single year, more than in any other year in the history of Brazil and possibly of any other country. Besides unprecedented economic growth and the sharp reduction of the inflation rates the "economic miracle" was also responsible for the extraordinary increase of Brazil's foreign debt and the drastic reduction of real wages, which exacerbated the historically perverse structure of income distribution. Moreover, the defeat of Egypt and Syria after their invasion of Israel brought with it the Arab nations boycott of oil exports to pro-American countries. The price of crude oil shot up from $3 to $11.50 per barrel. This was the first oil crisis and its effect on the Brazilian economy was devastating.

In response the working class began a long and painful process of reorganization. When an incipient strike movement occurred in the ABC region (São Paulo's industrial belt) in the early 1970s, it was rapidly stamped out and federal administrators intervened in the rebellious unions.

President Médici, following in the footsteps of Mexico's PRI, used the *"dedazo"* to handpick as his successor leading the organized opposition to protest by running Ulysses Guimarães, leader of the MDB, as the opposition presidential "anti-candidate". In spite of their protest General Ernesto Geisel, was appointed the fourth military president to take office since 1964.

The Winds of Change and Liberalization

The choice of General Geisel for president evidenced the return to power of Castello Branco's faction and mirrored the new international climate created by pressure from the Carter Administration for repressive regimes to respect human rights. The changing political circumstances were also a reflection of the U.S. military defeat in Vietnam, the end of Salazar's dictatorship in Portugal and the independence of its African colonies, and the 1975 Helsinki accords with the U.S.–USSR détente foreshadowing an end to the cold war.

In Brazil the political process was also transforming rapidly. The Catholic Church, which had actively supported the 1964 coup, turned against the regime, denouncing the systematic use of torture (Arquidiocese de São Paulo, 1985) and the widening gap between rich and poor as income distribution and misery deteriorated as a result of the regimes new economic policies (Pontifícia Comissão Justiça e Paz, 1976). Dom Paulo Evaristo Arns, the bishop who had blessed the military leaders after the coup in Minas Gerais, was now an oppositionist leader as the archbishop of São Paulo, the largest archdiocese in the country. The Catholic left had been collaborating with other progressive forces ever since the Second Vatican Council and the concepts of Liberation theology approved at the Second General Conference of Latin American Bishops held in Medellín in 1968 strengthened this position in Latin America. Catholic's played an important role in the struggle for a return to democracy and many left opposition leaders and militants owe their lives to the support of the churches' Commission for Justice and Peace.

In spite of the high levels of repression, growing popular discontent with the regime was increasingly expressed in the escalating electoral victories of MDB leading the regime to reluctantly and half-heartedly initiate a process of political liberalization. Similarly, liberalization was characterized by a negotiation process that led to political advances and imposed serious drawbacks. Torture continued in the dungeons of the army's intelligence and "internal defense" units (DOI-CODI), which many times ignored the chain of command in a genuine subversion of military hierarchy, Generals Geisel and Golbery were looking for ways to reform the regime in what was called the "gradual opening", that is, a highly controlled and limited process of political liberalization of the Brazilian political structure. Two points determined how this project panned out: the type of opposition allowed to legally function and the characteristics of the authoritarian structure to be conserved.

The process of liberalization proposed by the new Government had four objectives. Military leaders had to preserve the support of the armed forces for their political project, while at the same time lessen the influence of political hardliners who were entrenched in the "dungeons of the system", such as the network of torture that had been solidly established by the previous Administration. Next they had to limit the political capacity of the left opposition. Even though the armed struggle had been defeated, military hardliners saw the enemy on every street corner – thus the need for a "slow" process of change. The third objective was to reorganize the political system so that the pro-government party, ARENA, could retain a firm grip on power and impede any future electoral victory of the opposition. At his first cabinet meeting in March 1974, President Geisel promised "sincere efforts to bring about a gradual but secure democratic corrections" to the political system. He went on to declare that "creative political imagination" could help "exceptional powers" replace "efficacious safeguards" that were compatible with "the constitutional structure" (Geisel, 1974). Finally on the list of objectives was the need to maintain high levels of economic growth so as to achieve greater income redistribution and legitimatize the regime (Skidmore, 1988). The military leaders limited process of political liberalization seemed too little too late and in the elections of November 1974 the liberal democratic opposition in a united front that counted with the participation of the PCB inflicted a major defeat against the regime in the 1974 Congressional elections.

Brazil had entered a new stage of capitalist development with a more numerous and modern working class and an urban middle class that was increasingly being forced into salaried employment reflecting the domination of monopoly capitalism in articulation with the state. The qualitative transformation of Brazilian society had created a new role for these classes in national political life (Coletivo de Organização, 1984). The opposition scored a resounding victory in the major cities of the Southeast, South and Center-West where most industrial workers and the increasingly well educated middle class lived. The reminiscent activists of the armed struggle, Trotskyist groups and Catholic radicals who espoused liberation theology refused to join what they considered the "loyal opposition" and instead campaigned for voters to nullify their votes. They considered ARENA and MDB indistinguishable. The Government expected to win the 1974 election for Congress by a comfortable majority; however, the election in fact marked the beginning of the end for the dictatorship.

The repressive apparatus of the regime (the "men in cellars"), continued their work and between late 1974 and October 1975 the regime systematically hunted down the leadership of PCB, which they viewed as one of the reasons for the opposition victory even though the party was underground (Skidmore, 1988). More than one third of the CP's national leadership, including many members of the party's executive committee was murdered. The regime never admitted responsibility for the assassinations and the victims were considered "missing".

165

One of the most notorious cases was the assignation of Vladimir Herzog. In October 1975 Vladimir Herzog, a journalist and university teacher, was tortured to death by the DOI-CODI in São Paulo. The military authorities later declared that the journalist had "committed suicide". Herzog was a member of the PCB even though he was not part of its underground apparatus. A well-known intellectual because of his work for a public TV channel Herzog was at the peak of his career. His murder caused a massive outcry despite Brazil's airtight media censorship. The BBC (where Herzog had worked for several years), spread the story around the world and in an act of great courage, facing down pressures from military authorities as well as many of his colleagues, Rabbi Henry Sobel demanded that Herzog's body be buried inside the walls of the Butantã Jewish cemetery (which would not have been allowed had he committed suicide). A few days later Archbishop Dom Paulo Evaristo Arns, Rabbi Sobel and Reverend Jaime Wright, a Presbyterian pastor, led an ecumenical memorial service at São Paulo's main cathedral, the Catedral da Sé. Despite intense police intimidation approximately 10,000 people participated in the service making it the first mass public protest since Institutional Act no. 5 was issued almost seven years before (Markun, no date).

Geisel, however, proved unable to use the occasion to dismantle the network of torture and repression although he warned General Ednardo D'Ávila (commanding officer of the Second Army) responsible for the São Paulo region, that he would not tolerate any more occurrences of the kind. Then in early 1976 the São Paulo DOI-CODI committed another assassination. This time the victim, Manoel Fiel Filho, was a factory worker and grassroots PCB activist who distributed the party's newspaper *Voz Operária (The Workers Voice)*. Once again the official version was that he too had "committed suicide" which prompted Geisel to immediately remove General D'Ávila from his post without consulting Army Central Command. The decision was a blow to the military hardliners, as the torturers could no longer take it for granted that their superiors would cover up for them in the event of mass protest over physical abuse and assassination of political prisoners (Abreu, 1979). After this episode the "disappearances" in the dungeons of the dictatorship halted. A few months later, however, leaders of the PCdoB were surprised as they realized a clandestine meeting in São Paulo. During the police raid on a house two of the Party's leaders were shot to death.

Within the Latin American context Argentina, Chile and Brazil were all engaged in the same global project of "defending western values", symbolized by their participation in Operation Condor. This was a large network of cooperation among military regimes across the continent. In spite of this the Brazilian dictatorship was distinct from the Argentine and Chilean regimes. Compared with other South American repressive regimes the number of dead and missing did not exceed a thousand in Brazil, there was no "dirty war", no systematic extermination of political activists as there was in Chile and Argentina. One explanation for this may be that the Brazilian armed forces had a more democratic tradition when compared with the military in other countries of the region. Another reason was certainly the influence and pressure of progressive Catholics. The strategy and method of political repression in Brazil, however, was implemented in a far more intelligent manner focusing its actions primarily on the physical elimination of political leaders, intellectuals and popular organizers.

Giving continuity to the vision of Brazil as a "great power", Geisel responded to the oil crisis by making sure that the 2nd National Development Plan prioritized energy production. He initiated a state-subsidized program to produce and distribute ethanol derived from sugarcane as a fuel substitute, he developed a plan to build hydroelectric power plants along the Paraná River, and above all he accelerated the nuclear power program. In the authoritarian state, with Congress muzzled by the various "institutional acts", the Government had little difficulty passing the nuclear power program through the legislature without consulting the scientific community, let alone society. Billions of dollars were spent on a program that was drafted and approved in the restricted circles of the regime, which had neither political nor scientific legitimacy. Despite repeated statements that the Brazilian nuclear program was solely for peaceful purposes, there were indications that this was not the case. These claims are difficult to verify given the almost absolute secrecy in which the program was developed.

The development of the nuclear program was also an indicator that Brazil planned to distance itself from US foreign policy. For example when Brazil signed the 1975 nuclear agreement with West Germany, their relations with the United States became tense. The US distrusted Germany's intentions. Brazil's estrangement with US foreign policy also reflected the military regimes adoption of a foreign policy known as "responsible pragmatism". This new political view of the world led the regime to immediately recognize the victory of the Marxist MPLA and the subsequent creation of the People's Republic of Angola and by seeking to cultivate closer relations with the Arab world, resulting in Brazil's endorsement of the UN resolution denouncing "the racist nature of Zionism".

Economic growth during Geisel's term in office remained strong but with growth rates far more reduced than in previous years. The "economic miracle" was over. In addition to the mushrooming foreign debt, in part due to the nuclear program, the business community was increasingly discontent with the many forms of bureaucratic regulatory systems created by government technocrats. More and more segments of

167

civil society were becoming critical of the regime. The growing discontent by large sectors of the urban working and middle classes was increasingly evident as larger sectors of society pressured the regime to introduce greater measures of democratic governance and led Generals Geisel and Golbery do Couto e Silva to signal with the assuage the repressive political structure they had inherited, even if only briefly. The political effect of their actions was minimal and in the municipal elections held on November 15, 1976, while ARENA candidates won easily in rural regions the opposition, MDB, obtained large majorities in the key cities such as São Paulo, Rio de Janeiro, Belo Horizonte, Porto Alegre, Salvador, Santos and Campinas.

Concerned with the possibility of losing the upcoming 1978 election the Government responded with new repressive legislation that became known as the "April package". The measures were a series of decrees designed to guarantee ARENA'S victory in future political contests. To approve the measures Congress was once again shut down and several MDB congressmen were stripped of their mandates and political rights. The major changes brought about with "Package" allowed Constitutional amendments to be passed by a simple majority; state governors and one-third of the Senate were to be indirectly elected by an Electoral College and the number of congressmen would be stipulated based on the total population of each state rather than the number of registered voters. In this sense Congressional elections would no longer be proportional in terms of "one citizen, one vote" because all states, however small, were guaranteed at least eight deputies. This created a huge imbalance between large urban centers and rural regions with regard to their representation in Congress and facilitated a favorable electoral outcome for the Government. In addition to these measures, in 1976 another law known as Falcão's Law was introduced which severely limited a candidate for political office's access to the media.

Despite all of the repressive measures, popular protests and pro-democracy movements continued to gather momentum after the ecumenical memorial service for Vladimir Herzog. They included: the Movimento contra a Carestia (Movement Against the High Cost of Living); journalists protesting against censorship of the press; the reorganization of the student movement (after almost ten years of absolute silence), and the struggle demanding amnesty for exiles and political prisoners. The high point was a series of mass demonstrations and strikes by unionized workers demanding wage increases and democratic freedoms. The movement was initiated by metalworkers in the automotive plants of the ABC industrial belt and gave rise to "new trade unionism". The street protests evidenced growing popular impatience with the Government's strategy of promising liberalization while making frequent concessions to military hardliners.

Differently than what had happen with the appointment of Geisel to the presidency, his successor was not unanimously endorsed by the military. Hardliners in the regime preferred General Sylvio Frota but they were forced to accept General João Baptista Figueiredo. On October 15 the Electoral College confirmed General Figueiredo (the ARENA candidate), by 355 votes against 266 votes for the MDB candidate General Euler Bentes. In spite of the regimes stronghold on the presidency the results of the forthcoming congressional election on November 15, 1978, were an even greater defeat for the regime than in previous elections. The ARENA won 13 million votes for the Senate and 15 million for congress while the MDB won 17 million and 14.8 million respectively. The nationwide tally awarded a resounding victory to the MDB in every important state. The regime emerged severely weakened from this election. Before leaving office in January 1979 President Geisel repealed the AI-5. In practice, however, this meant little to transform the repressive political structure since all its provisions had been incorporated into the Constitution as well as the draconian National Security Law, which remained intact.

The Beginning of the End

João Baptista Figueiredo, the fifth general to occupy the presidency, took office in the context of a global crisis caused by the second oil shock and the resurgence of conservative governments led by President Ronald Reagan in the United States and Prime Minister Margaret Thatcher in Britain. The new political climate introduced neo-liberal economics and a renewed acceleration of the cold war with the threat of the anti-missile shield known as Star Wars; while in Poland increasing protests by the banned Solidarnosc ushered Jaruzelski to power with the support of the Soviet Union. In Central America political conflict was also rising to new heights. In El Salvador the left-led Farabundo Martí Front for National Liberation (FMLN) and the Nationalist Revolutionary Union of Guatemala (URNG) continued their armed struggle in spite of the US support for the "Contras" movement with the hopes of toppling the Sandinista Government in Nicaragua. Nevertheless, dictatorships gradually gave way to democracy in most of Latin America. The Argentine dictatorship collapsed after the disastrous Malvinas/Falklands War. Chile's military regime came to an end when the Socialists and Christian Democrats formed a united front without the support of the Chilean Communist Party.

Popular support for the general political amnesty in Brazil spread rapidly leading Congress to pass an amnesty law in 1979. Responding to organized pressure from society forced the government to review politically inspired "criminal investigation" levied against oppositionists, many of who had been stripped of their political rights, sent into exile or imprisoned. Shortly afterwards it reluctantly sent to Congress an amnesty bill. On August 28, 1979, after much debate, the bill was promulgated.

The law, however, was limited in its scope, that is, it was not extended to all victims of the military regime until ten years later when civilian rule had returned and Congress passed a new Constitution. Even so, however limited the law was, as communist senator Roberto Freire wrote: "But it fulfilled an important function, freeing dozens of prisoners of conscience and allowing back into the political arena thousands of citizens who had been proscribed for over a decade by the dictatorship. . . . Two hundred political prisoners were released immediately; 128 banned men and women and 4,877 politicians stripped of their mandates were able to recover their rights; 10,000 people who had been forced to leave Brazil were able to return from exile; and 263 students had punishments imposed by the dictatorship's decrees annulled. More than 500,000 people who had been prosecuted or politically penalized were given a clean criminal record. . . . The chains had been burst asunder and liberty was restored. It was a historic turning-point, a huge step toward the belief that authoritarianism would one day become a thing of the past" (Freire, 1999).

Despite all of the repressive political measures imposed to guarantee the electoral victory of the military regime, Figueiredo was not able to guarantee the survival of the regime in this "plebiscitary" contest between the ARENA and the MDB. The regimes arch-strategist Golbery set out to divide the opposition by relaxing the legal ban on the formation of new political parties. The MDB, which had been a broad united front against the dictatorship, now began to splinter. Liberal democrats led by Ulysses Guimarães, united with the pro-Soviet PCB, the Maoist PCdoB and the MR-8 argued against the breakup. In their view priority should be given to campaigning for a constituent assembly and parliamentary work to "clear away the authoritarian political structure", such as the Institutional Acts and the National Security Law, so that democracy could first be fully restored, thus creating the political conditions and ample freedom to organize new parties. Unable to keep the MDB united they created the Partido do Movimento Democrático Brasileiro (Party of the Brazilian Democratic Movement – PMDB).

But the attempts to keep the opposition united proved fruitless. Ivete Vargas (nephew of 1930s populist president Getúlio Vargas) resuscitated the PTB. Leonel Brizola, who considered himself Vargas's legitimate political heir, was forced to found his own party, which he christened Partido Democrático Trabalhista (Democratic Labor Party – PDT). The Partido Popular (Popular Party – PP), founded by Tancredo Neves and Magalhães Pinto, was short-lived. On the left the remains of small guerrilla groups, the catholic left, Trotskyites and trade unionists from the ABC founded the Partido dos Trabalhadores (Workers Party – PT). They counted with the firm support from the Cuban Communist Party as well as from the Swedish and German Social Democratic Parties. All the groups that had campaigned for voters to nullify their votes in the early 1970s joined this new-style party. For many of these groups democracy was not a fundamental question: they had no faith in parliamentary politics and did not see the struggle for a new democratic Constitution as essential. The PCB and PCdoB remained illegal. Significantly, the ARENA did not split.

Social movements and unions also split along roughly drawn ideological lines. There were basic disagreements about issues of the trade union movement, such as, the organizational structure and the priorities of the trade union movement in the struggle for democracy. The PT began by organizing parallel unions, that is, leftwing opposition caucuses inside the official unions. This policy ultimately led to the fragmentation of the trade union movement when workers in advanced sectors of the economy and civil service set up a new national labor federation of leftwing unions linked to the PT. Many workers in traditional industries remained in the old union structures that essentially dated from the Vargas era.

Despite the global economic crisis and deep economic recession at home, with an accelerating inflation rate, the burgeoning workers' movement forced the Government to restructure wage regulations that had been introduced early on in the dictatorship. The International Monetary Fund's (IMF) continued against and attempted to prevent lenient wages policies. The next step in the political liberalization process occurred in November 1980, when Congress passed a constitutional amendment reintroducing free elections for state governor and the entire Senate. This act of congress repealed significant aspects of the Geisel administrations "April package", however not everyone agreed with liberalization process in course. Golbery's adversaries, mainly from sectors of the military intelligence and counter-insurrection units, began using armed terrorist and clandestine actions of their own. In 1980 and 1981 newsstands that sold left and progressive newspapers were regularly threatened. Those who refused to heed the warnings had their kiosks bombed. These were covert actions carried out at night and initially there were no apparent deaths or registered casualties. The rightwing terrorists became emboldened sending a letter-bomb to the Ordem dos Advogados do Brasil (Brazilian Bar Association – OAB), one of the most combative organizations in the struggle for democracy. The device killed a secretary as she opened the package. The most scandalous terrorist attack occurred in April 1981. Two army officials attempted to place a bomb at a pop concert organized in support of leftwing causes at the RIOCENTRO complex in Rio de Janeiro. The bomb exploded in the parking lot, in the lap of one of the terrorists, an army sergeant was killed and a captain severely wounded.

The bomb was meant to explode in the crowd with the hopes of creating a panic and halting the concert. The Army took charge of the investigation, keeping their result totally undisclosed; however it was also a message that the military hardliners could still sabotage the political liberalization process. Leaders of Congress spoke out against the mounting rightwing terrorism, and Golbery, claiming he lacked support, resigned in protest of the Army's actions.

The question of political rights continued highly constrained. Despite the political amnesty, the right to assembly was restricted. In December 1982 the PCB attempted to hold a seminar to discuss their proposals for the crisis in Brazil. The organizers issued a public invitation to the meeting that was to take place in downtown São Paulo. Within hours of the meetings start the Army arrived commandeering a huge number of troops and vehicles and arresting approximately 100 of the meetings attendees.

The economic situation, however, continued to deteriorate, with an escalating disparity in the balance of payments, if Brazil had done without the IMF for 15 years that was to change as a result of the economic crisis driven by the mounting foreign debt.

It was in this complex economic and political context that the first direct elections for state governor were held; in fact they were the first elections for governor since 1965. The election was realized concurrently with elections for Congress and the state legislatures. Moderate opposition leaders such as Ulysses Guimarães, Franco Montoro and Tancredo Neves, among others, campaigned for expanding the right to vote to illiterates, increasing union independence and the right to strike, and improving the distribution of income. They also advocated the abolition of privileges that were enjoyed by multinational corporations and financial institutions.

The election outcome proved Golbery's strategy successful. The opposition won 59% of the overall vote but failed to obtain a majority in Congress because it had divided into several parties. The pro-Government party (which had changed its name from ARENA to the Partido Democrático Social (Democratic Social Party – PDS), won the majority of congressional seats, although it too failed to win an absolute majority. If the opposition parties joined forces they could veto the executive's proposals, but the Government was still strong enough to push its presidential candidate through the Electoral College.

In the statewide elections for governor the opposition won outright in the most economically developed regions and gained control of the key states, such as São Paulo, Rio de Janeiro, Minas Gerais and Paraná, while the PDS won the elections in the northeast and midwestern regions. Significantly, the first three had been the main base of support for the military coup in 1964. The centralized federalist political system set in place during the heyday of authoritarian regime left state governors little power to introduce significant change. The state governments depended largely on financial resources and other forms of assistance from the federal government. Even though General Figueiredo had no reason to be generous with the opposition, in any event he was already financially strapped because of the massive burden of the foreign debt (Skidmore, 1988).

As the economic crisis deepened the government found itself in greater difficulties. Indirect elections for president was now widely considered illegitimate leading Congressman Dante de Oliveira (PMDB) to propose a constitutional amendment restoring free and direct elections for the presidency. The PMDB leadership launched a national campaign for free elections, receiving the support of Luis Inácio Lula da Silva, leader of the PT, and Leonel Brizola, leader of the PDT. The campaign rapidly gained broad popular support as the campaign mobilized marches and rallies with millions of participants in all major cities across the country. In spite of the massive mobilization the amendment failed to pass in Congress by 22 votes; the next president would still be chosen by the Electoral College. At the same time the results were a clear indication that the official party was divided on their support for the right to freely elect the president and the conflict would continue into the selection process of Figueiredo's successor.

For the first time since 1964, the Government's candidate was chosen without being imposed by the president in power and the choice of candidate Paulo Maluf was far from unanimous. There were several other nominees and the selection process resulted in the emergence of a dissident group and the creation of the Partido da Frente Liberal (Liberal Front Party – PFL) by politicians who refused to support Maluf's candidacy. The opposition, however, was also divided: the PT refused to participate in the Electoral College, while the PMDB joined forces with other opposition parties to endorse the candidacy of Tancredo Neves, a moderate centrist. His candidacy attracted a broad spectrum of political forces from center-right to center-left, making him the best man to defeat Maluf.

This does not mean that military hardliners had not given up. In an attempt to discredit the opposition candidate posters of Tancredo Neves making the victory sign alongside the PCB's hammer-and-sickle appeared on the building wall of Brasilia as the campaign gained momentum. Rumors of a pending coup were reinforced when the Army High Command ordered a buildup of weapons, fuel and food supplies. In response to the pressure Neves promised influential officers of the armed forces that he would not allow a return to pre-1964 unrest nor would he prosecute military or police officials for torture or other human rights violations. Eventually Neves won the discreet support from several military leaders, including General Geisel, who enjoyed significant prestige in the Army. In another significant move General Newton Cruz, leader of the military hardliners, was forced to retire from the post of military commander of Brasília. The alliance of PMDB and PFL dubbed the Democratic Alliance ultimately endorsed Tancredo Neves (PMDB) for president and José Sarney (PFL) for vice president. The Democratic Alliance won a comfortable victory in the Electoral College. Neves was elected by 480 votes to Maluf's 180. There were 17 abstentions and nine congressmen absent during the election process including the congressional representatives of the PT.

The New Republic

Tancredo Neves was the first civilian president of Brazil since 1964. He received extraordinary demonstrations of public support and before taking office he made visits to the United States, Europe and several Latin American countries for talks with foreign governments and political parties. Upon his return to Brazil he worked intensely on the new government's program and was preparing to appoint a cabinet. Even though he was seriously ill he kept his health problems a secret so as not to give the military hardliners an excuse to create an institutional crisis or attempts to prevent the vice president from taking office. Unfortunately, one day before his inauguration Neves was rushed to hospital where he passed away some days later. With his death an institutional impasse soon emerged. Some argued that the constitutional solution was to swear in Vice President José Sarney, while others wanted Ulysses Guimarães (president of Congress) to assume the presidency since the candidates had officially been sworn into office. Furthermore there was no lack of people who predicted a return to military rule. Guimarães eventually stood down and Sarney was sworn into office, the New Republic had passed its first institutional test.

Sarney inherited Tancredo Neves' ministerial cabinet, which included representatives of all the political forces that had defended the parliamentary road to democracy. Practically a government of national unity, the newly elected government faced many difficulties due to lack of ideological consistency. The road to democracy in Brazil coupled the burdensome legacy of being the nation with the largest foreign debt in the world and the Latin American experience of the "lost decade".

Despite the worsening economic situation, Brazil remained the eighth largest economy in the world in terms of GDP even though it languished at the bottom of the social and human development hierarchy along with many African countries. The Sarney Administration attempted to improve real wages and introduced the "Cruzado Plan" with the hopes of reducing inflation. However, the plan was largely ineffective and early in 1987 the Government was forced to suspend interest payments of foreign debt. At the end of Sarney's term in office the inflation rate was a staggering 80% per month.

Even though Sarney's Administration was an economic failure, it achieved tremendous progress in the area of expanding political freedoms in Brazil. Both Communist parties (PCB and PCdoB) were legalized in 1985 and diplomatic relations with Cuba (which had been broken off in 1964), were restored in 1986. Despite economic difficulties, the PMDB continued with broad political support winning 19 of the 25 state capitals in the 1985 municipal elections. The party also won in 110 out of 201 other cities with over 200,000 voters, demonstrating confidence in civilian rule. In 1986, after the Cruzado Plan's inception, the PMDB obtained an even more resounding victory: all but one of the 23 state governors elected that year belonged to the party, which won an absolute majority in both the Congress and the Senate. Sarney's party, the PFL was defeated and left the coalition seriously undermining Sarney's legitimacy since the governors were elected democratically while he had been chosen by the Electoral College.

The most important achievement of the Sarney era was the "Citizens' Constitution" promulgated in 1988. The Congress elected in 1986 functioned as a de facto constituent assembly and despite disagreements among various political forces if congress had the constitutional power to do so, the new Constitution is the most democratic in Brazil's history. It repealed the National Security Law and all other authoritarian measures imposed in the previous 24 years that the military regime had been in power. The PT refused to sign the new Constitution, with the exception of two congressional representative, both were eventually expelled from the party.

Long before his four-year term as president was to expire, Sarney negotiated an additional year in office. This measure was opposed by several PMDB leaders who left in protest of the party's support for Sarney and organized the Partido da Social Democracia Brasileira (Brazilian Social Democratic Party – PSDB). Among the founders were influential oppositionist leaders such as Mário Covas, Fernando Henrique Cardoso, Franco Montoro and José Serra.

In 1989 the first direct election for president was held after 29 years. The candidates were Luiz Inácio Lula da Silva (PT), Leonel Brizola (PDT), Mário Covas (PSDB), Ulysses Guimarães (PMDB), Roberto Freire (PCB), Fernando Collor de Mello (PRN), Aureliano Chaves (PFL), Afif Domingos (PL) and Paulo Maluf (PDS). None of the candidates obtained an absolute majority of valid votes in the first round forcing Lula and Collor into a runoff election. The election polarized the country between left and right, and even though Collor won by a small margin both candidates tallied approximately 35 million votes.

Consolidation of Democracy

Collor was elected without a solid majority in Congress, mainly because he had campaigned as the leader of a small and newly organized political party with little political support. Fundamentally he was a populist demagogue, branding himself the "Savior of the Nation" and promising to sweep away corruption and reduce extravagant state spending while expanding assistance to the poor.

Even though it is not my intention to analyze Collor's presidency, but it is relevant to highlight that his short-lived term in office focused on expanding Brazil's participation in the tide of economic deregulation and liberalization that was emerging with force over Latin America. His economic stabilization plan and related initiatives proved a failure and he himself succumbed to charges of corruption. The true motive for his impeachment, however, was lack of congressional support. There have been many other presidents and governors throughput the history of Brazil who were not exactly stalwart guardians of the public good. Some even became legendary for their dishonesty but were never impeached from office. As in other periods of institutional crises, such as the suicide of Getúlio Vargas or the sudden resignation of Jânio Quadros (after only a few months in office), the real problem for Collor was his incapacity to govern without a solid political base in Congress. In contrast to previous cases, however, with the impeachment of Collor the Brazilian democratic system guaranteed the transition of power to Vice President Itamar Franco without further political upheavals or the fear of a military coup.

Fernando Henrique Cardoso was elected president in 1994. During the first year of his first term, the Congress passed a law to "make moral amends" to political activists killed or declared missing during the period of the military regime and pay reparations to their relatives. In this sense the state recognized its responsibility for the disappearance of 136 missing persons that were in fact dead. The state took responsibility for their kidnapping, imprisonment, torture and death, and officially condemned this barbarous form of human rights violation that became commonplace in Brazil and throughout Latin America. The law also set up an official special commission comprised of seven members appointed by the president to examine case by case allegations of other disappearances and deaths of militants "on police premises or the like" (Miranda, 1996). This raised other problems, for example, the difficulty of defining the meaning of "police premises or the like", not to mention the suppression of information by the Federal Police and groups working within the armed forces. On September 11, 1996 the Commission acknowledged the assignations of Carlos Marighella and Carlos Lamarca, two of the leading symbols in the armed resistance to the military regime (Miranda, 1996). This moment marked the end of the transition to democracy.

Relatives of the victims, lawyers, jurists, human rights advocates, former political prisoners and congressmen involved in the issue demanded a more comprehensive law – a law that would force full disclosure of the circumstances in which the victims had died. They also wanted the law extended to deaths caused by other forms of political violence, such as the case of Frei Tito, a Dominican priest who committed suicide unable to live with his memories of torture and the torturers. They also wanted recognition for those who died in firefights, killed themselves to avoid capture while actively organizing the resistance to the dictatorship, or those assassinated by participating nations of Operation Condor in other countries of the Southern Cone. The movement did not succeed, all the amendments submitted to Congress to extend the parameters of reparations were defeated arguing that any extension of the Act could provoke an institutional crisis with sectors of the military.

Comparison of Several Transitions

Finally, it is worth making a brief comparison with democratic transitions in other countries. Just as in Portugal, Spain and Greece, the transition in Brazil reflected a top-down controlled process in which the main actors were the political parties and where the popular sectors of society were marginalized. In this process the tutelage of the Western powers was also a key element of the scheme. In the case of Greece and Portugal, however, there was a radical rupture with the dictatorial regime so that politicians with ties to the old regime were ostracized and isolated from the political process. In contrast, in Spain and Brazil only a partial break with the past occurred and as a result the transition to democracy was a process of continuous negotiations with the very forces that embodied the repressive system. There was a fear of extolling the rupture and a concern to avoid confrontation with the military, which could bring about a return of the dictatorship. The transition became a mask and an alibi for self-transformation of the authoritarian regime and the political actors linked to it. Everyone from the President of the Republic to the political police donned new clothes and acquired a new legitimacy, which enabled them to share in the glory of having brought democracy back (Vidal-Beneyto, 2000).

Notes

1 The switch to a parliamentary system in 1961 was designed to neutralize Goulart, elected vice president when Jânio Quadros won the presidency in a landslide vote. Quadros resigned only months after taking office and Goulart became president. Opposition to his leftwing sympathies created an institu-

tional crisis. Moderates thought giving real power to a prime minister would solve the problem.

2   "Communists" as a blanket term covering nationalists and the left generally was widely used by Latin American conservatives in the cold-war years. For example, both Juan Bosch (Dominican Republic) and Jacobo Arbenz (Guatemala) were branded communists.

References

Abreu, H., *O Outro Lado do Poder*, Rio de Janeiro: Nova Fronteira, 1979.

Almeida, F. I. (ed), *O Último Secretário – a luta de Salomão Malina*, Brasília: Fundação Astrojildo Pereira, 2002.

Arquidiocese de São Paulo, *Brasil Nunca Mais*, Petrópolis: Vozes, 1985, 9a edição.

Carneiro Pessoa, R. X. (ed), *PCB: vinte anos de política, documentos (1958–1978)*, São Paulo: Ciências Humanas, 1980.

Castañeda, J. G., *Utopia Unarmed: the Latin American Left After the Cold War*, New York: Vintage, 1993.

Coelho, M. A Tavares, *Herança de um sonho*, São Paulo: Record, 2000.

Coletivo de Organização, *Uma alternativa democrática para a crise brasileira*, São Paulo: Novos Rumos, 1984.

Costa, J.C. Zorzenon, *As crises do início dos anos de 1960 e o desenvolvimento brasileiro*, Tema no. 41, Jul/Dec 2002, São Paulo.

Debray, R., *Revolution in the Revolution? Armed Struggle & Political Struggle in Latin America*, New York: Grove Press, 1967.

Dreifuss, R., *1964: A Conquista do Estado, Ação Política, Poder e Golpe de Classe*, Petrópolis: Vozes, 1981.

Frederico, C., *A Esquerda e o Movimento Operário (1964–1984)*, Belo Horizonte: Oficina de Livros, 1990.

Freire, R., extracts from a speech at a ceremony to commemorate the amnesty's 20th anniversary, in Diário do Senado Federal, page 20623, 19/08/99.

Gaspari, E. (a) *A Ditadura Envergonhada*, São Paulo: Schwarcz, 2002.

—— (b) *A Ditadura Escancarada*, São Paulo: Schwarcz, 2002.

Geisel, E., *Discursos*, vol. 1, Assessoria de Imprensa da Presidência da República, Brasília, 1974.

Hobsbawm, E. *Age of Extremes: the Short 20th Century*, London: Michael Joseph, 1994.

Markun, P. (ed), *Vlado: retrato da morte de um homem e de uma época*, São Paulo: Círculo do Livro, no date.

Miranda, N., *O desmonte das "versões oficiais"*, Revista Teoria e Debate no. 3, São Paulo: Fundação Perseu Abramo, 1996.

Pöerner, A. J., *O Poder Jovem*, Rio de Janeiro: Civilização Brasileira, 1968.

Pontifícia Comissão de Justiça e Paz da Arquidiocese de São Paulo, *São Paulo 1975, Crescimento e Pobreza*, São Paulo: Loyola, 1976.

Skidmore, T., *Brasil: de Castello a Tancredo*, Rio de Janeiro: Paz e Terra, 1988.

Vidal-Beneyto, J., *Pourquoi la droite triomphe en Espagne*, Paris: Le Monde Diplomatique, April 2000.

9

TRANSITION AND DEMOCRATIC CONSTRUCTION IN POST-FUJIMORI PERU

Rafael Roncagliolo

Twenty-five years ago in Ecuador and the Dominican Republic, the authoritarian regimes, which had started with the Brazilian coup of 1964 and had spread throughout Latin America, began to dismantle. The wave of democratization initiated 25 years ago had no precedents. Now we have more democratic regimes and more democratic government turns in office than ever before. And this is not only in Latin America. Today, for the first time in history, the majority of countries worldwide have governments elected in universal and secret, free and fair elections. As López Pintor notes, "In the last decade of the 20th century approximately fifty armed conflicts from civil to territorial wars have ended, the majority of these related to the decreased tensions between the superpowers of the Cold War and the collapse of the Soviet Union. Simultaneously, a democratizing wave has begun without historical precedents. Considered one of the bloodiest centuries in the modern era, it came to an end fortunately with more than two thirds of the national governments based on free elections. Twenty years ago during the transition in Spain, there were a little over thirty democracies all over the world. While writing these lines, the number of democratic regimes in different phases of consolidation numbered fifty-five. The contradiction between violence and negotiation squares up in favor of the pact" (López Pintor, 1999, p. 15).

It's not just about a numerical predominance. The universality of the democratic model is one of the consensuses of globalization. In other words, globalization is not only advancing at the economic, neo-liberalist pace, but also it seems to be developing with two other additional consensuses: democracy as the form of government and the universal adherence to human rights. A global society is built on the dimensions of market, political democracy and human rights.

In these dimensions, we find that national sovereignties yield to supranational bodies. In the case of the market, it is obvious. In terms of human rights, the surrendering of sovereignty is illustrated clearly by the events concerning General Pinochet. However, along with the expansion and consolidation of the formal democratic regimes, we also witness the emergence of international bodies founded on the adherence to democracy.

It is not simply coincidence that the OAS as well as Mercosur and the Andean Community define themselves as democratic clubs, which place the responsibility for democratic regimes upon its members; and in its absence, a casual expulsion. This is why it was the OAS who set the stage for negotiations between the government and the Peruvian opposition, prior to the overthrow of the Fujimori regime in 2000. It is no coincidence that on September 10, 2001 in the Extraordinary Assembly in Lima the OAS adopted the Inter-American Democratic Charter. Furthermore, the Heads of State and the Rio Group (the first club of democratic countries formed in the region), met in Cusco in May 2003 to study precisely how to strengthen and secure democratic governance.

Peru and the Andean Region

Oftentimes, when speaking from outside Latin America, the Southern Cone is the privileged first to be analyzed and followed by Central America. The Andean region (comprising from north to south, Venezuela, Colombia, Ecuador, Peru and Bolivia) maintains certain opacity towards the outside world. This is attributed, undoubtedly, to numerous factors; one being that this area did not experience the armed conflicts of Central America, or the brutal dictatorships of the Southern Cone. Two of the five Andean countries (Venezuela and Colombia) were not affected by the wave of authoritarian regimes that extended throughout almost the remainder of the region, between 1964 and 1978. In fact, Venezuela did not have a military coup in the second half of the 20th century. Colombia had only two military coups in all its Republican history (1854 and 1954) and has continued being governed by two political parties (conservative and liberal), which were founded in the 1830s.

However, democracy is particularly fragile in this part of the region, with Colombia in a civil war, Venezuela undergoing a polarization the outcome of which is still uncertain, while Ecuador and Bolivia with their civil governments threatened by instability.

Peru had two *sui generis* military governments, between 1968 and 1980, during the nationalist and reformist general Juan Velasco Alvarado (1968–1975), and later with the restorer of democratic order, Francisco Morales Bermúdez (1975–1980). Immediately after, during the 1980s, the country was shaken up by the expansion of the subversive movement,

180

Shining Path (Sendero Luminoso), which was completely different from all existing Latin American guerrillas, and which was characterized by the use of terror on a grand scale. From 1987 the threat of the Shining Path, extended practically throughout the country, and inflation reached record levels in Peru, as well as in the entire region. Under these circumstances, the engineer Alberto Fujimori Fujimori was elected for the first time in the 1990 elections.

The liberal, authoritarian regime of Fujimori and Montesinos

Why can the Peruvian transition be considered pertinent and eventually even interesting? No doubt because of the never before seen characteristics of the Peruvian authoritarian system, as well as because of the peculiarities of transition during the last decade. Those characteristics could very well repeat themselves in Latin America. The peculiarities, for their part, shed light on the conditions for the success of any transition towards democracy.

Certainly during the 1990s in Peru, a specific kind of political regime developed, which was liberal, economically speaking, and formally democratic, politically speaking. However, this democratic formality hid an exercise of power profoundly authoritarian and sophisticatedly repressive, making it a liberal-authoritarian regime.

Similar regimes also seem to have existed in other parts of the world. The most similar cases are Malaysia in Asia and Zimbabwe in Africa. In Latin America, Fujimori's Peru has sometimes been compared to the Uruguayan regime of Bordaberry. However, Fujimori's regime shares with Bordaberry's its civil origins as well as its main military support, but differs substantially in its mechanisms of control and repression.

On the other hand, the term liberal-authoritarian was used before by the Chilean regime of Pinochet, who like Fujimori, was obsessed with establishing a new legality. However, the differences between the two refer to their origins (a coup in Chile; elections in Peru); closely connected to legalistic obsession (founding of legality by Pinochet; procedural and judicial control of legality, in the case of Fujimori).

As British electoral expert Rebecca Cox noted in her report of the early stages of the electoral process in 2000, what is relevant in the case of Peru is that "Peru in 2000 had the institutions and the appearance of democracy, but neither the norms nor the essence" (Cox, 2000, p. 1). This regime sustained itself through the control and the manipulation of the Judiciary Power, Parliament, and the Armed Forces, but above all, through the control of the media in general, and of television in particular. Control, and this is the peculiar element, was practiced in the name of "democratic" and liberal freedom of press. Authoritarian Peru was an extreme case of the destruction of the democratic life and of the public spaces in the name of liberalism, namely, a caricature, a "happy world" of Huxley, almost an Orwellian "1984".

The peculiarities of Peruvian transition

Manuel Antonio Garretón (2000, pp. 77ff.) distinguished between three types of political democratization: (a) foundation of democracy in places where a genuine democratic life didn't exist previously (Central America); (b) the "transition", a concept that appears restricted to the cases of negotiation between the exiting authoritarian regime and the entering democratic forces (Spain, The South Cone); and (c) the "reform" as the expansion of the democratic exercise (Mexico).

What occurred in Peru doesn't correspond to any of these types. Instead of negotiation, there was a kind of collapse, with the flight of the President and seven general commanders, as well as incarceration or flight of all television station owners, and everything else in between. Thus, in the Peruvian transition there was neither negotiation nor impunity.

Perhaps this explains that until October 2000 (date of publication of his book), Garretón expressed a certain pessimism towards the democratization of Peru, thus confirming that there weren't nor were then any true political parties in this country (" . . . it is not possible to think that civil society itself will end with the dictatorship and govern a country", p. 136). The most notable is the sentence which concludes the paragraphs dedicated to the Peruvian case: " . . . Peru is going to have to confront its Achilles' heel: having a constitutional authoritarian rule of the most difficult kind to overthrow, instated after an election – regardless of the frauds committed – and recognized by other governments, as well as lacking a political party system to channel, organize and project an opposition and change in regime" (p. 137).

Thus, few of the preexisting theories and models of "the democratic transitions" can be applied to Peru's recent history. In fact, the idea that the elections were enough to consolidate a regime and expects its stability was the same viewpoint of several Latin American chancelleries concerning the Peruvian situation in 2000.

The uniqueness of the Peruvian transition is that the ousting of the authoritarian regime wasn't produced by one of the known processes of transition, in which the old and the new order negotiate the transition. Here, the old order didn't have any claim to negotiate or any spokesmen. Instead of negotiation there was destruction.

Even though the authoritarian regime was overthrown, the long, complex, and indispensable task of dismantling the authoritarian culture

182

was left pending, which is understandable in a country that never had a stable, political system of democracy, and where everyone demands a national accord for the reconstruction of democracy. Today Peru faces the challenge of creating a genuine democratic culture – the basis of a lasting, democratic political system – whose possibilities of success or frustration are beyond the present reflections. These are even more dramatic given the fact that a governance crisis could motivate the citizenry to "kick them all out" (as occurred recently in Argentina and Bolivia).

The paradoxes of democracy

As stated at the beginning of this study, never before have there been so many democratically-elected regimes in Latin America. It is necessary to add, however, that democracy has never been so weak in Latin America (and worldwide). This is explained by two paradoxes:

1. First Paradox: Disaffection with Democracy

It would seem that as democracy spreads in Latin America, there is a parallel growth in discontent. Thus, the index of confidence and satisfaction in democracy has decreased greatly in the last period, as shown by the following figures:

Index of Democracy: More Support and more Satisfaction

	1996	2001
Uruguay	66	67
Costa Rica	66	61
Venezuela	46	49
Honduras	31	46
Argentina	53	39
Peru	46	39
Mexico	32	36
Bolivia	45	35
Nicaragua	41	34
Chile	41	34
Panama	52	28
Ecuador	43	28
Brazil	35	26
Guatemala	34	25
El Salvador	41	23
Paraguay	41	23
Colombia	38	22
Average	**44**	**36**

Source: Latinobarómetro 2001.

Only in Uruguay and Costa Rica did the index exceed 50% of support and satisfaction. And in Costa Rica, it has also diminished in the last 50 years.

At the same time, there has been a decrease in the preference for democracy: from 61% to 41% in 2001; the principal institutions that are part of the democratic frame do not enjoy the confidence of the majority of the population. The Church has the leading percentage (72%), followed by television (49%). However, neither the Armed Forces, the President, the Police, the Judiciary Power, Parliament, nor political parties go beyond 40%. In the case of parties, there is a revealing piece of information: 95% of Latin Americans believe parties are indispensable to democracy, but only 15% trust the existing parties. We are facing a grave deficit in legitimate democracy.

Trying to discover the causes of this dissatisfaction with democracy, a group of experts called together not long ago by the Rio Group and International IDEA came up with the following list of factors: (a) insufficient economic and social results of democratic regimes; (b) the crisis and the disparagement of the State itself; (c) the lack of a solid democratic culture; (d) the effects of political corruption; (e) the difficulties in the relationship between political parties and the rest of civil society; (f) the subordination of political life to the powers that be of national and transnational origin; (g) the increase in political violence without politics; and (h) in some countries, the difficulties in the relationships between the Armed Forces and institutional democracy (Rio Group – International IDEA, 2003).

What is certain is that there is a profound disaffection of citizens *vis a vis* democracy and its institutions. The risk of the establishment of an authoritarian culture is high, even more so if the support of a democratic system is secondary concerning economic conditions and attention to other social problems, such as unemployment and poverty, which increasingly typify Latin American societies.

2. Second Paradox: De-democratization of Democracy

However, that is only the tip of the iceberg. It is important to add that our democracy is less and less democratic. And undoubtedly this de-democratization is rooted in disaffection and in the deterioration in the aforementioned legitimacy.

In 2000, Jose Nun published a convincing study about the risks and problems of the understanding inherent in democracy, under the suggestive and forceful title of *Democracy: Government of the People or Government of the Politicians?* (Nun, 2000). It is wise to pause and reflect on this book due to its extraordinary relevance to Latin Americans today.

Nun starts by relating that Greece not only held the seeds of democracy, but also contained two antagonistic models that may serve as perspectives for analyzing contemporary democracies. The first and classic one is the model of Athens, where citizens met to deliberate directly on public issues; the second model is that of Sparta, where the members of the City Council were nominated according to the intensity of applause from the assembly received by each candidate.

Athens can be considered as the great, historical antecedent of direct democracy and Sparta as a caricature of representative democracy. Moreover, prepared against any possibility of manipulation, "the Athenians did not consider voting democratic because they said that it was a method whereby the rich, those born to noble families, and the successful were favored" (Nun, 2000, p. 21). This is the reason behind the lottery system. In Athens, democracy was born as a deliberation among citizens, while in Sparta citizens were reduced to the condition of spectators, barely apt to express their approval or disapproval. Athens inspired the idea of democracy as the government of the people, while Sparta nurtured the practice of democracy as the government of politicians.

According to Nun, this Hellenic dichotomy between the deliberating citizen and the mere voter repeats itself in the 20th Century, in the antagonistic pair which appear in the book *Capitalism, Socialism, and Democracy,* published by Schumpeter in 1942, and the Universal Declaration of Human Rights, approved by the United Nations in 1948. For Schumpeter, "democracy simply means that the people have the opportunity to accept or refute men who will govern them" (cited by Nun, 2000, p. 26), since "citizens only get to applaud or not to applaud, like in Sparta" (Nun, 2000, p. 27).

In contrast, the Declaration of 1948 ties the three types of corresponding citizenry to the three types of human rights established by the Declaration and systematized by Marshall in 1949 (civil rights, political rights and social rights). It also restores the integral notion of democracy as the government of the people, the bearer of rights that must be attended to by the administration of politicians.

The aforementioned fundamental dilemma of the political condition of the citizen (debater or mere voter), vastly transcends the dichotomy between representative and direct democracy, since the original idea of representative democracy itself was born from the vindication of human beings as citizens and no longer as subjects.

The universal deterioration of democracy in the last decades consists in that, following an originally American practice, the confrontation of ideas was replaced by publicity. Citizens have been turned into consumers, who must be seduced and no longer convinced, to use the paradigm of Regis Debray (1991, 1992, 1995). This can be developed in the following manner:

185

	Democracy Originally	Democracy Today
Voter Conception	citizen	consumer
Conception of leader	hero	star
Function of leader	interpreter	interpreter
Purpose of Communication	needs	sensations
Politics	convince	seduce
Types of relations	face to face	media
Predominant Base of Message	word	image
Type of Message	proposals	publicity spots

Thus, the competition between ideas has become a mercantile competition between publicity mechanisms. Content (electoral options) is no longer as important, as form (the appearance of the candidate, the modulation of the voice, the publicity spot, etc.). The statistician's job is replaced by the role of the actor. The combined effect of video-politics and opinion polls (which end up being crucial to the electoral options) has contributed, in all senses, in producing an electoral game characterized by the absence of ideas, by localism and by the privatization of public spaces. Giovanni Sartori (1998) has noted this, undoubtedly with exaggerations not shared by the present author. By this route we arrive at the antipodes of representative democracy, since one of the forms (elections) is observed at the cost of sacrificing all of its fundamental contents.

Sinesio López (1997) has worked on the history and the meaning of the concept of citizenship (corner stone of democracy), its limited vigilance and the dispersion of maps of the Peruvian citizenry. The result of his extensive inquiry indicates that we are far from crossing the frontier between subjects and citizens.

According to the classification of Marshall, also used by López, Nun and many others, it is important to distinguish between civil citizenship, political citizenship, and social citizenship. The first means equality before the law, which includes freedom of speech, thought and religion, the right to engage in contracts, work and ownership of properties, and the right to obtain justice ruled by egalitarian laws. In the strict sense, the second means the right to elect and be elected, the right to vote, which only became truly universal during the 20th century. The third, which became internationally endorsed in the mid-20th Century (with the Declaration of Human Rights), includes free and obligatory education, minimum wage, social security, and the combined gains corresponding to the welfare state (appearing in post-war and denominated welfare state, precisely in opposition to warfare state).

These social rights are binding to the democratic State *vis a vis* its members, and correspond, historically speaking, to compensation for the special effort citizens lent during the war, according to the explanation given by Giddens (1985). The minimum result of this formulation is that "there can be no democratic citizenry without social rights" (Nun, 2000, p. 65). "In contrast to Schumpeter and his followers," Nun states, "this perspective of politics promotes, then, the active idea of citizenship and of its implication in the communal life, which goes so much more beyond the vote." (Nun, 2000, p. 68).

What is certain is that true democracies only last where there are social rights and economic development. There are no stable democracies without the existence of a certain degree of social equality between citizens. This leads to prioritizing the fight against poverty as an essential task for democratic construction, even in the more political and electoral meaning of "democratic construction". Democracy cannot be stable if it is not framed by an efficient process of poverty alleviation.

We mustn't forget that the inherent rights granted to social citizenry emerge as the responsibilities and obligations that the State has to assume to allow democracy to work. In other words, the exercise of citizenship, even if only political citizenship, demands a certain level of education, which is why the abusive and discriminatory vote *censitaire* was formally established.

We now know that democracy demands a cultural environment of a democratic nature. An antidemocratic culture corresponds to and serves as the base of an antidemocratic regime. Political democracy does not flourish where familiar, scholarly, media, labor and all other types of relations remain strongly authoritarian, discriminatory, and *machistas*, as was explained by Giddens (1998), when he invoked the task of democratizing democracy.

In short, the universal paradox of contemporary democracy is that political democracy has never been so extensive and at the same time never less intense. In other words, we live in a time when political and electoral democracy has spread geographically, but has diminished in terms of quality of democratic life. Peru under Fujimori is a good example of the extremes that could be reached: a State of formal democracy without any democratic content whatsoever. In addition, the Peruvian transition reveals that it is not enough merely to recover the forms of political democracy. Instead it is necessary to deal with the task of constructing a real democracy to overcome the institutional precariousness of the Latin American countries.

What is important to emphasize in the Peruvian case, and with the former disquisition, is that democracy was born as the government of the people, etymologically and historically speaking. When the sole focus is on technically legitimizing a government of politicians, then we are no longer talking about democracy, but technocracy.

The challenge of democratization in Latin America no longer consists solely or principally in holding free and fair elections. Above all it means constructing legitimate, democratic regimes accountable to the citizenry. It also must be capable of maintaining the methods of participation and must attend to the popular needs that allow for the solidity of political democracy through its crystallization as an economic and social democracy.

References

Ames, Rolando *et al.* (2001), *Situación de la democracia en el Perú* (2000–2001), PUC, Lima.
Bourdieu, Pierre (1996), Sur la télévision, Liber, París.
Bowen, Sally, El expediente Fujimori. El Perú y *su Presidente 1990–2000*, Lima, Perú Monitor, 2000.
Briggs, Asa and Burke, Peter, *De Gutenberg a Internet, una historia social de los medios de comunicación,* Taurus, Madrid, 2002.
Castells, Manuel (1998), *La era de la información, economía, sociedad y cultura,* 3 volumes, Alianza Editorial, Madrid.
Cox, Rebecca (2000), *Evaluación de la coyuntura electoral en el Perú,* Electoral Reform International Services, Londres (typewritten).
Debray, Régis (1991), *Cours de médiologie générale,* Gallimard, París.
—— (1992), *Vie et mort de l'image,* Gallimard, París.
—— (1995), *El Estado seductor, las revoluciones mediológicas del poder,* Manantial, Buenos Aires.
Ferry, Jean-Mar *et al.* (1989), *El nuevo espacio público,* Gedisa, España.
Flychy, Patrice (1993), *Una historia de la comunicación moderna, espacio público y vida privada,* GG Mass Media, Mexico.
Fowks, Jacqueline (2000), *Suma y resta de la realidad, medios de comunicación y elecciones generales 2000 en el Perú,* FES, Lima.
Franco, Carlos, *Acerca del modo de pensar la democracia en América Latina,* Friedrich Ebert Stiftung. Lima, 1998.
García Canclini, Néstor, *Consumidores y ciudadanos, conflictos multiculturales de la globalización,* Grijalbo, Mexico D.F., 1995.
Gargurevich, Juan, *La prensa sensacionalista en el Perú,* Catholic University of Peru, Lima, 2000.
Garreton, Manuel Antonio, *Política y sociedad entre dos épocas, América Latina en el cambio de siglo,* Homos Sapiens, Rosario, 2000.
Giddens, Anthony (1985), *The Nation State and Violence: Volume Two of a Contemporary Critique of Historical Materialism,* Cambridge, Polity.
—— (1998), *Más allá de la izquierda y de la derecha, el futuro de las políticas radicales,* Cátedra, Madrid.
Grupo de Río – Idea Internacional (2003), *El papel de los partidos políticos en el fortalecimiento de la institucionalidad democrática,* International IDEA, Lima.
Habermas, Jürgen (1989) , *The Structural Transformation of the Public Sphere: An Inquiry into a Category of Bourgeois Society,* Polity, Cambridge.
López pintor, Rafael (1999), *Votos contra balas,* Planeta, Barcelona.
López Sinesio (1997), *Ciudadanos reales e imaginarios,* IDS, Lima.
Marshall, T.H. (1963), *Sociology at the Crossroads and other Essays,* Heinemann, London.

Nun, José (2000), *Democracia, ¿gobierno del pueblo o gobierno de los políticos?*, FCE, Buenos Aires.

Patrón, Pepi (2000), *Presencia social, ausencia política, Espacios públicos y participación femenina*, Agenda Perú, Lima.

——, "Democracia y nueva articulación entre privado y público. El problema de los 'espacios públicos'", en Urzúa, Raúl y Agüero, Felipe, *Fracturas en la gobernabilidad democrática*, Centro de Análisis de Políticas Públicas, Universidad de Chile, Santiago, 1998.

Popper, Karl (1992), *La lección de este siglo*, Temas Grupo Editorial, Buenos Aires.

Roncagliolo, Rafael, "La crisis de la modernidad y la cultura de la paz", in *Paz* No. 361, Centro de Estudios y Acción para la Paz, Lima, september 2,000.

——, "Los espacios culturales y su onomástica", in *diálogos*, No. 50, october 1997, FELAFACS, Lima.

——, "Pensar o dispensar la democracia", in *Socialismo y participación* # 82, CEDEP, Lima, september 1998.

Sartori, Giovanni (1998), *Homo videns, la sociedad teledirigida*, Taurus, Madrid.

Schumpeter, Joseph (1961), *Capitalismo, socialismo y democracia*, Aguilar, Mexico D.F.

Thompson, John (1998), *Los media y la modernidad, una teoría de los medios de comunicación*, Paidós, Spain.

Transparencia (2000), *Balance de las elecciones del año 2,000*, Lima.

Vargas Gutiérrez, José Luis, *Adiós a la vergüenza, los talk shows en el Perú*, Universidad Nacional de San Agustín, Arequipa, 2000.

10

HOW THE ARGENTINE MILITARY INVENTED HUMAN RIGHTS IN ARGENTINA

David Sheinin

The last dictatorship in Argentina (1976–1983) was a catastrophe in the sense intended by Marc Bloch and Walter Benjamin.[1] It punctuated Argentina's recent past, dramatically ending some historical processes. It brought others to light by underlining transitions from democracy through dictatorship. In many areas it marked the starting point for subsequent historical developments and continued to function as a reference point for change. One such area, perhaps the most important, was human rights. The period of dictatorship transformed how Argentines understood human rights. The state violence that followed the coup d'état of 24 March 1976 had no precedent. Nor did the human rights abuses the military visited upon civil society, both in the numbers of those who suffered and in the extent of the brutality. While the military rampantly disregarded human rights, a small number of individuals and human rights groups in Argentina, accompanied by a growing chorus of foreign critics, fought the generals. What emerged from this conflict was the first and only human rights regime in Argentina, where "regime" is meant to suggest three key components beyond simply what Argentines came to understand as "human rights." First, the regime of the late 1970s marks the first broadly based (though not popular) understanding of human rights as a comprehensive set of standards on basic civil rights. That set of standards remained in place through the 1980s and 1990s, long after the return of democracy.[2]

Second, the definitions of what constitute human rights in Argentina quickly emerged as conceptually narrow. While in United Nations and other international forums at the time human rights was a rapidly expanding set of concepts that went well beyond state violence under dictatorships, in Argentina human rights encompassed relatively little. For obvious reasons, in light of the destruction being wrought on civil society, definitions were tightly focused on the most blatant representations of state terror – disappearances, torture, and clandestine incarcerations. Third, during the dictatorship and after, the human rights regime was highly charged ideologically and politically. This is most evident in how human rights groups chose to emphasize and publicize violent government wrongdoing in an effort to topple the regime. But its most lasting impact is likely that the creation of a human rights regime in Argentina further marginalized a majority of poor Argentines. Those protesting human rights abuses were by and large from the communities most affected by the internal war, white urban middle class Argentines. For that reason in part, and unlike the experience in Chile, Guatemala, and other Latin American countries under dictatorship, the human rights regime came to have only limited relevance to a majority of poor Argentines in the sprawling urban "villas miserias" and in rural zones. In many regards, the human rights regime was defined and established by the military itself after 1975.

Before 1970, while aspects of what came later to be understood popularly as "human rights" were present in Argentine political cultures, human rights were not. Human Rights were addressed sporadically, as a legal or diplomatic problem, often in the abstract as it related to rights issues in Argentina. The 1949 Constitution, for example, defined a range of workers' rights that, much later, would be considered basic human rights. But during Juan Perón's first term, neither Peronism backers nor civil society understood the government's guarantees of social security, the well-being of all Argentines, and improved living conditions for the poor, as part of human rights. With the start of the *proceso* there was a transformation in what society understands as human rights.[3]

The ways in which Argentine authorities conceived defenders of human rights as dangerous antagonists, and then fought them, shaped the definition of human rights with profound implications for what would remain a relatively static understanding of human rights after 1983. A majority of poor Argentines had little sympathy for the very limited armed revolutionary struggle of the *Montoneros* and other leftist insurgent groups; the military understood this and had little difficulty convincing many Argentines that violent suppression was a necessary measure to restore order. For a majority of poor Argentines, the *proceso* did not mark the cataclysm it represented for the urban middle classes. Nor did it come to signify in their historical memory after 1983 a particularly violent historical period compared to other periods in the past four decades highlighted by police and judicial violence, growing poverty, and abysmal living conditions.

This chapter argues that the ways in which the military government confronted foreign criticisms of human rights violations had a crucial impact on the creation of the Argentine human rights regime. By and large, the international community quickly sympathized with how Argentine groups characterized human rights violations during the dictatorship and identified remarkably quickly a broad range of accurate details on torture, executions, and other forms of repression. Argentine authorities identified a conspiratorial web of critics. These included "leftists" in the United States and other western governments; human rights organizations (like Amnesty International and the Washington Office on Latin America); powerful representatives of the liberal international media (like the *Washington Post* and the *New York Times*); and dozens of other groups including the American Bar Association and the National Press Association.

Believing that with the support of allies abroad, it could reverse an immediate and lasting perception of the dictatorship as *pinochetista*, the military devoted enormous energy to denying the extensive human rights abuses, accusation by accusation. The strategy itself was perhaps not misguided. Argentina faced mounting hostility on a range of foreign policy issues from the United States, France, Canada, and many other countries over human rights violations. Because massive human rights violations represented an essential and apparently non-negotiable component of military governance, the *junta* had no policy alternative but to deny all accusations. But the ways in which the military denied and contradicted the accusations failed to convince most foreign and many domestic middle class observers. They contributed to the comprehension of how human rights were understood in Argentina. Irrational denials by the military in the face of overwhelming evidence to the contrary; an ideologically driven insistence that the ongoing use of military force was necessary in Argentina; repeated efforts to suggest that Argentina was a leading international defender of human rights; and the reprehensible failure of members of the non-aligned movement (and in some cases, members of the Soviet bloc) to hold Argentina to account for human rights violations, all helped reinforce a widespread international perception of Argentina as a human rights violator in the specific terms outlined by pro-human rights activists in Argentina.

During 1976 and 1977, there was an exponential increase in foreign pressures on the Argentine *junta* over reports of widespread human rights abuses. These attacks came principally from Canada, the United States, and Western Europe. Argentina's military rulers made the defense against these attacks a priority. They labeled them communist-inspired and responded through an increasingly convoluted combination of justifications, denials, and lies. Even as the military built a public mythology suggesting their supposed active support for human rights domestically and internationally, the generals entrenched a political culture of deliberate and methodical dishonesty and concealment.[4] In international forums, the *junta* adopted several tactics to show Argentina to be pro-human rights. Like the government of Augusto Pinochet in Chile, for example, Argentine authorities trumpeted their supposed commitment to aboriginal rights, including the return of communal lands and water rights to native peoples. At international conferences, the Argentine government took a vigorous interest in the rights of women. But most of the Argentine military's defense of its human rights record was targeted at foreign claims of human rights abuses. After the coup, the first problem that reached the international stage was the thousands of refugees from military violence who crowded the embassies and consulates of Buenos Aires and other Argentine cities. By the middle of 1976, there were hundreds of foreign inquiries over what humanitarian actions the military might take to alleviate the situations of the asylum seekers. As early as July, the Argentine government recognized that it would have to develop a command center to coordinate the official response to foreign accusations on human rights. Mandated to explain to foreigners the "real Argentina," the command center would be composed of representatives from a number of ministries and government departments. Its priority, based on what the military believed correctly to be the strong ties between human rights and a range of foreign and domestic problems, was to create the impression that there were no human rights violations in Argentina.[5]

Ironically, in light of Cold War politics and the conviction of the Argentine military that the Soviets were behind the Argentine revolutionary left and the growing international "conspiracy" to invent a human rights problem in Argentina, the *junta* was not pressured by Communist states on human rights. Shortly after the coup, for example, the Cuban government assured the Argentine military that while Cuba had intervened in the domestic politics of some countries in the Americas, Argentine military intelligence would never find links between the Argentine revolutionary left and Cuba. Cubans told the Argentine military secretly that their country had had and would have nothing to do with Argentine insurgents. Cuban authorities understood that such links would jeopardize valued, friendly Argentine–Cuban relations (in the field of nuclear medicine, for example) and told the Argentines so. While they opposed Argentine coup d'état, they considered it a "necessary change" in that some "bandits" (meaning the previous Peronist government) had taken over before and had eliminated security for the general public.[6]

By early 1977, the Argentine military and its civilian allies had designated the problem of defending its human rights record against foreign attacks as a top priority in the United Nations, the International Nuclear Regulatory Agency, and in other venues. In raising its enemies in the context of human rights, military propaganda, spectacle, constitutional law and other areas defined human rights through the early 1980s. A variety of national and international factors contributed to the creation of a human rights regime in Argentina after 1976. In part, the historical extremes of the violence itself are notable. There had been dictatorship in Argentina before 1976. But the extent of state sponsored torture and assassination had no precedent; the extent defined what was meant by human rights violations. Another factor was the emergence in the preceding decade of a handful of international human rights organizations, notably Amnesty International.[5] With the coup d'état in 1976, Amnesty had established a reputation in many quarters for a politically impartial identification of human rights violations in different countries. While the Argentine military viewed Amnesty as a dangerous ally of international communism, the human rights organization played a major role in pressuring Argentine authorities on human rights and in pressing a variety of already sympathetic governments to make human rights a central foreign policy focus. A third context for the definition of an Argentine human rights regime was the strengthening of pro-human rights Catholic groups. In Argentina, such groups as the Santiago-based Vicario de la Solidaridad had little impact. Even so, the role of Church groups in defining human rights in Chile, Brazil, and elsewhere helped prompt the discovery by people in wealthy nations of human rights as a Latin American problem, at the time of the fall of Salvador Allende in 1973. This in turn focused tremendous international attention on the Argentine coup and its aftermath.

At first, the Argentine military believed it could manage the internal and foreign criticisms of its human rights record. In 1977, despite that the Inter-American Human Rights Commission (CIDH) had visited a number of countries and had issued a stinging indictment of the Pinochet regime, the Argentine government believed it could talk the Commission out of a serious investigation of human rights in Argentina. The Foreign Ministry believed that if Argentina invited the Commission to visit judicial, police, and penitentiary facilities *in situ*, it could avoid a more hostile visit later. In addition, the government worked for months to try press the Commission to reject the option of a specific investigation of human rights in Argentina alone and to do so, tried to create a dialogue with Commission members.[7] Amnesty International, on the other hand, was immediately perceived as an enormous threat to Argentina. A late 1976 report by the Secretaría de Inteligencia del Estado (SIDE) identified Amnesty as planning a very dangerous campaign against the country, with the backing of the "forces of Marxism." At least in part, SIDE's linking of Amnesty International to subversion and Marxism was tied to Amnesty's defense of members of terrorist organizations such as the Baader Meinhof gang. But there was more to it:

Esta pretensión humanitaria e imparcial llega como queda dicho hasta una fecha meridiana: 1968. A partir de este año sus actividades en pro de la subversión marx-

ista se tornan una realidad tangible a través de una prédica unilateral en pro de los
elementos que, actuantes en el mundo libre, están enrolados en la subversión marx-
ista sea a niveles combatientes, periféricos o 'kriptos'.[8]

Evidence for Amnesty's danger included its supposed ties to Comisión
Argentina de Derechos Humanos, the Montoneros, and the International
Red Cross (infiltrated by international Communism, according to the
SIDE). The Argentine regime also believed the so-called international
Marxist conspiracy had won hold of dozens of other agencies and govern-
ments critical of Argentina's human rights record including UNESCO and
the United Nations Commission on Refugees.[9]

When Amnesty representatives Robert Drinan (a Jesuit priest) and Lord
Avenbury (president of the British Parliamentary group on human rights)
visited Argentina in November 1976, they asked for information on and
access to those detained for political reasons. Argentine authorities simply
pretended that there were no illicit detention centres, torture, or disappearances in the country. They got away with this in part because the
Amnesty delegates, still unaware of the scope of the violence, asked only
for information on those detained as part of the Poder Ejecutivo Nacional
(PEN), the constitutionally mandated detention apparatus. The Amnesty
representatives were taken to the Villa Devoto federal prison on their first
day, part of the above ground judicial system where prison conditions
were much superior to those of the clandestine detention centers. They
were lectured on Argentine pro-human rights legislation, refugee laws, the
right of *habeas corpus*, as well as other judicial and civil rights guaranteed under the military government. In keeping with the military's view
that those well-meaning foreigners critical of the human rights situation
in Argentina simply did not understand the threat of subversion, government representatives spent hours "explaining the general situation" in the
country both before and after 24 March 1976.[10]

The military tried to manage Amnesty as it managed others who questioned the legitimacy of the internal war. On November 10, Col. Ricardo
Flouret and Capt. Eduardo Andújar, representing the Interior Ministry,
explained to the Amnesty representatives that many of the so-called disappeared were in fact members of the guerrilla who had simply gone
underground. They also cited examples of so-called subversives who had
left the country clandestinely, then surfaced in other nations. Amnesty was
also told that many of those listed as disappeared had in fact died in
action. As part of the Argentine government's ongoing effort to conceal
the numbers of dead, according to the Sub-Secretary of Foreign Relations,
Capt. Gualter O. Allara, there were 20 deaths that could be documented,
as though this number represented of the destruction taking place in
Argentina. Allara went on to note that all disappearances were investigated but that some reports on these cases took a long time to complete

"y que muchos de los desaparecidos entran en la categoría que normalmente desaparece en una ciudad de la dimensión de Buenos Aires, como ocurre en todas las grandes urbes del mundo."[11] Lord Averbury confirmed that he had seen no cases of prisoner mistreatment during his visit to the Villa Devoto prison. But when he raised reports of brutality that Amnesty had received in anticipation of the visit, Flouret acknowledged that there were certainly isolated incidents of prisoner mistreatment. Indeed, on the basis of two such cases at Villa Devoto, the prison director had been sacked.

Where the Amnesty visitors presented their most explosive evidence, the military simply lied. In response to questions about the whereabouts of Mónica Mignone, who would become one of the most prominent cases among those disappeared during the *proceso*, the Interior Ministry simply indicated that Mignone was not in the hands of any of the armed services (one of the few documented admissions during the visit that the military was holding prisoners outside of the PEN). It also pointed out that Mignone's father, Emilio, an internationally known human rights activist had had personal access to the highest authorities in Argentina and had been given full opportunity to express his concerns.[12]

The military managed the Amnesty visit as a propaganda campaign for the consumption of domestic media, the international press, and the visitors themselves. The government was under no illusions that it could engender a serious change in Amnesty's views of human rights violations in Argentina. But the military did believe it had registered some important successes in how it had managed the human rights problem with the world looking on for ten days. Lord Avebury and Robert Drinan expressed their thanks to the government for their free access to detention centers and for the "ample information and patient explanations" they received in response to their questions. They also promised to make the *junta* aware confidentially of the report they would write prior to publication so that the Argentine government could respond to any criticisms. The Foreign Ministry counted as another positive result of the visit the government's success in projecting an image of Argentine strength and conviction, though privately it recognized the government's inability to locate quickly some of those identified by Amnesty as having disappeared.

Despite the generals' conviction that they had managed the visit effectively, Amnesty remained unconvinced. As a result of the visit, it issued a scathing attack on the *junta*. The absurdity of the generals' protestations of innocence served only to confirm in the minds of foreign critics what Argentine human rights groups were asserting. Two years later, the Argentine military faced a still more dangerous site visit. Early in 1979, the CIDH announced its plans to visit Argentina to investigate the state of human rights. Three years into military rule in Argentina, much more was known about those who had been incarcerated and disappeared. The

CIDH had much more detailed and specific information it wished to confirm in Argentina. Facing growing isolation in the international community, Argentina had no choice but to accept the visit. Based on three years of experience and in light of a perceived higher level of danger than the Amnesty visit, the regime's response was more sophisticated than it had been in November 1976. The Commission had a wide variety of specific requests that disturbed the Argentine military. It asked, for example, to visit the province of Tucumán on 14 September 1979 for what Edgardo Paz Barnica, CIDH Executive Secretary, called preliminary work. Argentine officers responded by cracking down on human rights groups, further alarming foreign critics, and by gathering whatever potentially useful intelligence they could on the problems they might face. In September 1979, for example, Argentine Naval Intelligence reported with concern that one high ranking CIDH official, Edmundo Vargas Carreño, had recently visited ex-president Frei in Chile at which time the two men had discussed human rights in a manner critical of the Argentine regime.[13]

Argentina had received a generally positive CIDH assessment in 1976, whose annual report had cited Argentine responses to a questionnaire as evidence of the country's support for the American Human Rights Declaration.[14] But Argentine authorities refused to cooperate in the drafting of the following annual CIDH report. The country's human rights-related relations with the Organization of American States (OAS) deteriorated. Scrambling to improve its image at the OAS before the visit, Argentina proposed a new inter-American agreement to make torture an international crime. In Argentina, the military's adversaries tried to capitalize on the CIDH visit. In a missive of August 6 the Montoneros urged the print media to take advantage of the international scrutiny the commission's visit would afford. Instead of the usual excuses for not publishing information on human rights abuses ("inconvenience," "the lack of space," and so on), the Montoneros enjoined the media to report faithfully the statements of Argentine human rights organizations. The military cracked down hard. An Interior Ministry decree, for example, banned the distribution of a popular underground pamphlet, "¿Dónde están? 5581 Desaparecidos," produced by the Asamblea Permanente por los Derechos Humanos and other human rights groups.

Planning for the visit included what the government called psychological factors. According to the Interior Ministry:

> [La] población argentina, cuyo abordamiento se efectuará, principalmente, a través del método 'sugestivo' implementado por los medios de comunicación masiva. Integrantes de la propia CIDH, que serán abordados mediante una acción psicológica 'persuasiva' pero que también serán impregnados por la precitada propaganda 'sugestiva.'[15]

The CIDH was to see only what the government wished it to see. *In loco* visits would proceed only with Commission members respecting Argentine sovereignty. This meant that they would not be permitted to question what Argentine authorities offered as evidence of the state of human rights. The visitors would be permitted to interview whomever they wished in federal or provincial police custody. This was meant to reinforce the Argentine position that illegal detentions, executions, and torture did not exist. But as had been the case for the 1976 Amnesty International visit, no military facilities or detention centers would be accessible. And while the CIDH would be allowed to review documentation relating to detentions, they would not be given access to anything other than so-called "public" records.[16]

The control and suppression of information on human rights extended to provincial military governors who were given explicit orders to limit what the international community would learn through the CIDH. Were a CIDH representative to reach a particular province, the governor would assign the provincial Ministro de Gobierno to track them. The Interior Ministry ordered that provincial authorities were not to give the impression that they were there to control CIDH activities, but rather to suggest they were available to facilitate their work. No visit to a police station or prison would take place without the chief of police or penitentiary warden present. Though wardens and police chiefs were charged by the government with answering any questions the CIDH might have, such questions would have to be submitted in writing twenty-four hours in advance. Questions would be forwarded to the Interior Ministry in Buenos Aires for the correct response. New, dedicated telephone lines were opened in the Interior Ministry to receive emergency phone calls at any hour from officials faced with CIDH questions.[17]

As was frequently the case, the *junta* planned to suggest lawful calm to the international media covering the CIDH visit:

> Es conveniente transmitir la imagen de un país serio, con clara división de los Poderes, con instituciones responsables, respetuosas y respetadas en su competencias de un gobierno eficiente al servicio de la población.[18]

The use of the term "imagen" and other similar language pointed to what the military wished to conceal about daily life under the dictatorship. "Se evitará la acción represiva policial," wrote Interior Minister General Albano Harguindeguy: "La Justicia actuará de acuerdo a las responsabilidades que le son propias" – or in another statement, "los periodistas nacionales y en particular los extranjeors no serán limitados en sus accionar. En caso de vulnerar la Ley será la Justicia quién actúe." The state then, would conceal what it termed commonplace police repression. It would try deliberately to create the false impression that political protest was allowed, and when such protest went beyond what the law allowed, the justice system – as opposed to military thugs – would act, leveling charges and affording a fair trial. It maintained conditions for freedom of press and treated foreign and domestic journalists equally.[19]

The military was suspicious of Commission members, particularly the American jurist Tom Farer whom the junta identified derisively as an American liberal – tantamount to a leftist and a dupe of international Communism. But the Colombian Monroy Cabra was a Commissioner the junta believed it might trust to paint a positive picture of Argentine human rights. Cabra spoke the language of the generals. He expressed his concern to Argentine authorities that so-called leftist extremists might try to assassinate him while he visited Argentina. He also stated his confidence in the Argentine judges, many of whom he said he knew personally and as friends. The Interior Ministry brought military precision to how the government would respond to specific cases that CIDH jurists had raised. To a commission accusation that Jorge San Vicente was being detained, the Justice Department offered that the government might argue that the case was still before the courts – despite that it was not. On the more high profile case of Dagmar Hagelin, the government proposed to stonewall with continued promises of a formal judicial inquiry. In a meeting with US State Department official Viron Vaky in March 1979, the Argentine military made over a dozen promises on improved human rights in anticipation of the CIDH visit. But each promise, from continual medical attention to very good food, identified so-called delinquent terrorists in federal prisons, not those being held in clandestine detention.[20]

The campaign in response to the CIDH visit fooled few in the international community, and perhaps not many more in Argentina. But like other foreign attacks on human rights violations in Argentina between 1976 and 1983, the 1980 CIDH report, strongly critical of Argentina, seemed to galvanize military resolve to defend its human rights record both at home and internationally. The government simply continued to deny human rights violations and to find explanations for foreign criticisms other than the obvious – that such violations were taking place. A series of Venezuelan criticisms of the Argentine human rights record, for example, was met in the Argentine Foreign Ministry with an accusation that the Venezuelan government was still touched by the lingering influence of the Carter administration in Washington. Through 1982, military authorities held firm that what foreigners and human rights activists in Argentina viewed as violations were a legitimate response to subversion, while knowingly concealing the vast extent of their repression.

Some military government initiatives in Argentina failed to define human rights in keeping with dictatorship ideologies – but frequently contributed to the construction of a human rights regime. For example, in international forums, *proceso* diplomacy pressed for a recognition of "terrorism" as the military saw it. These initiatives generally failed in the community of nations, and also to sway many Argentines to reject so-

199

called terrorist views of human rights as invalid. In 1981, for example, Argentine diplomats lobbied colleagues at the United Nations Commission on Human Rights to make language changes to document 1603a outlining definitions of human rights. Specifically, the military pressed for language that rejected human rights violations complaints from "terroristas en actividad asociados para un fin determinado."[21] In response to Commission language that identified human rights abuses in Argentina, the dictatorship asked for appended language to highlight the violence of the revolutionary left – for example, that:

> A fines de 1975 las bandas Ejército Revolucionario del Pueblo y Montoneros realizaron una operación conjunta contra un arsenal en Buenos Aires que implicó la participación de centenares de terroristas en la acción. El accionar terrorista y el descalabro social y econónico obligó a las fuerzas armadas a asumir el podre en el mes de marzo de 1976.[22]

While this initiative failed, others were more successful. Also in 1981, the Committee on Union Freedom of the International Labour Organization (ILO) adopted a series of recommendations based on a report on conditions in Argentina (case 842). Argentine delegates convinced the ILO to modify its language on human rights violations considerably. Initially, the ILO observed that "una proporción importante de sindicalistas no han sido todavía procesados. Al tiempo que señala a la atención del Gobierno el interés que reviste para la mejora del clima social la liberación de los dirigentes sindicales detenidos, el Comité ruega al Gobierno que informe sobre la situación de las personas sobre las que todavía no ha enviado respuesta, asi como de manera mas general, sobre toda medida que fuera adoptada con miras a la liberación de los sindicalistas todavía en prisión."[23] Argentine ILO delegates convinced the organization to eliminate specific human rights criticisms in the above statement; there was no reference in the final document to the important proportion of union members still lingering in Argentine prisons but not charged.

Some of the military's most important human rights propaganda, and the role of that propaganda in the creation of a human rights regimes, came in the response to foreign government attacks. The Argentine government was deeply aware of the isolation experienced by Chile, South Africa, and Israel. The generals hoped to avoid such isolation. The attacks intensified steadily and, for the Argentines, came to exhibit identifiably specific political objectives. The governments most invested in the criticisms, according to the regime, were the United States, Great Britain, France, and Holland. Argentina depended on its membership in the Non-Aligned movement and its good ties with Eastern European governments to counter the attacks. It also relied on the support of other Latin American countries. For Argentine authorities, the question of human rights was intimately tied to such problems as the Soviet invasion of

Afghanistan, the conflagrations in Central America, and tensions between Iran and Irak. Defending the regime and the nation against accusations of human rights violations dovetailed with the military's vision of a larger, titanic Cold War struggle that placed Argentina on the front lines of a war against subversion.[24]

Ironically, in 1979 and 1980 the Argentine government worried about being associated with the Soviet Union and its invasion of Afghanistan in the minds of those decrying human rights abuses in the United Nations. Argentine officials believed that wealthy western nations and their allies, including Amnesty International, were intent on destroying the influence of the non-aligned movement within the United Nations in order to discredit Argentina as violator of human rights. According to the Argentine Foreign Ministry, unlike Africa, where there was solidarity among nations across the continent, in Latin America there was no such support for Argentina in the face of these attacks. Argentina was exposed. In response, Argentina strongly backed the worst human rights violators in the hemisphere. In March 1980, for example, Jaime Barrios Peña, Guatemalan Ambassador in Buenos Aires, asked the Argentine government for its support in the United Nations in confronting a Cuban resolution condemning Guatemala's human rights record. Argentine Foreign Minister Carlos Washington Pastor wrote back to indicate that Argentina had already decided to support Guatemala's position in the United Nations.[25]

As a diplomatic problem, defending the nation's honor against human rights-related American accusations became an obsession equivalent to Kremlin watching. Throughout the *proceso,* Argentine diplomats and military leaders continually assessed and reassessed how the United States government approached human rights in order to identify the best possible strategies to debunk the increasingly well-researched accusations against the military. For Argentine leaders, the American position on human rights in Argentina was attributable to a complicated range of factors. In 1980, a still tougher American human rights stand had various components. Argentines attributed the strength of a new wave of United Nations criticisms to American leadership at the Thirty-Sixth meeting of the United Nations Human Rights Commission. At the meeting, the Americans had pressed particularly hard for the establishment of permanent international mechanisms for the verification of human rights, with special regard to Argentina. Argentina also "blamed" the United States representative at the meeting, Jerome Shestack, whose positions the Argentines described as extremely virulent and aggressive.[26] In December 1980, the Human Rights Department of the Argentine Foreign Ministry posited that significant "damage" had done to Argentina by the sway over the Carter administration by human rights "hawks" in the State Department led by Patricia Derian. While Argentina might expect a favorable policy shift from the incoming Reagan administration, "la mentalidad impuesta por la administración Carter hará muy difícil que cualquier cambio sustancial de orientación sea puesto en práctica sin inconvenientes."[27]

On hundreds of occasions, the military itself helped conceive the coup d'état as a catastrophic moment in the creation of a human rights regime. The country was living through a period of "great anarchy" through 24 March 1976, the government explained in 1979 to the United Nations Sub-Commission on the Prevention of Discrimination and the Protection of Minorities. This justified the state violence that followed the coup. Had the military not responded with overwhelming force, the country might well have disintegrated. Faced in late 1975 with an ambiguously defined subversion characterized by what the military called indiscriminate violence, the state was no longer able to meet its primary responsibility of maintaining order. Worse still, the state had been infiltrated at high levels by subversives undermining any efforts to restore order. The judicial branch of government was paralyzed by the threat of violence against judges and the legislative branch wallowed in inactivity. The economy had entered a catastrophic phase of intense recession and uncontrollable inflation. Crucial to the military's justification of post-coup d'état political violence was the argument that there had been no one left to act:

> Todos los sectores sociales representativos, incluídos los que conformaban internamente el partido en el poder, se mostraban impotentes para aportar remedios, o soluciones que salvaran a la Nación del caos y anarquía. Las más notorias figuras políticas del país confesaban públicamente su incapacidad para contribuir a sostener el orden institucional tambaleante.[28]

Based on the argument that violent measures were needed to confront the crisis, the military government mounted a ludicrous constitutional defense for its human rights violations. That defense simply contributed at the time and later, to a sense among Argentine and non-Argentine critics of the regime that human rights abuses had been entrenched by government. At the same time, foreign critics rightly concluded that the military's position on human rights was contradictory. While implicitly defending the necessity of torture in light of what it called the anarchic violence that pervaded Argentina through March 1976, Argentine authorities repeatedly denied that the state used torture. Among other repeated points cited was Argentine legislation that expressly prohibited torture – as though this legal precedent, in and of itself, meant that there was no torture on behalf of the state in Argentina.[29]

The military also commonly justified its actions with reference to Article 23 of the 1853 Constitution that referred to internal disruptions or foreign attacks likely to endanger the exercise the Constitution and the authorities whose duties were mandated by it. The article justified the denial of individual rights guaranteed by the Constitution with what the military interpreted as references to "armed terrorist organizations." The regime often simply ignored the fiercest criticisms of Amnesty International and other groups by defending the record of the country's legal system. In 1978, for example, the government pointed out that many of those detained by the PEN had had their cases submitted to the UN Human Right Commission – as though this somehow showed the commitment of the government to human rights. In response to foreign criticisms of *habeas corpus* denials, the government noted that where judges had issued denials, these had been appealed to higher courts in Argentina, supposedly confirmed the existence of a legitimate judiciary.[30]

Argentine authorities took the defense of a legitimate judiciary one step further by insisting that, where called for in international law, any foreign human rights critics appeal first to Argentine law. In 1979, the French chapter of the Comisión Argentina de Derechos Humanos presented a denunciation to the United Nations Subcommission on the Prevention of Discrimination and Protection of Minorities. In the case of Haydée Orazi, the report alleged massive human rights violations against the Argentine dictatorship. According to Argentine officials, like hundreds of similar testimonials from groups and individuals, this was simply an effort to denigrate the Argentine government and state institutions. Argentina made a case to the UN for the document's dismissal based on the Comisión de Derechos Humanos not having exhausted juridical avenues for recourse within Argentina. Because Argentina had legal norms governing the protection of human rights, any group or individual might demand those protections. International legal precedent proscribed UN intervention until internal judicial processes had been explored thoroughly by the complainant.[31] In this case and others, the fantasy of judicial recourse was transparent. It simply strengthened the role of external forces in the structuring of the human rights regime in Argentina.[32]

Other public military protestations of Argentina's adherence to a pro-human rights policy unwittingly reflected the moral rigidity of the dictatorship. In a speech to the Thirty Seventh World Assembly on Aging, the Argentine delegate highlighted Argentina's good treatment of the elderly as evidence of its strong support for human rights. The country's elderly benefited from a "Latin and Christian" approach to family and community. One would assume, based on the Argentine delegate's speech, that Argentina's care for aged citizens was equivalent to that of any western European country. In this post-Peronist fantasy, all Argentines supposedly had available to them home visits, immediate attention for emergencies, free hospital care and prosthetics, and wheel chairs.[33] In response to United Nations General Assembly resolution 35/200 (15 December 1980) on measures adopted by countries against Nazis, fascists, neo-fascists, racial intolerance, hatred, and other totalitarian practices, the Ministry of Justice confidently identified Argentina as an antagonist of each of these. It held up a host of supporting legislation that included Law 16,478 (20 June 1963) designating murder motivated by racial or religious hatred as a punishable offense as well as various provisions against those who violate public peace and order.[34]

In public statements, the dictatorship gave the appearance of a broad and unflinching support for human rights. However, its back room policy making, reflected a more ambiguous position. In negotiations for a United Nations Convention on the protection of migrant workers and their families, the Argentine government refused to support the labor rights of undocumented workers. The military also wanted to exclude refugees or those that had received asylum from those defined as migratory workers (and able to benefit from associated United Nations human rights provisions). Argentina refused also to support the freedom of thought, freedom of conscience, and freedom of religion of migrant workers where these freedoms might impinge on public security, public order, and public morality. It opposed undocumented workers having the right to disseminate information and ideas in writing, orally, or in art forms. Furthermore, to a proposed UN guarantee that migratory workers have the right to life saving medical care, Argentina suggested appending a provision that such care would not abrogate a government's right to expel such workers from the country "if appropriate."[35]

Most commonly, the Argentine government simply denied foreign accusations as though the thousands of reports of human rights violations were invented. In 1978, Amnesty International documented 6,000 people illegally detained in Argentina. The Grupo de Abogados Argentinos Exiliados en Francia described as illegal and arbitrary the military's appeals to the Argentine Constitution as grounds for the coup d'état. According to the military government, the data and statements of these and dozens of other human rights organizations were nonsense. They reflected the infiltration of human rights groups by "subversives." Also in 1978, the SIDE issued a report accusing the Rome-based press agency Inter Press Service (IPS) of having the backing of the Montoneros. This, in turn, explained its unrelenting criticism of the dictatorship's human rights record.[36]

The blanket denials of human rights abuses were effective in prompting the redoubling of foreign and domestic criticisms of the regime, and the ongoing fervency of Argentine accusations of a conspiracy against the government had a similar effect. The 1981 version of the conspiracy linked the UN Human Rights Commission (which had criticized Argentina), to having orchestrated international press attacks on the Reagan administration's failure to pressure Argentina on human rights issues, and a European press insistence that the Soviet Union backed Argentine human rights abuses. Proof of the conspiracy for the Argentine government was the annoying association made between itself and international Communism. On several occasions, the military attempted to convince American authorities that Argentina was on track to democratic reform, particularly once Roberto Viola assumed the presidency. Here again, the military's arrogant and wrong-headed conviction that foreigners could be talked into what they themselves believed or wanted others to believe contributed to building the human rights regime in Argentina. In Washington, they increased the skepticism of officials like Patricia Derian, already convinced that Argentina was a human rights violator. They reinforced the complacency of those officials already supportive of the Argentine government on human rights.[37]

When Viola visited the United States in 1981, Argentine officials were concerned with his statements being misunderstood and misrepresented by the media. They challenged reports that Viola intended to make known a list of "desaparecidos" because for Argentine authorities there were no disappeared for whom the government was responsible. They bristled at what they viewed as the efforts of the international media to tie the credibility of the Viola presidency to the non-existent list. This, in turn, highlighted what the military identified as the threat of responsibility for the disappearances, and the proposal from many quarters of an amnesty for political prisoners. The danger here was that the international community would both define and impose on Argentina what the military maintained publicly was a false set of definitions around human rights violations.

What proved especially damaging to Argentina's foreign relations were the thousands of well-documented cases of the disappeared. The Argentine military viewed Germany as among the less threatening of the western democracies on human rights. Many German political leaders had visited Argentina after the March 1976 coup d'état; unlike many of the Americans who came, Argentine leaders found that German visitors were not primarily concerned with fact-finding on human rights. Argentines believed that the German visits had helped dampen the growing isolation Argentina faced in the international community over human rights. Moreover, unlike France and the United States, German foreign policy stressed a low key emphasis on human rights that highlighted private diplomatic approaches to Argentine authorities in regard to particular cases.

In 1980, the German government protested the detention in Argentina of Ricardo Otto, Oscar Ricardo Bader, and Inés del Valle Lugones. The petition was hardly moderate. The German Chargé d'Affaires made it clear to Argentine authorities that the failure to release these three prisoners would have damaging consequences for Argentine-German relations. He stressed specifically that for the upcoming visit to Argentina of the Prime Minister of Baden-Wurttenberg to have a positive impact on

DAVID SHEININ

bilateral relations, the three would have to be released. In March 1980, the German Foreign Secretary, Gunther van Well, spoke with the Argentine Interior Minister about the prospect of an amnesty for Germans detained in Argentina. Six months later no action had been taken on this request. Van Well made clear to the Argentine government that poor progress by the dictatorship on the question of German detainees was adversely affecting the political prospects of the German government domestically. He threatened that Argentine intransigence on human rights would likely impact on several areas of bilateral ties including nuclear cooperation, technology transfers, and financial relations. In bilateral ties with many countries, the long-term and intense focus on disappearance and torture in Argentina played an important role in building Argentina's human rights edifice.[38]

After the dictatorship fell in 1983, despite the profound political changes that shook Argentina, the perception of activists and others of human rights remained remarkably unchanged. Through the end of the century, for example, the most prominent human rights groups in Argentina continued to stress the relatively narrow legal and political definitions of human rights violations that had defined violence against the urban middle class during the *proceso*. These groups frequently cited the *proceso* itself as the origins of current human rights problems, often at the expense of a range of other considerations.[39]

The coup d'état as a catastrophic historical moment begins with the construction of historical memory that reinvents connections between past, present and future. That continuity defines the post-dictatorship democratic state. According to the historian Hugo Vezzetti, "con la reconstrucción de la democracia, en 1983, las responsabilidades de la memoria y las demandas de justicia se encontraban y se enlazaban, por asi decirlo, con las tareas de la reconstrucción del Estado y el nuevo pacto con la sociedad." Like other historians working on memory in Argentina, Vezzetti combines his analysis with an activism that favors the remembrance of dictatorship in very strict terms.[40]

The human rights regime defined during the *proceso* has multiple terms. After 1983, for example, the most important cases of the application of international norms to Argentine national law were based in large measure on dictatorship era cases. The agreement between Ragnar Hagelin and the Argentine State, in 2000 represented an unprecedented integration of an Inter-American Court of Justice decision and Argentine legal precedent. As never before, the pact underlined the acceptance in Argentina of the San José Pact (1969) as a relevant and applicable juridical instrument.[41] For many poor, rural Argentines, human rights remained an abstract concept. For the urban middle class, human rights were still focused on the *proceso*, on punishment, and on victims of state terror. In political terms and in the media, much more so than in Bolivia,

206

Guatemala, or in other Latin American countries, there is still a strict association between human rights and the abuses of the last dictatorship. Human rights groups that established themselves during the dictatorship to combat the abuses of the state continue to be the strongest pro-human rights groups in Argentina and continue to understand the problem of human rights through a *proceso* era prism.[42]

With the election of Ronald Reagan in 1980, Argentine military leaders correctly anticipated a new order on human rights in the United States though as early as the preceding year the strength of Patricia Derian and other human rights advocates within the Carter administration had been on the wane. In the early 1980s, the Argentine dictatorship cooperated extensively with the US government in support of repressive regimes in Central America. A 1981 Argentine intelligence report characterized the Reagan administration's struggle in Central America as a national security priority for Argentina. For the Argentine military, the key distinction between Carter and Reagan was that the latter had redefined US foreign policy in a manner that had ceased to "contemplate the advances of subversives with disinterest and had begun, with no uncertain measure, to support friendly governments threatened . . . by Nicaragua." This Argentine approval of the US escalation of military aid to El Salvador, Guatemala, and Honduras was less telling than what the Argentine military now believed was a set of global connections to Central America that Washington both faced and, according to Argentine intelligence, understood. US support for right-wing repression in Central America was directly tied to Cuban and Soviet expansionism, the kidnapping of General James Dozier by Red Brigades operatives in Verona, the threat to NATO from Warsaw Pact countries, the possible revival of the Weather Underground in the US, and a variety of other international leftist threats. These were precisely kinds of chilling, and far-fetched connections that had shaped Argentina's internal war since 1976, and that the Argentines now believed Ronald Reagan, a kindred spirit, was making. The substitution of democratic values and the rule of law for an extreme ideology of terror was complete and would shape Argentine society for two decades through the human rights regime.

By the early 1980s, society's understanding of human rights had been radically transformed. Argentina's first post-dictatorship president, Raúl Alfonsín, was elected in some measure because of his professional role as a human rights lawyer – a position he and a handful of others defined in the Argentine context during the preceding decade. Moreover, not only did Argentines develop a working definition of human rights associated with the dictatorship, but that definition shaped how many Argentines understood the problem of human rights in the two decades that followed. Specifically, and for example, just as the military dictatorship directed its internal war primarily against urban middle class Argentines, it was members of that class whose experiences as victims of state terror defined the Argentine human rights problem – often to the exclusion of the experiences of poor Argentines. Since 1983, largely as a result of the experience of the dictatorship and the legacies of that experience, unlike Chile, Guatemala, or Bolivia, there has been no popular political movement based around human rights issues in Argentina that has defined and redefined what people understand as human rights.[43]

In Argentina, a generation of analysts worked to differentiate between the *proceso* and the Alfonsín government, with ample attention to change in how the state applied human rights norms.[44] After 1983, the key point of reference with which to assess the state of human rights in Argentina remained the period of dictatorship. The dictatorship not only defined human rights as a global problem in Argentina after 1983, but has continued to define what human rights means until now. There is a different discourse that defines human rights beyond the touchstones of torture, disappearances, and state violence, and that includes a wide ranging notions of what human rights constitute, including questions of health, poverty, and prison conditions, among other themes. But as a cultural, political and ideological regime, human rights remain norms established during the dictatorship.[45] As the country emerged from military rule late in 1983, Argentines were seized by optimism. Through the late 1970s, as an outspoken human rights lawyer, the newly elected president, Raúl Alfonsín, had decried military rule and had contributed to the creation of the human rights regime during the *proceso*. He came to power in part on the promise of a democracy founded on the human rights regime now in place. But like other countries where human rights violations had been massive under repressive dictatorial rule, Argentina could not shake its authoritarian legacy. While middle class Argentines became dismayed over the state's inability to mete out just punishments to repressors, poor Argentines remained ambivalent about the late 1970s. Alfonsín and other political leaders saw the early euphoria of the post-military period quickly fade away.

Argentina was the first Latin American nation to set in place a truth commission charged with investigating and documenting the abuses of the dictatorship. Under the direction of the distinguished author Ernesto Sábato, the commission produced a thick volume, *Nunca Más*, which quickly became a best seller; many middle class Argentines were hungry for the details of what had happened between 1976 and 1983.[46] The book defined the human rights regime. The commission's findings helped lead to the prosecution and imprisonment in 1985 of a handful of the dictatorship's most senior generals. These included the first *de facto* president Jorge Rafael Videla and Leopoldo Galtieri, the leader responsible for the foolhardy 1982 war against Great Britain over the Malvinas.[47] Two years after the collapse of the dictatorship, these convictions and the commission report pointed to Argentina's having turned a corner on its past.[48]

But the turn was incomplete. *Nunca Más* proved unsatisfactory as a mechanism for bringing conciliation, memory, and justice to a society shaken by years of violence. The document was incomplete. Despite the wealth of information it provided on many of those who had been tortured and executed, *Nunca Más* left too much unanswered. It gave no explanation for how or why the country could have descended so quickly into such extreme violence. It offered no clarification of the motivations or decision-making of the military leadership, or the mechanisms by which society accepted the supplanting of legal and constitutional norms. More problematic still was that those who drafted the document insisted that this was the final word on a now-closed chapter in Argentine history. Because the human rights regime made sense only in the context of dictatorship, it seemed reasonable to some that with the end of the *proceso*, there should be no loose ends as far as crime and punishment were concerned. Each time a set of details trickled out and a better understanding of the dictatorship developed in the years that followed, Argentines found the information both welcome and troubling – troubling in part because the promise of *Nunca Más* as an end to the dictatorship was further undermined. In the mid-1990s, a handful of ex-soldiers stepped forward to provide evidence as to how the military had dumped live, drugged torture victims from airplanes into the Río de la Plata. The result was an outpouring of discussion, analysis, and artistic interpretation of these flights. The journalist Horacio Verbitsky wrote a book on the subject, while the rock group Bersuit released a song that spoke in the first person voice of a flight victim. The rocker Charly García planned a concert whose backdrop would be the dumping of simulated bodies into the Río de la Plata. It took the leader of the Mothers of the Plaza de Mayo to talk him out of the performance that in the view of some people would have exacerbated the cultural crisis of the dictatorship's unresolved legacy.[49]

Even though *Nunca Más* led in part to the conviction and imprisonment of a handful of top generals, the political and judicial systems of the new democracy could not bring justice for the majority. Dozens of reported incidents reminded Argentines that murderers and torturers walked among them. The journalist Jacobo Timerman and the writer Alicia Partnoy, both held and tortured during the dictatorship, were among many Argentines who ran into their former torturers on the streets of Buenos Aires. Far from being tense encounters, these meetings often showed the facility with which human rights violators lived and worked in post-1983 Argentina.

In late July 2000, a group of human rights activists came face-to-face with the torturer Julio "El Turco Julián Simón" in a downtown Buenos Aires café. El Turco was recognizable to the small crowd that surrounded him because the former soldier had made a career of appearing on television talk shows defending his actions during the recent dictatorship and dismissing as inconsequential the concerns of those who sought to prosecute human rights violators. In the café, the police arrived to save Simón from a violent beating by the crowd. For some, the fact that the crowd had confronted El Turco marked an important step forward for Argentine society, a metaphor for Argentina confronting its past. For others, the episode was a reminder that the country could not put its past to rest. Later, in the fall of that year, El Turco Julian was arrested and charged with crimes relating to his activities during the dictatorship. But why now? Though heartened by the arrest, many Argentines perceived the prosecution as a function of the café incident. Like the period of military rule itself, and in contrast to the more centralized and more hierarchical Chilean equivalent under Augusto Pinochet, Argentine justice has been and continues to be capricious and anarchic. The human rights regime established in the late 1970s continues to hold sway, unresolved and seemingly unable to integrate larger human rights problems that impact upon groups beyond the urban middle class.[50] In the 1990s, a new human rights activist group emerged composed principally of children of disappeared Argentines. HIJOS pioneered the *escrache,* an often impromptu, mass protest in front of the home of a suspected human rights violator. Far from reshaping the nation's human rights regime, HIJOS reinforced twenty-five year old perceptions of human rights problems.

To a certain extent, the persistence of the *proceso* human rights regime relates to the inability of post-dictatorship governments to set aside unresolved dictatorship cases of human rights violations. The thousands of foreign and domestic complaints about disappearances and torture during the dictatorship declined sharply after 1983, but did not end. In 1986, for example, the Argentine embassy in Switzerland reported that 791 people had signed complaints against the Argentine government with regard to the unresolved case of Mariana Zaffaroni-Islas, an 11 year old daughter of an Uruguayan refugees in Argentina who disappeared in September 1976. That same year, the Italian government asked the Alfonsín government for information on dozens of disappeared Italian citizens. The Armed Forces set about showing that a number of those supposedly listed as having been executed by the repressor Luciano B. Menéndez had, in fact, turned up in Mexico.[51]

Perhaps the most troubling indicator of the persistence of Argentina's *proceso* era human rights regime was the political success of Aldo Rico and Jorge Bussi. In the 1990s, the people of the poor, northwestern province of Tucumán elected retired General Jorge Bussi as their governor. Bussi had previously been the appointed military governor of the state during the recent dictatorship. In addition, human rights groups had produced evidence of his personal involvement in illegal arrests, torture, and assassinations. The election of an unrepentant Bussi was hardly a frivolous gesture. Clearly, for many poor Argentines the problem of a legacy of human rights abuses under military rule was far less important than other issues. Even so, the election highlighted profound social divisions that were now exacerbated in the context of a cultural crisis relating to human rights.

In another similar case, cashiered colonel Aldo Rico, a leader of the 1987 Easter Weekend uprising and an outspoken defender of military atrocities between 1976 and 1983 was elected mayor of a town in the province of Buenos Aires, then appointed to an important post in the provincial government. The elections of Rico and Bussi reflect the strength of a military ideology carefully constructed before 1984 as well as the rigidity and limitations of Argentina's human rights regime.

Notes

1 Carole Fink, *Marc Bloch: A Life in History* (Cambridge: Cambridge University Press, 1989), 112–113.
2 J.L. García *et al.*, *Fuerzas armadas argentinas: el cambio necesario* (Buenos Aires: Galerna, 1987), 45–53; Ernesto López, *Seguridad nacional y sedición militar* (Buenos Aires: Editorial Legasa, 1987), 55–77; Horacio Verbitsky, *La última batalla de la tercera guerra mundial* (Buenos Aires: Legasa, 1987); Alipio Paoletti, *Como los Nazis, como en Vietnam* (Buenos Aires: Contrapunto, 1987), 143–160.
3 Eduardo Ángel Russo, *Derechos humanos y garantías* (Buenos Aires: Plus Ultra, 1992), 57–60; Elías Neuman, *El abuso de poder en la Argentina* (Buenos Aires: Espasa Hoy, 1994), 56.
4 Asociación Madres de la Plaza de Mayo, *Massera el genocida* (Buenos Aires: Editorial La Página, 1998), 59; Lois Wilson, *Turning the World Upside Down* (Toronto: Doubleday, 1989), 91–92; Bill Fairbairn, "The Inter-Church Committee on Human Rights in Latin America," in Christopher Lind and Joe Mihevc, *Coalitions for Justice* (Ottawa: Novalis, 1994), 169–173.
5 "Proponer Establecimiento 'Unidad de Trabajo' Sobre Derechos Humanos," 5 July 1976, 149, Argentine Government Documents (AGD). See Hilda López Laval, *Autoritarismo y cultura* (Madrid: Espiral Hispano Americano, 1995).
6 Ezequiel F. Pereyra, Director of External Politics, Argentine Foreign Relations Ministry (MRE), "Entrevista del Director General de Política Exterior con S.E. el Embajador de Cuba," 24 April 1976, 479 AGD.
7 See for example Amnesty International, London, "Carta abierta de Amnistía Internacional a los Jefes de Delegación participantes en la XII Sesión Ordinaria de la Asamblea General de la Organización de los Estados Americanos," 21 October 1982.
8 SIDE, "Visita al país de representantes de la organización Amnesty International, entre el 5 y el 15 Nov. 1976," nd [1976], 4382; MRE, "Entrevista con el Secretario General de la OEA, Embajador Orfila, celebrada en Granada el 13 de junio de 1977; No. 1442, Jorge Aja Espil, Argentine Ambassador, Washington, to Foreign Ministry, 20 May 1977; No. 391, Ambassador Julio César Carasales, to Vicealmirante César Augusto Guzzetti, Foreign Minister, 26 April 1977, 4001, AGD.

9   Martin Ennals, Secretary General, Amnesty International, to Jorge Rafael Videla, de facto president, Argentina, 20 October 1976, 4382, AGD.

10 "Visita de representates de Amnesty International del 5 al 15 de noviembre de 1976," nd [1976], 4382, AGD.

11 MRE, Memorandum, 10 November 1976, 4382, AGD.

12 MRE, "Reunión con visitantes de Amnesty International," 8 November 1976, 4382, AGD.

13 Servicio de Inteligencia Naval, "Chile: R/Secretario Ejecutivo de la CDHA," 7 September 1979, 239, AGD.

14 CIDH, *Informe*, 1976 (doc. OEA, Ser. L/V/II 40 doc. 5 del 11 de febrero 1977).

15 "Campaña de Derechos Humanos," 1979, Ministry of the Interior, AGD; Daniel Barberis *et al.*, *Los derechos humanos en el 'otro país'* (Buenos Aires: Puntosur editores, 1987), 42–43.

16 "Aspectos Básicos para la Visita de la Comisión Interamericana para los Derechos Humanos" August 1979, Ministry of the Interior; Foreign Relations Minister to D. Andrés Aguilar M., President of the CIDH, 10 October 1978; Foreign Relations Minister to Lieutenant General Jorge Rafale Videla, 3 January 1978, 479, AGD; Elizabeth Jelin, "The Politics of Memory: The Human Rights Movement and the Construction of Democracy in Argentina," *Latin American Perspectives*, vol. 21 (1994): 38–58.

17 Albano E. Harguindeguy, Minister of the Interior, "Instrucciones a los Señores gobernadores e intendente municipal de la ciudad de Buenos Aires con motivo de la visita al país de la Comisión Interamericana de Derechos Humanos," 1978, Ministry of the Interior, 479, AGD.

18 *Ibid.*

19 Enrique I. Groisman, *La corte Suprema de Justicia durante la dictadura (1976–1983)* (Buenos Aires: CISEA, 1987), 35; Enrique I. Groisman, *Poder y derecho en el "Proceso de Reorganización Nacional"* (Buenos Aires: CISEA, 1983), 11–21; Jerry Knudson, "Veil of Silence: The Argentine Press and the Dirty War, 1976–1983," *Latin American Perspectives*, vol. 24 (November 1997): 93–112.

20 Ministry of the Interior, Memorandum, nd [1979]; Ministry of the Interior, "Entrevista con Secretario Vaky," March 1979, 479, AGD.

21 UN Human Rights Commission E/CN.4/SR.1603, 1981.

22 MRE, Sección de Edición de los documentos oficiales de las Naciones Unidas, 7 April 1981, 192, AGD.

23 MRE, Memorandum, nd, [1981], 192, AGD.

24 MRE, "La acción diplomática en el terreno de los derechos humanos," April 1980, 104, AGD.

25 No. 13, Barrios Peña to Washington Pastor, 12 March 1980; Washington Pastor to Barrios Peña, 21 April 1980, 104, AGD.

26 Ignacio Pico Estrada, "Apreciaciones sobre los hechos mas recientes de la política de los Estados Unidos de América en relación con el tema derechos humanos en la República Argentina," 25 July 1980, 104, AGD.

27 MRE, Departamento de Derechos Humanos, "Actualizar memorandum no. 8 de fecha 25 de julio de 1980 con apreciaciones sobre los hechos más recientes de la política de los Estados Unidos de América en relación con el tema derechos humanos en la República Argentina," 30 December 1980, 104, AGD.

28 MRE, "Respuesta del gobierno de la República Argentina a la Comisión de Derechos Humanos en materia de Comunicaciones sujetas al procedimiento

de la Resolución 1503 (XLVIII) del ECOSOC," 28 December 1979, 123, AGD.

29　Legislation cited included the Article 18 of the 1853 Constitution, Law 94 (1864), Article 144 of the Argentine Legal Code, and Federal Court decisions in Chaco (19 May 1964) and Entre Ríos (19 June 1969). MRE "Antecedentes Legislativos y Jurisprudenciales sobre condena de la tortura," 14 November 1980, AGD; Norma Fóscolo, *Los derechos humanos en la Argentina* (Mendoza: EDIUNC, 2000), 124–129.

30　No. 243, Argentine Mission Before the International Organizations, Geneva, to Secretary General, United Nations, 7 August 1978, 3132, AGD.

31　MRE, Misión Permanente de la República Argentina ante los Organismos Internacionales en Ginebra, Memorandum, 7 January 1981, 426, AGD.

32　MRE, Misión Permanente de la República Argentina ante los Organismos Internacionales en Ginebra, Memorandum, 7 January 1981, 381, AGD.

33　Asamblea Mundial Sobre el Envejecimiento, Discurso de la Delegación Argentina, August 1982, 3841, AGD.

34　Adolfo Tamini, Executive Secretary, Comisíon Ordenamiento Legislativo, Ministry of Justice, 27 March 1981, 3841, AGD.

35　"Recomendaciones a efectuar con relación al proyecto de `Convención Internacional sobre la Protección de los Derechos de Todos los Trabajadores Migratorios y de Sus Familias' aprobado provisionalmente por el grupo de trabajo," nd [1982], 3841, AGD.

36　SIDE, "Conexiones entre la BDS Montoneros y la Agencia Noticias I.P.S," May 1978, 1561, AGD.

37　MRE, Misión Permanente de la República Argentina, Naciones Unidas, "Campaña de Prensa Anti-Argentina," 16 April 1981, AGD.

38　MRE, Departamento de Europa Occidental, "Solicitud de la República Federal de Alemania con relación a tres personas detenidas," 22 September 1980, 104, AGD.

39　Wolf Grabendorff, "De país aliado preferido? Las relaciones entre la Argentina y los Estados Unidos: 1976–1981," El poder militar en la Argentina, 1976–1981, compiled by Peter Waldmann and Ernesto Garzón Valdéz (Buenos Aires: Editorial Galerna, 1983), 157–161; David Pion-Berlin, "The National Security Doctrine, Military Threat Perception, and the `Dirty War' in Argentina," *Comparative Political Studies*, vol. 21 (October 1988): 382–407.

40　Hugo Vezzetti, *Pasado y presente: guerra, dictadura y sociedad en la Argentina* (Buenos Aires: Siglo veintiuno editores Argentina, 2002), 24. See also Cathy Caruth, "Parting Words: Trauma, Silence and Survival," in Michael Rossington and Anne Whitehead, eds., *Between the Psyche and the Polis* (Burlington: Aldershot, 2000), 77–96; Lindsay DuBois, "Past, Place and Paint: A Neighborhood Mural Project in Suburban Buenos Aires," *Anthropologica*, vol. 39 (1997), 9; Linsay DuBois, "Valiant Ladies: Gendered Dispositions in Argentine Working Class Memories," *Social Analysis*, vol. 43 (1999), 20.

41　Juan Antonio Travieso, *Derechos humanos y jurisprudencia* (Buenos Aires: EUDEBA, 1998), 35–39; Jorge Reinaldo Vanossi, *La Constitución Nacional y los derechos humanos* (Buenos Aires: EUDEBA, 1985), 83–115.

42　See Alison Brysk, *The Politics of Human Rights in Argentina* (Stanford, CA: Stanford University Press, 1994); Raúl Veiga, *Las organizaciones de derechos humanos* (Buenos Aires: Centro Editor de América Latina, 1985); Juan Carlos Vega, *La justicia en la transición democrática argentina* (Córdoba:

Marcos Lerner, 1998); Carlos Santiago Nino, *Radical Evil on Trial* (New Haven, CT: Yale University Press, 1996).

43   Luis Roniger and Mario Sznajder, *The Legacy of Human-Rights Violations in the Southern Cone* (Oxford: Oxford University Press, 1999), 58–63; Andrew McAdam, Viktor Sukup and Claudio Oscar Katiz, *Raúl Alfonsín: La democracia a pesar de todo* (Buenos Aires: Corregidor, 1999), 66–71.

44   See for example, Alipio Paoletti, *Como los nazis, como en Vietnam* (Buenos Aires: Contrapunto, 1987); Horacio Verbitsky, *La última batalla de la tercera guerra mundial* (Buenos Airest: Legasa, 1984); J. L. García *et al.*, Fuerzas armadas argentinas: el cambio necesario (Buenos Aires: Galerna, 1987).

45   Daniel Barberis, *et al.*, *Los derechos humanos en el oro país* (Buenos Aires: Puntosur, 1987); Matilde Bruera, *SIDA, sistema penal y derechos humanos* (Buenos Aires: Homo Sapiens, 1997); Martín E. Vázqeuz Acuña, *Derechos humanos y sida* (Buenos Aires: EUDEBA, 1995). Buenos Aires, Oficina del Ombudsman, *El Ombudsman de la Ciudad de Buenos Aires y los derechos humanos* (Buenos Aires: Oficina del Ombudsman de la Ciudad de Buenos Aires, 1994).

46   Comisión Nacional Sobre la Desaparición de Personas, *Nunca Más: Informe de la CONADEP* (Buenos Aires: EUDEBA, 1985); Jorge L. Ubertalli *et al.*, *El complot militar: un país en obediencia debida* (Buenos Aires: Ediciones Dialéctica, 1987), 54–55; Salvador María Lozada, *Los derechos humanos y la impunidad en la Argentina (1974–1999)* (Buenos Aires: Nuevohacer, 1999), 141–148.

47   See Carlos J. Moneta, "El conflicto de las Islas Malvinas en el contexto de la política exterior argentina," *América Latina y la guerra del Atlántico sur: experiencias y desafíos*, compiled by Roberto Russell (Buenos Aires: Editorial de Belgrano, 1984), 1–59.

48   *Argentina: The Military Juntas and Human Rights* (London: Amnesty International Publications, 1987).

49   Horacio Verbitsky, *El vuelo* (Buenos Aires: Planeta, 1995).

50   Marguerite Feitlowitz, *A Lexicon of Terror: Argentina and the Legacies of Torture* (New York: Oxford University Press, 1998), 209–213.

51   No. 280/86, Argentine Embassy, Switzerland, to Dante Caputo, Minister of Foreign Relations, Argentina, 5 June 1986; Italian Embassy, Buenos Aires, to Caputo, 6 November 1986; Col. Timoteo Gordillo, Military Court Judge, to Maria Teresa Marciadri de Morini, Subsecretaria de Derechos Humanos, Foreign Ministry, 21 July 1986, 523, AGD.

11

EDUCATIONAL REFORMS IN TRANSITIONS TO DEMOCRACY
THE CASES OF CHILE, ARGENTINA AND PARAGUAY

Batia Siebzehner

In the process of social and political change, debates take place about educational reforms that challenge basic premises and goals of the educational system. During transition periods discussions arise regarding the causes of the countries' problems as well as the strategies of change and development concerning increased participation, strengthening of national identities, economic expansion and creation of greater equity. Educational reforms try to offer alternative visions and policies that require conscious consideration of change in the educational system. Most reforms stem from national laws and are promoted by the state itself, in the belief that it is working toward its own transformation. The state attaches to reform a critical role in the modification of social and economic conditions and in the consolidation of new regimes.

This paper analyzes the educational discourse of several Latin American countries in transition to democracy. The main argument of this paper is that new notions, ideas, practices and contents concerning the change of education systems, formulated by policy makers and intellectuals, reflected existing institutional characteristics. Prevailing political conflicts and institutional characteristics also influenced the mode of accomplishment of reforms and the extent of their impact. In other words, trends and tendencies regarding state, economy and civil society that distinguished different regimes before transition to democracy shaped the role of education and mode of implementation of new ideas and policies. Argentina, Chile and Paraguay, three different regimes that went through a process of democratization and adopted similar educational notions will be compared. The paper focuses on the first steps of the transition, illuminating the initiatives towards the world of education while shaping democracies.

Towards new educational proposals

Intellectual, political and economic currents sweeping over national boundaries shaped changes in the educational field. Most proposals elaborated in Latin America during the '80s and '90s by agents of the new regimes were inspired by similar sources, mainly paradigms from Europe and the USA (Braslavsky, 1999). The adopted models suggested ideas of decentralization and competitiveness as central objectives while upholding concepts of commitment to democratic participation and equity. The prescriptions that emerged from adopting such notions in a changing reality recognized the immanent tensions between equality and competitiveness, consensus and autonomy, universalism and the different nature of social groups (Coraggio, 1993). The similarity of principles guiding reforms was explained by the "regional tendencies" approach, related to the effects of global economy in the educational system (Braslavsky, 1999; Tedesco and Schiefelbein, 1995), and by the "domination" approach, namely neo-colonialism and cultural domination exercised by international agencies (Coraggio, 1997; Martinez Boom, 2000). Another suggestion was that the "Latin American educational discourse" created a closed discursive frame that inspired common ideas, while limiting the production of *other* ideas and practices (Beech, 2002).

In Argentina, Chile and Paraguay transitions to democracy aimed to reestablish the rule of law, respect for human rights, to restore civil society, change economic markets, hold elections, and build political and other institutions. In all these spheres of action change was preceded by a hierarchic military regime that retained prerogatives while imposing conditions on the transitional political process (Linz and Stepan, 1996). However, Chile had a stronger democratic tradition and institutionalized party system than Argentina, which underwent several democratic experiments intercalated with military regimes. Paraguay had no experience with political democracy. These three countries had weak civil societies that gave the state and political elite great autonomy, Paraguay being the most extreme case (Oxhorn and Ducatenzeiler, 1999). Chile avoided the populism and the extreme politicization of the state that characterized Argentina, while in Paraguay clientelism and corruption shaped the functioning of the repressive military regime. The three countries had, albeit at different rates, high income inequality and regressive public expenditure. Education, like other policies designed to develop human resources, suffered from budget cuts mostly due to government budget deficits (Williamson, 1990c; CEPAL, 1988).

Economic and political liberalization was ruled by contrasting social logics. In Chile, privatization, deregulation and open economy preceded democratization. In Argentina, economic liberalization and the consolidation of democracy took place more or less at the same time (Waisman, 1999), while in Paraguay, the idea of political liberalization preceded any idea of economic liberalization. The opposed logics of transition received institutional expressions in most social spheres as well as in the educational discourse. In all three countries there were discussions concerning the expected role of education in shaping the new rules of the game and in all of them proposals reflected opposing orientations. Chile began a program of compensatory policies and later on developed a change in the plan of studies. Paraguay proposed a change in the national curriculum without formulating a Law of Education.

Educational projects formulated at the beginning of transition, reiterated the belief in the power of education to consolidate the new regimes. Government and elites agreed that knowledge, organized around new contents and methods, could stimulate new ideas, attitudes and practices that would create new subsystems capable of communicating future goals and serving as linkages between existing and new structures. The projects expressed new visions and formulated policies capable (as declared in the conference of Ministers of Education) of dealing with "poverty, hunger, political instability, and social imbalances" and of changing relations between social, economic, cultural and political spheres. Many of these orientations echoed modernization perspectives, which assumed that education could contribute to sustained economic growth and stabilize political democracy (Kohli, 1993; Leftwich, 1993). From this perspective, the educational discourse was about equal opportunities, strengthening national identity, producing cultural consensus, expanding pre-school education, teaching and developing science and technology. Issues dealing with social and political integration of groups were redefined in societal categories and sectors with the potential of creating new modes of inclusion. Discourse on reforms attempted to integrate some ideas that characterized the "second wave" of world reforms and included interrelations between different institutions involved in the educational sector. A salient characteristic of the new tendencies implied creation of mechanisms for evaluating and controlling institutional models and practices (Popkewitz and Pereyra, 1994). In most cases, agents involved in elaborating reforms immediately adopted the jargon without, however, clarifying the role of the state in its relation to society or how to deal with state reform and modernization (Garreton, 1999). The omission was evident in educational laws and proposals at the end of the 90s as will be shown below.

The structures of transitional projects in Chile, Paraguay and Argentina included similar aspects:

1. Diagnosis of economic underdevelopment, social inequalities and political instability (over-stability, in the case of Paraguay). This type of analysis, presented in the different educational programs, implied the acceptance of a modern vision that attributed to education the capacity of transforming relations between different social spheres. The discourse delineated the expected contribution of the components of the educational system to the changing future. Curricular changes and the teachers' new roles were elaborated according to goals capable of producing labor market competencies.

2. The discursive practice in Chile and Argentina reflected new concepts of possible modes of power distribution in the educational realm. The programs imparted to the state an active role in the administrative and economic regulation of the educational system, while supporting the autonomy of schools in defining their own pedagogic strategies. These differential trends were related to the adoption of models of decentralization that implied a movement from the state to the provinces in Argentina and from the states to the local councils in Chile. Although they faced very dissimilar decentralization reforms, which took place within two different sets of regulatory frameworks, they achieved similar results in the socio-economic field. (Narodowski and Nores, 2002). In Paraguay the issue of decentralization was much more marginal than in the other two countries.

3. The educational discourse reflected new concepts of participation and authority. According to most proposals, groups representing diverse population sectors were expected to take an active role in the advancement and regulation of education. This trend, although differently applied in each country, implied a break with concepts and mechanisms regulating educational policies under authoritarian regimes; all countries legitimized schools as sources of self-regulation and direction, although they still prescribed goals, contents and teaching methods.

4. Transforming authoritarianism entailed the introduction of systems and procedures capable of creating a social space where groups accepting common meanings, could negotiate their demands. Hence, in all three countries reforms discourse dealt with issues of consensus-building and social democratization aimed at consolidating collective action (Ratlif, 1999).

5. In all three countries, as in most of Latin American countries, reformative trends reflected the recommendations of several international agencies such as the United Nations, the Organization of American States, the World Bank and the International Monetary Fund. Under such influences the organization of the educational systems internalized symbols and practices that characterize modern markets (Brunner, 1994).

6. In Argentina, Chile and Paraguay, transitional governments named committees to develop new notions and policies; groups representing civil society activists sent representatives: teachers' union delegates, intellectuals, priests and clerics, community groups, government officials, school heads, parents and students. The formulation of educational reforms by different groups ensured that all actors would contribute concepts stemming from their specific frameworks and interests resulting at the end of the process in common collective action strategies. None of the political groups struggled for imposing a hegemonic educational project. The idea was that the proposed plan would be the result of an agreement achieved among all consultation groups. Proposals were expected to reflect their constituencies and result in different versions of democratic states (Braslavsky and Gvirtz, 2000).

While the three countries were influenced by similar models, their respective projects as expressed in symbols, images and practices were different; in other words each country created an education system reflecting its own preexisting tendencies and characteristics, as will be seen in the case analyses below.

Chile: a pact for continual changes

In 1988, after fifteen years in power, the army was united; the authoritarian regime had a solid core of supporters in civil society, and the president, General Pinochet, planned to rule by constitution for at least another decade. However, in the plebiscite he received only 44 percent of the votes (and not the 50.1 he needed). Subsequently, following the 1989 presidential election, power was transferred to President Patricio Aylwin. He was head of the "Concertacion" of Parties for Democracy, a coalition of center and left-wing political parties. Pinochet remained as Commander-in-Chief of the Armed Forces until 1998 at which point he briefly entered the Senate, as stipulated in the1980 constitution. During the first phase of transition, parties agreed to begin government with important parts of the authoritarian regime's constitution still in effect. This was considered as one of the most controlled transitions to democracy in Latin America (Munck 1994; Portales, 2000). The incoming democratic government had to share power *de jure* with individuals and institutions whose bases had no democratic origin, leading researchers to attribute an unchanging nature to the state, beyond its institutional apparatus (Barton, 2002; Moulian, 1997).

In August 1991 the elected president announced that the Chilean transition had been completed and the new task was to consolidate democracy. Backed by a coalition of a coherent majority, the government was able to formulate and implement a set of programs in all areas (Linz and Stepan, 1996). Some programs, rather than seeking a rupture with the authoritarian regime, appeared as part of "a strategy of continuity" (Barton and Murray, 2002). In the educational realm Chile's military government launched in 1980 a profound reform based on market competition (Munck, 1994). The reform aimed to promote efficiency through administrative decentralization, per-capita financing, labor deregulation and open competition between public and privately administered schools. The regime's education authorities decided to decentralize the administration of state schools by turning them over to municipal governments. Presumably, schools would become more responsive to local demands and needs, although the Ministry of Public Education continued to issue basic curricula guidelines, approve textbooks, and control certification of teachers. By the end of 1988, the proportion of students in state-run schools (by then under municipal control) had dropped to 60 percent, private state-subsidized school enrollment rate increased to 33 percent, and fully private schools continued to enroll 7 percent of the students. Other data suggested that the number of primary and secondary students in private schools increased from 27 percent in 1981 to 56 percent in 1986. The authorities also transferred administration of the state's vocational, industrial, and agricultural schools to employer associations, although public funding of these schools continued (Arellano Marin, 2001; Eyzaguirre and LeFoulon, 2001; MINEDUC, 1999).

The ambiguities and inconsistencies that characterized the plans and programs of the military regime allowed reinterpretation and acceptance of new ideas, without necessarily detaching themselves from past practices. Proposals of the new regime in the 90s did not break away from authoritarian government policies, but followed premises of modernity and development introduced by the military. In Aylwin's words in 1989 "The institutions of state have a mission to guarantee the historical continuity of the nation" (La Epoca, 16 December, quote by Barton and Murray, 2002). The idea of the market as a quasi entity regulating relations between groups, and the emphasis on "individuals" as carriers of change, hinted at continuity in structure and means of both regimes rather than re-conceptualization of education (Magendzo, 1988; Munck, 2001). The changes allowed complementary sources of school funding from the private sector, parents or tax-deductible donations. In the privately subsidized sectors and in the municipal schools students results improved, narrowing differences between them (Narodowsky and Nores, 2002).

The proposals of the transitional regime supported the idea of decentralization as a mechanism to promote coverage, quality and equity in education. Two very important changes were introduced in the organiz-ation of the educational system: a system of subsidies to finance private education and the transfer to municipalities of all educational establish-ments belonging to the central government. The proposals gave the state (Ministry of Education) the responsibility of paying a monthly fee for every student attending classes in a municipal or private school chosen by his parents. The policy of subsidies, which shares some commonalities with "the voucher system" known in other countries, has a long-standing tradition in Chile. Ever since the nineteenth century, private schools have received assistance from the government (Parry, 1997). During the twen-tieth century different measures were introduced to assure continuity of the system. In the1980's the financial support per pupil attending class was set at a uniform level. The educational plan followed international organizations (mainly the World Bank) that encouraged decentralization as an institutional mechanism converging with market mechanisms (Impacto, 1999). The discourse under the military regime had already emphasized education as an instrument for building competitive human capital and promoting social mobility. The Aylwin government doubled funding for education by 1992, and adopted a new educational strategy aimed at reorienting public investment toward greater quality and equity, while maintaining most of the previous administrative and funding frame-work. Administration of primary and secondary schools systems remained to a large extent in the hands of local governments, with ongoing efforts to provide increased funding to poorer municipalities and regions. These policies show a consistency between proposal and mode of implementation, unlike the Argentinean case, where more inconsistencies were detected.

The Aylwin administration maintained the free-market model inherited from the military, but launched a program to invest in human capital, which would promote long-term growth. The government argued that economic growth was a necessary, but not sufficient condition for achieving greater equality in Chile. In addition to political goals, the administration was interested in enhancing social democratization, epit-omized in the notion of "growth with equity". Thus, it proposed to continue policies promoting economic growth and stability, to be comple-mented with social policies designed to achieve greater equality. Emphasis on equity did not stem from an ethical concern for social justice; it was based on the idea that equity was important for the consolidation of Chile's newborn democracy. Although the program increased the complexity of the role of the state, it indicated a pragmatic attitude about the role of education rather than an evaluative or ideological approach. Reformulation of the state's role in the process of change did not mani-fest itself in tension between authoritarianism and democracy in matters concerning the bases of legitimacy; the Constitutional Law of Education

(1990) did not mention the word "democracy"; it referred to the contribution of education to reframing national identity and preparing the individual for improved "active participation in the community."

The term "community" introduced by advocates of change had a different meaning from that elaborated in Paraguay. To promote the idea of deregulation that characterized the Chilean transition, distinct communities were organized around specific problems. Each educational community had to define its own project on the basis of its particular diagnosis. Accordingly, despite state regulation, the teaching team was autonomous enough to design appropriate actions for students, lay down objectives, deadlines and evaluation strategies as well as innovative teaching and management methods. Such dynamic approach contributed to shape the educational discourse as a site for "continual changes" contributing to its ability to mobilize consistent political support from all levels of the democratic coalition government. Only later on, during the Frei government, were the educational changes presented in terms of "reform", and the discourse elaborated premises that emphasized the limited role of the state in the process.

Argentina: a space for generalized goals

In Argentina, the military government that ruled from 1976 to 1983 and created more authoritarian situations than an institutionalized regime, marked the transition to democracy. The military held elections in October 1983; in December 1983 Raul Alfonsin, of the Radical Party, was inaugurated as Argentina's new president[1]. He was followed by Carlos Menem of the Peronist Party in June 1989. In contradistinction to Chile, where a political pact existed, in Argentina there were few agreed-upon restrictions and a weak, almost inexistent, pact among political parties that participated in the transition (Linz and Stepan, 1996). Educational proposals defined broad goals without clear principles of implementation, revealing a narrow range of consensus concerning the political and social basis upon which the reforms were to be based. The ongoing discourse attributed the crisis of the state to conflicting tendencies and disagreements about modes of participation in society and lack of agreement about state priorities and preferences.

Public debate was a central strategy in redesigning educational policy. These debates resulted in programs and methods to be implemented in the educational system, which until then had been unable to meet the challenges of the new situation. Formal committees attempted to identify the causes that brought about the need for profound institutional change in the educational system. Analysis of the discourse shows that most causes were presented in functional rather than evaluative terms; similar to the

Chilean case, this did not mean de-legitimizing or ignoring the previous military regime and its policies, on the contrary, " . . . contribution of the past is considered very important for reaffirming the common basis of the entire nation". (Bases para la transformacion educativa, 1991: 11).

The desire to strengthen consensus and increase participation was manifested in the Pedagogical Congress in which various social groups, local, provincial and national assemblies participated. The Congress lasted from 1984 to 1988 and discussed contents and planning, attempting to create a wider basis of agreement among participants. Many of their arguments were translated into the Federal Education Law, passed in 1993, the first law in the history of the country that regulated all areas of the educational system.[2] However, beyond matters of design, the Law did not reflect widespread popular participation nor did it define a strong basis of common goals (Braslavsky and Tiramonti, 1990). It emphasized the importance of " . . . national unity and the need to enhance national consensus for consolidating democracy and achieving social solidarity". (Ley Federal de Educacion, art.6, b). The Law also included broad concepts of decentralization and equity but left details of implementation to provincial authorities (Pini and Ciglutti, 1999); this made it difficult to understand the role of the state in the regulation of the process of change. For example the Law recommended scholarships for poor students with special academic or artistic talents, but it did not identify funding sources (Hanson. 1996).

Consistent with its desire to increase participation, the Congress promoted educational community as a primary force of social mobilization, and called on it to participate in the governance of schools. Families and schools were considered agents capable of institutionalizing participation. However the mode of their involvement, the support and regulation offered by the system were vaguely defined. Tiramonti (1989) argued that the ambiguity of scope and content of participation convinced administrators to go along with the reform, since no significant redistribution of power was spelled out.

In a country characterized by opposing and conflicting interpretations of collective identity, the consolidation of democracy depends, *inter alia*, on the existence of a pluralistic political culture and the development of an effective state. In such a context, education can be considered an integrative mechanism capable of reconstructing common boundaries while maintaining diversity. This ability was translated in the educational realm by a quest for unity – not necessarily cultural homogeneity – while respecting regional diversities, historical and cultural peculiarities (Braslavsky and Gvirtz, 2000). The proposed programs considered "cultural diversity and richness of our country" as one of the prime goals of education, while maintaining an inclusive framework for the construction of the collective identity (see Alfonsin statement, 1988 and Menem's

"Unidad Nacional y Transformacion Educativa", 1991). The translation of broad goals into practice requires definition of a common denominator concerning contents and specific guidelines on how the cultural and social distinctiveness of various groups should be manifested in the national framework. The proposals failed to address the course of action for shaping and legitimizing attributes of minorities. Recognition and representation of diversity implied that the geographical framework, rather than other fundamental characteristics, would serve as the base line for both unity and pluralism, thus emptying the concept of pluralism of content, since minorities do not necessarily live in concentrated areas. A rhetorical emphasis on multiple identities implied an attempt to avoid "preconceived scenarios" (Braslavsky, 1999).

Menem's government assumed that the state's effectiveness could be improved by a well-elaborated national policy defining educational activities capable of bringing about structural transformation. The state "has to define the political lines of the scientific, cultural and educational activities . . . for achieving the goals of the productive revolution in the process of national development . . . (Menem, 1989: 35); " . . . it is the state's responsibility for the common good that allows constructing educational institutions as means for advancing justice for the entire population."(A. Van Gelderen en homenaje a McKay Bs As 1990). The same proposals, however, did not deal with the institutional means capable of assuring more equitable modes of sharing economic resources between the various areas of the country, leaving the proposals in the realm of recommendations.

According to premises of liberal democracy, effectiveness entailed reduction in size and power of the state and a policy of decentralization that required a redefinition of relations between the state and different sectors of the population. From an institutional point of view, this implied redefining relations between the state and the provinces, a process begun under the military regime, which transferred most primary schools and a large portion of secondary schools to the provinces and municipalities. Since 1979, under the military regime, the " Consejo Federal de Cultura y Educacion" was in charge of planning, coordinating and counseling the implementation of the gradual transference of the national schools. (Tedesco, Braslavsky and Carciofi, 1987: 111). The Pedagogic Committee dealing with educational reforms during transition was convinced that bureaucratic centralization of the national system and the narrow space for manifestation of regional differences paralyzed social initiatives. Decentralization became a device to encourage institutionalization of autonomous arrangements, implying that different units had to assume responsibility about educational outputs (Acevedo, 2001). During the first stages of transition the primary education system was under provincial jurisdiction while secondary and vocational education remained mostly under the national Ministry of Education, which was supposed to transfer authority gradually to local units (Vieytes and Zanga de Ravinale, 1995).

The proposed modes of regulation differed from those in other countries adopting decentralization policies where state regulation became marginal and allowed influence of other groups (Popkewitz, 1996). The model elaborated by people working to consolidate democracy in Argentina assumed a strong involvement of central government in prescribing guidelines yet did not specify its role. Bargaining among units was regulated by the state, in charge of "orienting, evaluating and facilitating the exercise of responsibilities that it proposed to schools." (Jerarquizacion de la escuela . . . 1990: 23). The state guideline aimed to avoid atomization and "to preserve among teachers and students their sense of belonging to one educational system . . . " (Idem: 18). Although the laws establishing the different modes of negotiation between the provinces and the Ministry allowed certain degrees of flexibility while emphasizing education governance as a federal rather than a national entity, they limited the possibility of a cohesive planning (Tiramonti, 1988); self-definition of school purposes was expressed in generalized goals, not in specific aims. For example, the Federal Education Law allotted a budget increase of 20% of the GNP in five years, but did not point out the source of this substantial amount.

The idea of participation in Latin America in general and in Argentina in particular was conceived as access to education (Garreton, 1999). The educational discourse proposed extension of participation through practices that assumed inclusion of all community agents, while creating conditions for free choice by individuals who would encounter a wide range of opportunities (Seminario, 1992). The reformist perspective viewed education as capable of creating links that help increase solidarity and maintain "the substantive unity of the system". Educational agents, the family, the local community, labor organizations, businessmen and others were expected to create networks sustaining a strong commitment to the nation. Access to knowledge was thus identified not only as a developmental tool but also as a mode of extending solidarity between teachers, students and the entire community. This tendency was manifested, for example, in proposals dealing with the introduction and extension of investigation and information. One of the main topics at the "National seminar about education and information" in 1992 was investigation as a tool facilitating educational change through the creation of a framework consolidating horizontal relations between researchers, teacher-researchers, officials, students and parents. The proposals assumed that a common basis of knowledge in the community would create a local focus of decision-making and evaluation of the educational process. Furthermore, it was assumed that the production and diffusion of information through a participatory framework could contribute to the development of expressive and instrumental bases capable of creating the need and the feeling for sharing. The idea implicit in the discourse was that the process of creation of knowledge would be transformed into an attitude encouraging political action thus transforming symbolism into reality (Seminario, 1992). However, participatory arrangements preserved some characteristics of the corporate model, namely that the state coordinates activities with different bodies in the community such as teachers, the Army, the Church, industrial and business sectors, political movements etc. For example, during elaboration and implementation of the reforms, the Church and political parties constantly pressed to have representatives with key roles in the system. This mode of participation opened the system to short-term influences of officials who left office with unfinished projects, thus increasing instability in the senior ranks (Hanson, 1996).

Expectations of change in the new political order were not limited to organizational reforms in the educational realm, which was also considered capable of ensuring national independence and political sovereignty. New horizons were built on a broader perception that attempted to establish moral and cultural bases upon which the new regime would act. Proposals and programs from the "periphery" were designed to change the country's place in the international arena. The belief was that in that process a strong commitment to the Argentinean collective would develop and this would liberate the country from the marginal position where history had placed it (Ley Federal de Educacion. 1993). Plans focused on the need to protect Argentina 's independence and internal stability, to develop the country's economy and to free it from external influences so as to enable it to find its independent path and rightful place in the world. The discourse did not de-legitimize the authoritarian regime or the internal forces supporting it; external powers were viewed as unfriendly entities, obstacles and menacing forces against which the country had to defend itself. Inequality was attributed to external dependence and economic dependency was extended to the political, social and cultural realms. Since education was perceived as a practical instrument for strengthening national identity, the "nation" became an important axis around which knowledge had to be organized. In this framework, the critical sense, achieved through rational logic (an idea implicit in modern pedagogy), was designed to develop the provisions for limiting the penetration of foreign ideologies that promote domination and destroy national independence.

Paraguay: Reframing Social Inclusion

Paraguay presents a unique case. From 1954 to 1989 the State was identified with General Stroessner and the Colorado Party apparatus. Before Stroessner the country operated in an almost chaotic state, hence he was credited with unifying the nation while consolidating his own political position. The regime succeeded in creating a strong sense of collective identity while limiting participation and sustaining political integration through the exclusion of popular sectors. In such a structure of power and inequality, the educational system operated on a concept of nationality that went beyond particularities and differences thus reducing public debate concerning the role of education.

The *coup d'état* led by General Rodriguez in 1989 ousted General Stroessner and offered a unique case of political liberalization initiated by a section of the army, a segment within the regime itself (Linz and Stepan, 1995). Processes of change in neighboring countries, in Spain and other European countries emphasized democracy as the most viable alternative for change. Since Paraguay had no democratic tradition, history was no source of inspiration for a reconstruction process. In contrast with Argentina and Chile, where national and provincial constitutions were significant in policy regulation (although put aside by the military whenever convenient), Paraguay knew only a hierarchical, command-and-control structure of governance. Establishing democracy implied elaboration of new concepts and creation of new structures to implement mobilizing policies (Arditi, 1992; Miranda, 1990).

In Paraguay, as in Chile and Argentina, a committee created by the new government made in charge of the Educational Reform. Aside from technical collaboration with US University of Harvard to prepare the diagnosis, the committee opened the floor to a variety of groups at the regional and national levels. The formation of the council was accompanied by political tensions, manifesting Paraguay's social cleavages. Due to public opinion pressure (a new phenomenon in the Paraguayan context), thousands of citizens were invited to participate in the council. Considering the lack of tradition of public debates, participants in the process had difficulties in developing a dialogue based on consensus. A reduced committee attempted to formulate educational goals, detaching themselves from the party and ministry guidelines, creating broader liberal public discourse. The Colorado Party reacted immediately by changing the main actors with others more loyal to existing principles of social and political order. The discourse reflected the idea that "educational policy concerns the state", a line of thought that legitimized continuation of state control in all areas of education (Interview, 1993).

Like in other Latin American countries, reforms in Paraguay attributed to the state an important role in defining goals, policies and orienting administrative and curricular contents. The expected functions were defined as regulations, attaining diversity and controlling educational outputs. Regulations included practical considerations dealing with technological development and modes of productivity and the search for " .. . new roads of training for work and productivity" (Montero Tirado, J.S.I., 1993). The idea of the state's role was not redefined in the proposals. When discussing intervention, the manner of dismantling the repressive state was not mentioned and, as in the other countries studied, educational discourse assumed the option for democracy without de-legitimating the former regime.

Educational discourse emphasized a 'logic of identity' according to which the main problems of the country were attributed to fragmentation of the population and the exclusion of the indigenous majority from the process of change and modernization. Collective goals were reframed in terms of inclusion, emphasizing primary criteria as a central mark of membership. In the words of Wasmosy, the first president after the fall of Stroessner, education was considered the means for "widening the basis of participation in the national enterprise". In this design, bilingualism was proposed as a central device facilitating the absorption of marginal groups into the state organization. Article 140 in the Constitution promulgated in 1992 by the elected government established that "Paraguay is a bilingual and multi-cultural country". Discourse emphasized implementation of a bilingual program, which would have a crucial role in eliminating illiteracy, dropout, and absenteeism that was crippling the educational system especially in rural areas. One of the assumptions behind these proposals was that teaching the Guarani child in his own language would facilitate learning Spanish, thereby simplifying access to the public sphere, achieving academic and technical preparation and competence in the international market (Reforma, 1992). The use of Guarani as a symbolic device for social inclusion was meant to avoid instilling abstract values such as development, advancement and productivity, which were alien to the indigenous culture. The National Congress of Education reinforced the role of the state in advancing the linguistic policy arguing that "the linguistic body of the Guarani needs state support for avoiding conflicts between two modes of planning" (Corvalan, 1991).

Emphasizing the role of community in the process of educational change further enhanced the role of the state. Unlike Chile, where the role of the community came to life in practical and immediate terms, proposals in Paraguay, strongly influenced by the Church, enhanced the role of the community as a key agent in ensuring advancement of the common good. The political communities were perceived as ideal entities for the development of individual and collective action. Encouragement of participation in collective formations comprising the entire community thereby renewed one of the crucial goals traditionally associated with the state. In addition to winning the good will of the people, it implied control of disintegrative forces, enhancement of transcendental aims and harmony of the entire community. This approach to restructuring frameworks of participation were similar to those established by the authoritarian regime, where unity was identified with unanimity, a trend that limited diversifying forces from impinging on institutional arrangements and in the construction of national identity.

Conclusions

The discourses elaborated in Chile, Argentina and Paraguay during the transition to democracy were influenced by paradigms that presented new goals and practices in the educational realm. The new programs promoted ideas meant to modernize the educational system, create wider basis of social consensus, reduce inequality and diminish state involvement in daily activities. Reforms were considered effective for improving the structure of the educational system and consolidating a new social order. A first reading of the new programs points to similarities in basic assumptions underlying the reformative texts in the three countries. A "second reading", in Bourdieu's words (1992), points to differences emerging from the mode of interpreting the initial concepts and assumptions. The comparative analysis presented here shows that differences stemmed from institutional characteristics prevailing in each of the countries analyzed. Without resorting to the specific constellations that influenced implementation of new programs, the analysis of the educational discourse shows that reforms are not necessarily factors of change, but on the contrary, can contribute to strengthening several non-democratic orientations and practices of regimes seemingly in transition to democracy.

Notes

1 Since 1946 this was the first time that a non-Peronist candidate won the elections.
2 From 1894 to 1993 Argentina operated under the same "organic law", which structured the educational system. Attempts to change the law in 1918, 1939, 1946, 1969, 1974–75 and 1979 failed.

References

Acevedo, C. 2001 *Secondary Education Reforms: Responding to Demands for Equity, Quality and Relevance*. Pittsburgh: Institute for International Studies in Education.
Arditti, B. 1992 *Adiós a Stroessner. La reconstrucción de la política en el Paraguay*. Asunción: RP Ediciones.

229

Arellano Marin, J.P. 2001 "Educational reform in Chile", *CEPAL Review*, 73: 81–91.

Barton, J. R. and W.E. Murray 2002 "The end of transition? Chile 1990–2000" *Bulletin of Latin American Research*, 21,3: 329–338.

Beech, J. 2002 "Latin American education: perceptions of linearities and the construction of discursive space" *Comparative Education*, 38, 4: 415–427.

Bourdieu, P., and L. J. D. Wacquant 1992. *An Invitation to Reflexive Sociology*. Chicago: Chicago University Press.

Braslavsky, C. 1999 *Re-haciendo escuelas*. Hacia un nuevo paradigma en la educación latinoamericana. Buenos Aires: Santillana.

Braslavsky, C. y G. Tiramonti 1990 *Conducción educativa y calidad de enśenanza*. Buenos Aires: Ed Mino y Dávila.

Braslavsky, C. and S. Gvirtz 2000 "Nuevos desafios y dispositivos en la política educacional latinoamericana de fin de siglo" en M. Puelles Benítez (coord.) *Política y educación en Iberoamérica*. Cuadernos de la OEI. Educación Comparada, 4: 41–72.

Brunner, J.J. 1994 *Bienvenidos a la modernidad*. Planeta: Santiago.

CEPAL (Comisión Económica para América Latina y el Caribe) 1988 *Equidad, transformación social y democracia en America Latina*. Mimeo. Santiago:United Nations

Coraggio, J.L. 1993 *Economía y educación en America Latina: Notas para una agenda de los 90's*. Santiago: CEAAL.

Coraggio, J.L. 1997 "Educational policy and human development in the Latin America city" in Torres, C.A. and A. Puiggrós (eds.) *Latin American Education: Comparative Perspectives*. Boulder, CO: Westview Press.

Corvalán G. 1995 *Bilingüalismo y comunicacion*. Asunción: Seminario Nacional sobre Bilingüalismo.

Eyzaguirre, B. and C. Le Foulon 2001 "La calidad de la educación chilena en cifras" *Estudios Públicos*, 84: 85–204.

Garreton, M.A. 1999 "Social and economic transformations in Latin America: the emergence of a new political matrix?" Pp. 61–77 in Oxhorn, P. and P.K. Starr(eds.) *Markets and Democracy in Latin America: Conflict or Convergence?* Boulder: Lynne Reinner Publishers.

Hanson, E.M. 1996 "Educational change under autocratic and democratic governments: the case of Argentina" *Comparative Education*, 32, 3: 303–317.

Interview in 1993 with a high-ranking member of the Colorado Party at the Ministry of Education.

Kohli, A. 1993 "Democracy and economic orthodoxy: trends in developing countries", *Third World Quarterly*, 14, Nov: 671–689.

Leftwich, A. 1993 "Governance, democracy and development in the Third World", *Third World Quarterly*, 14, 3: 605–624.

Linz J.J. and A. Stepan, 1996 *Problems of Democratic Transition and Consolidation. Southern Europe, South America and Post-Communist Europe*. Baltimore: The Johns Hopkins University Press.

Magendzo, A. 1988 *Desarrollo de las normativas curriculares bajo el régimen militar (1973–1987): un análisis crítico*. Santiago: Academia de Humanismo Cristiano.

Martínez Boom, A. 2000 "Políticas educativas en Iberoamerica" en M. Puelles

Benítez (coord.) *Política y educación en Iberoamérica*. Cuadernos de la OEI. Educación Comparada, 4: 73–26.

Miranda, C.R. 1990 Paraguay y la era de Stroessner. Asunción: RP Ediciones.

Montero Tirado, J. S.I. 1993 "La escuela como instrumento del poder" *Diario Opinión*, 13 enero.

Moulian, T. 1997 *Chile actual: anatomía de un mito*. LOM ARSIS: Santiago.

Munck, G.L. 1994 "Authoritarianism, modernization, and democracy in Chile" *Latin American Research Review*, 29, 2:188–211.

Narodowski, M. and M Nores 2002 "Socio-economic segregation with (without) competitive education policies. A comparative analysis of Argentina and Chile" *Comparative Education*, 38, 4: 429–451.

Oxhorn. Ph. And G. Ducatenzeiler, 1999 ""The problematic relation between economic and political liberalization: some theoretical considerations" pp. 13–42 in Oxhorn, P. and P.K. Starr (eds.) *Markets and Democracy in Latin America: Conflict or Convergence?* Boulder: Lynne Reinner Publishers.

Parry, T.R. 1997 "Theory meets reality in the education voucher debate: some evidence from Chile". *Education Economics*, 5,3: 307–331.

Pini, M. and S. Ciglutti 1999 "Participatory reforms and democracy: the case of Argentina" *Theory and Practice*, 38,4: 196–205.

Popkewitz, T.S. y M.A. Pereyra 1994 "Estudio comparado de las prácticas contemporáneas de reforma de la formación del profesorado en ocho países: configuración de la problemática y construcción de una metodología comparativa" Pp. 15–91 en T. S. Popkewitz (compilador) *Modelos de poder y de regulación social en pedagogía*. Barcelona: Ediciones Pomares-Corredor.

Popkewitz, T.S. 1996 "Rethinking decentralization and state/civil society distinctions: the state as a problematic of governing" *Journal of Educational Policy*, II,1: 27–51.

Portales, F. 2000 *Chile: una democracia tutelada*. Santiago: Sudamericana.

Ratlif, W. 1999 "Development and civil society in Latin America and Asia", *Annals of the American Academy of Political and Social Science*, 565: 91–112.

Reforma educativa, compromiso de todos. informe de avance del consejo asesor de la reforma educativa. Asunción: Fundación en Alianza.

República Argentina. Ministerio de Educación y Justicia. 1988 *Discursos del presidente de la Nación Dr. Raúl Ricardo Alfonsín en el centenario de la muerte de Domingo Faustino Sarmiento*. Buenos Aires

——. Ministerio de Educación y Justicia 1989 *Unidad nacional y transformación educativa*. Discursos del Sr. Presidente de la Nación Dr. Carlos Saúl Menem. Buenos Aires.

——. Ministerio de Educación y Justicia 1991 *Programa: transformación de la educación secundaria*. Documento Base. Buenos Aires.

——. Ministerio de Cultura y Educación. 1991 *Bases para la transformación educativa*. Buenos Aires.

——. Ministerio de Cultura y Educación. 1992 *Seminario nacional de investigación e información educativas*. Buenos Aires: Centro Nacional de Información Educativa.

——, Ministerio de Cultura y Educación de la Nación 1993. *Ley Federal de Educación*. Buenos Aires:

República de Chile, Ministerio de Educación de Chile 1993 *Sistemas educativos nacionales.* Madrid: OEI.

——. Ministerio de Educación, 1999. *Reforma en marcha: buena educación para todos.* Santiago: MINEDUC.

——. Ministerio de la Planificación y Cooperación 1999 *Impacto de la política educacional, 1990–1996.* Santiago: División Social.

Tedesco, J.C., Braslavsky, C. & Carciofi, R. 1987 *El proyecto educativo autoritario, Argentina 1976–1982.* Buenos Aires: FLACSO.

Tedesco, J.C. y E. Schiefelbein 1995 *Una nueva oportunidad. El rol de la educación en América Latina.* Buenos Aires: Santillana.

Tiramonti, G. 1988 *¿Hacia dónde va la burocracia educativa?* Buenos Aires: Mino y Dávilas Editores.

Torres, C.A. 2002 "The state, privatization and educational policy: a critique of neo-liberalism in Latin America and some ethical and political implications." *Comparative Education,* 18, 4: 365–385.

Vieytes, M.R. Pentimalli de y A.M.Zanga de Ravinale, 1995 *Ley Federal de Educación.* Acuerdos sobre su implementación. Buenos Aires: Editorial C&C.

Waisman, C. 1999 "Civil society, state capacity and the conflicting logics of economic and political change". Pp. 43–60 in Oxhorn, P. and P.K. Starr (eds.) *Markets and Democracy in Latin America: Conflict or Convergence?* Boulder: Lynne Reinner Publishers.

Williamson, 1990 (ed.) *Latin American Adjustment: How much has happened?* Washington, D.C.: Institute for International Economics.

THE CONTRIBUTORS

Juan Avilés is a history professor in the Universidad Nacional de Educación a Distancia (UNED), Madrid, and Director of the Instituto Universitario de Investigación sobre Seguridad Interior (IUISI). He has published several books and articles on the political history and foreign relations of Spain in the twentieth century, including *La izquierda burguesa en la Segunda República* (1985), *Pasión y farsa: franceses y británicos ante la guerra civil española* (1994), *La fe que vino de Rusia: la revolución bolchevique y los españoles, 1917–1931* (1999) and *Pasionaria: la mujer y el mito* (2005). An expert on terrorism, he writes for the Real Instituto Elcano de Estudios Internacionales y Estratégicos.

Tamar Groves earned her M.A. degree in contemporary Spanish history in the History Department of Tel Aviv University. She is a doctoral student at both Tel Aviv University and the UNED, Madrid. Her dissertation deals with the Teachers' Movement during the Spanish transition to democracy.

Ander Gurrutxaga is Head of the Sociology Department in the Universidad del País Vasco. He is the author of several books, including: *El Código nacionalista vasco durante el franquismo* (1985), *La refundación del nacionalismo vasco* (1996), *La perplejidad sociológica* (1996), *Las transformaciones del nacionalismo vasco* (1997), *La mirada difusa. Los dilemas del nacionalismo* (2002) and *El malestar en la democracia* (2005). He has published numerous articles in both Spanish and international journals, and was a visiting professor in several universities in Spain and abroad. He also served as University and Research Vice-Minister in the Basque Country government.

Dina Lida Kinoshita is a professor at the Universidade de São Paulo, Brazil. She is a member of the UNESCO Chair of "Education for Peace, Human Rights, Democracy and Tolerance" at the Institute for Advanced Studies in the same University. Member of the editorial boards of *Política Democrática* and *Novos Rumos*, she has published more than 40 articles

233

and chapters in books and scientific journals, and delivered lectures in universities, trade unions and other social movements.

José María Marín Arce is a lecturer in modern history at the UNED, Madrid, as well as a visiting professor at the Political Studies Institute of Paris. He has done research on comparative political history, the political party system in Spain during the first third of the 20th century and political and economic aspects of the Spanish transition to democracy. He has published articles in Spanish, French and Italian journals, and his books include *Santiago Alba and the Restoration Crisis* (1991), *Unions and Industrial Restructuring during the Transition* (1997), *A Political History of Spain.1939–2000* (2001). He also contributed to *The Reign of Juan Carlos I* (2003), volume 42 of Menéndez Pidal's *History of Spain*.

Xosé-Manoel Núñez obtained his Ph.D. from the European University Institute, Florence, and is currently professor of modern history at the University of Santiago de Compostela. His research interests focus on comparative nationalism and migration studies.

Raanan Rein is director of the S. Daniel Abraham Center for International and Regional Studies at Tel Aviv University and editor of the journal *Estudios Interdisciplinarios de América Latina y el Caribe*. He is the author of numerous books and articles on modern Spain and Latin America. His recent books include *Argentina, Israel, and the Jews: Perón, the Eichmann Capture and After* (2003), *Peronismo, populismo y política: Argentina 1943–1955* (1998), and *In the Shadow of the Holocaust and the Inquisition: Israel's Relations with Francoist Spain* (1997).

Rafael Roncagliolo Orbegoso is a sociologist and journalist. He served as General Secretary of the Asociación Civil Transparencia from its establishment in 1994 until the end of 2002 and as Technical Secretary of the Acuerdo Nacional (2002). He is also Director of the Peru Program of IDEA (Institute for Democracy and Electoral Assistance). He was a visiting professor in various academic institutions in Peru and abroad, as well as consultant to the Interamerican Institute for Human Rights, UNESCO, the Organization of American States, and the Interamerican Development Bank, among many others. In addition, he is the author of numerous books and articles.

Luis Roniger, a comparative political sociologist, is Reynolds Professor of Latin American Studies and Political Science at Wake Forest University and Associate Professor of Sociology and Anthropology at the Hebrew University of Jerusalem. His publications include *Patrons, Clients and*

Friends (with Shmuel N. Eisenstadt, 1984), *Hierarchy and Trust in Modern Mexico and Brazil* 1990), *The Legacy of Human Rights Violations in the Southern Cone: Argentina, Chile and Uruguay* (with Mario Sznajder, 1999), *The Collective and the Public in Latin America* (co-edited with Tamar Herzog, 2000), and *Globality and Multiple Modernities. Comparative Perspectives on the Americas* (with Carlos Waisman, 2002).

David Sheinin is professor of history at Trent University. He has published five books on inter-American relations. His sixth, *An Alliance Contained: Argentina and the United States, 1800-2000,* is forthcoming from the University of Georgia Press.

Batia Siebzehner is a research fellow of the Truman Institute for the Advancement of Peace at the Hebrew University of Jerusalem and a Senior Lecturer of Sociology at Beit Berl College. She has published *Social Change in Latin American Societies* (co-edited with S.N.Eisenstadt and Fred Bronner, Jerusalem, 1986) and *La Universidad Americana y la Ilustración. Autoridad y Conocimiento en Nueva España y el Río de la Plata* (Madrid, 1994). She has recently completed, with David Lehman, a manuscript entitled "Religious Awakening: The Shas Movement and the Politics of Identity in Israel".

Enric Ucelay-Da Cal received his Ph.D. in history from Columbia University. At present, he is professor of contemporary history at the Universitat Autònoma de Barcelona. He is author of numerous articles in specialized journals, as well as many contributions to collective works. Among his books are *La Catalunya populista: Imatge, cultura i política en l'etapa republicana, 1931–1939* (1982) and a biography of Francesc Macià (1984). In collaboration with Francisco Veiga, he wrote *El fin del segundo milenio (Un siglo de miedos apocalípticos, 1914–1989)* (1994), a general interpretation of the twentieth century. His most recent book is *El imperialismo catalán. Prat de la Riba, Camó, D¹Ors y la conquista moral de España* (2003).

Carlos H. Waisman (Ph.D., Harvard University) is professor of sociology at the University of California, San Diego. He specializes in comparative political sociology. He has worked on the incorporation of the working class into the political system, the development of Argentina in a comparative perspective, and transitions to the market economy in Latin America and other regions. He has published *Modernization and the Working Class, Reversal of Development in Argentina, Institutional Design in New Democracies,* and other books, articles, and essays.

INDEX